Social Security in Britain

Stephen McKay and Karen Rowlingson

First published in Great Britain 1999 by
MACMILLAN PRESS LTD
Houndmills, Basingstoke, Hampshire RG21 6XS and London
Companies and representatives throughout the world

A catalogue record for this book is available from the British Library.

ISBN 0–333–72978–1 hardcover
ISBN 0–333–72979–X paperback

First published in the United States of America 1999 by
ST. MARTIN'S PRESS, INC.,
Scholarly and Reference Division,
175 Fifth Avenue, New York, N.Y. 10010

ISBN 0–312–22348–X

Library of Congress Cataloging-in-Publication Data
McKay, Stephen F.
Social security in Britain / Stephen McKay and Karen Rowlingson.
p.   cm.
Includes bibliographical references and index.
ISBN 0–312–22348–X (cloth)
1. Social security—Great Britain.   I. Rowlingson, Karen.
II. Title.
HD7165.M35   1999
368.4'00941—dc21   99–18739
                                                                                CIP

This book is printed on paper suitable for recycling and made from fully managed and sustained forest sources.

10   9   8   7   6   5   4   3   2   1
08   07   06   05   04   03   02   01   00   99

Editing and origination by
Aardvark Editorial, Meudham, Suffolk

Printed in Hong Kong

For Alexandra

Contents

List of Figures	x
List of Tables	xi
Preface	xii
Acknowledgements	xiii

1 The Aims of Social Security — 1
Introduction — 1
Insuring against risk — 6
Alleviating poverty — 10
Other objectives of social security benefits — 14
A mixed economy of social security? — 16
Benefits in cash and in kind — 17
Other areas of government policy affecting income maintenance — 19

2 The International Context — 22
Introduction — 22
Why look at other countries? — 22
Results from comparative and related studies — 27

3 The Historical Context — 44
Introduction — 44
The Poor Law and industrialisation — 45
Early twentieth-century reforms — 49
Beveridge, full employment and the post-war consensus — 54
The 1950s and 60s: the rediscovery of poverty — 61
The 1970s and 80s: the end of consensus — 64
The 1990s: towards a new consensus? — 69

4   The British System Today   72
Introduction   72
Different types of benefit   72
Expenditure and number of people on different
      benefits   84
Benefit levels and adequacy   87
The benefit unit   89

5   Who Receives Benefits?   92
Introduction   92
Pensioners   93
Benefits for sickness and disability   100
Families with children   109
The unemployed   115

6   Benefits to Meet Specific Costs of Living   125
Introduction   125
Help with housing costs   127
Help with the costs of local taxes   132
Benefits to help meet 'special needs'   133

7   Delivering Benefits   142
Introduction   142
The administration of benefits   142
Claimants, customers or recipients?   150
Equal access to benefits for all?   151
Decision-making and appeals   153
Non-take-up of benefits   154
Fraud and error   158

8   The Effects of Social Security   165
Introduction   165
Disincentives to work: is it worth working?   166
Disincentives to marry? Incentives to have larger
      families?   177
Disincentives to save?   180

9 Social Security Reform **182**
Introduction 182
Problems facing the social security system 182
Possible radical reforms 188
New Labour and social security: a developing agenda 193
Conclusion **199**

10 Conclusions **201**

Appendix: Data Sources Relevant to Social Security **207**
Information provided by the government 207
Non-official sources 209
Useful websites for social security information 210

References 211

Index 224

List of Figures

1.1 Government spending 1996–97   2
2.1 Social protection expenditure as a percentage of Gross Domestic Product   32
2.2 Social assistance spending relative to social security   38
2.3 Social assistance recipients as a proportion of the total population, 1992   38
2.4 Additional disposable income of a couple with two children over a childless couple (at average male earnings)   40
2.5 Low incomes pre- and post-transfer, and direct tax   42
4.1 Expenditure on contributory and other benefits   85
4.2 Spending on different groups   86
5.1 The changing composition of social security spending   93
5.2 State statutory pensions as a proportion of previous earnings, by earnings level and country   99
5.3 Numbers receiving Child Benefit   111
5.4 Family Credit (Family Income Supplement) recipients   113
5.5 Age distribution of unemployment in 1996   117
5.6 Real spending on the unemployed   120
5.7 Benefits received by claimant unemployed in 1996   120
5.8 Claim duration of unemployed people receiving Income Support   121
6.1 Number of lump-sum grants for special needs   137
6.2 Expenditure on the Social Fund in 1996   140
8.1 The effects of earnings on net income: schematic picture   176
9.1 Elderly dependency ratios in the G7 population aged 65 and older as a percentage of the working-age population   187
9.2 Pension expenditure as a percentage of Gross Domestic Product   189

List of Tables

2.1 International comparisons of the mix of different types of benefit   29

4.1 Weekly Income Support rates, 1998–99   88

7.1 Benefits Agency performance targets in 1996–97   145

7.2 Take-up of means-tested benefits   155

7.3 Fraud in the Benefits Reviews   159

7.4 Main types of fraud of means-tested benefits   160

7.5 Chief Adjudication Officer comments on benefit decisions   163

Preface

This book explores the structure of social security. It concentrates on Britain but seeks to apply a comparative perspective and a knowledge of other systems to provide a less parochial viewpoint. The importance of this subject is simply illustrated. In Britain, total government spending on social security is close to £100 billion, more than the spending on health and education put together. Some three-quarters of households receive one or more social security benefits.

This book is designed both as a textbook for undergraduate and post-graduate courses, and for the more general reader interested in matters relating to social security. It grew out of our general dissatisfaction with the books currently available in this field. Existing material seeking to explain social security in Britain (such as Alcock, 1987; Hill, 1990; Spicker, 1993), while good in many respects, was either becoming rather dated or tended to link social security so closely with the alleviation of poverty that many of its wider objectives and functions went overlooked. The subject of poverty is already well covered by existing books (for example Roll, 1992; Alcock, 1993), and we do not attempt any detailed discussion here. Existing books also seemed to make little use of graphic material in helping to bring this area to life, and while comparative research is increasingly common, it was less frequently integrated with texts on social security in general.

This book aims to provide a comprehensive explanation of all aspects of the social security system in Britain. It begins by providing a guide to the context of social security in terms of the aims of the system, comparative perspectives and historical perspectives. It then gives details about the current system: an overview of the structure; the different types of benefit; how the system is administered; and how the system affects behaviour in terms of working, saving and forming particular family types. A final substantive chapter discusses the challenges facing the current system and how the system might change to meet those demands, including developing New Labour policies.

STEPHEN McKAY
KAREN ROWLINGSON

Acknowledgements

The comments of Pete Alcock (Department of Social Policy and Social Work, Birmingham University) and Jane Millar (Department of Social and Policy Sciences, Bath University) on the initial outline of this book were helpful in shaping the contents of this book, and we thank them for their advice. Pete also provided essential advice on the full draft.

That we were in a position to write this book is testimony to the advice and guidance of many of those we have worked with over the years. Our final thanks are to Macmillan for agreeing to publish this book, particularly to Catherine Gray for her support and efficiency while it was being written.

Crown copyright is reproduced with the permission of the Controller of Her Majesty's Stationery Office.

Table 2.1 is reproduced with the permission of IPPR. Figure 5.2 is reproduced with the kind permission of Kluwer Law International. Figures 9.1 and 9.2 are reproduced with the permission of the OECD.

Every effort has been made to trace all the copyright holders but if any have been inadvertently overlooked the publishers will be pleased to make the necessary arrangements at the first opportunity.

Any remaining errors or omissions are the responsibility of the authors.

1

The Aims of
Social Security

Introduction

This chapter outlines what is meant by social security, and the main aims that it is generally regarded as trying to achieve. It also draws attention to other mechanisms, both state and private, that may meet similar ends. This forms essential background to the rest of the book. A few simple facts illustrate the size and importance of the social security system in Britain:

- Government spending on social security is £100 billion per year – about one-third of all government spending and more than is spent on health, education and social services combined (Figure 1.1). This represents about £2,000 each year for every man, woman and child in Britain, and is more than the total raised each year through income tax.
- One-third of dependent children live in households receiving the main safety net benefit, Income Support, which is often regarded as an income insufficient for 'normal' participation in society.
- Three-quarters of British households now receive at least one social security benefit, with one-fifth of non-pensioner households (double the proportion in 1979) receiving one or more means-tested benefits.
- People are spending more time on means-tested benefits. More than two-thirds (67 per cent) of the 1996 Income Support caseload had been on benefit for at least a year, compared with less than one-half (45 per cent) as recently as 1980.

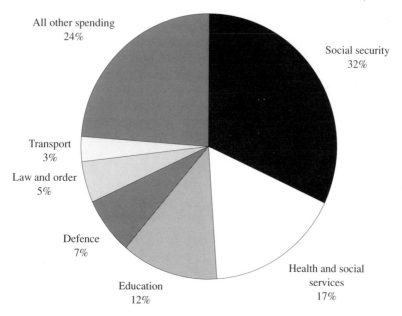

All other spending
24%

Social security
32%

Transport
3%

Law and order
5%

Defence
7%

Education
12%

Health and social
services
17%

Figure 1.1   Government spending 1996–97 (DSS *Focus File 01*, 1998b)

Defining 'social security'

Social security clearly plays a central role in Britain, as it does in most modern industrialised societies. But what is meant by social security? There is no universally accepted neat definition of 'social security'. Indeed, the financial flows underlying social security have been described as 'so central to the welfare state that attention is seldom given to its precise definition' (Hill, 1996: 61).

The term 'social security' can be defined in a number of ways. Starting with the very widest definition, it is sometimes used to refer to all the ways in which people organise their lives in order to ensure access to an adequate income. This wide concept includes securing income from all sources, such as earnings from employers and self-employment, financial help from charities, money from a family member and cash benefits from the state. A slightly narrower definition would include within social security all types of financial support except those provided by the market system. In this way, reliance on the immediate or extended family would still be classed as helping to achieve social security. However, it is increasingly usual to adopt an even narrower definition and to regard social security as those sources of immediate financial support provided by the state. Michael Hill has put forward a rather pragmatic definition that 'social security may be identified with the range of policy responsibilities of the government's Department of Social Security' (Hill, 1990: 1), in some respects a narrower definition than all payments from state funds (see below).

The definition of 'social security' as the system of cash benefits paid by the government to different individuals appears to be fairly simple and unproblematic. But it is inadequate or at least does not include the same range of activities that most people would regard as being social security. This is because some 'benefits' are not paid for by the state, or need not be. Statutory Sick Pay used to be paid by government. While it remains a legal requirement, it is now a cost mostly met by firms. There are also occupational schemes for sickness, widowhood and retirement that are similar to Department of Social Security benefits, that have a similar function, but are organised by employers. One could also envisage the government finding ways to 'privatise' what are currently state benefits, or instigating new compulsory private provision, perhaps for pensions. Thus, both voluntary employer schemes and some programmes mandated by government may also be classed as social security – neither of which neatly fits the above definition.

There are also several ways in which the government pays people money that are not generally regarded as 'benefits' and hence not usually classified as 'social security', including the following:

- Victims of crime may receive money under the Criminal Injuries Compensation Scheme.
- Local education authorities may give grants to help purchase clothing.
- Higher education students receive grants.
- People may receive financial assistance to help to improve their homes, including providing loft insulation.
- The Children Act 1989 permits social services to give financial assistance to families.
- The Family Fund Trust, funded through government, may give grants to families with severely disabled children.

Some of these sources involve payment for fairly specific needs, while student grants are a more general form of support. Most social security benefits may be used for any purpose, but some involve specific rights to free health-related goods such as dental care, and in some countries the equivalent of social security may be paid as vouchers rather than cash. Low-income families with children may also have some or all their costs of childcare met through social security arrangements.

Another rather grey area is the distinction between cash benefits and systems of tax allowances and tax credits, which are the responsibility of Inland Revenue. There are important areas in which taxes and benefits perform similar roles. While only 'benefits' are typically regarded as social security, elements of the tax system may need to be considered in looking at all the ways in which people assemble a package of income.

For the reasons mentioned above, it is difficult to give a precise definition of social security. In this book, we take a fairly narrow, pragmatic approach but put social security within the context of other related forms of government and employer financial provision.

It is worth mentioning here that the use and definition of terms varies across different countries. In the USA, the 'social security' label is generally reserved for benefits based on an individual's previous financial contributions (often termed 'social insurance' or the 'contributory system'), the more negative and separate term 'welfare' being reserved for benefits based on alleviating low income and not requiring people to have paid into the system (a part of social security often called 'social assistance' or 'means-testing' elsewhere). In contrast, in the UK, reform to all aspects of social security, including contributory benefits, is increasingly called 'welfare reform'. In some European Union countries, the term 'social security' has a wider scope than it does in Britain and may include access to their systems of health care.

The aims of social security

But what are the aims of social security? The answer is complex. As elsewhere, the system in Britain has evolved over time so is not necessarily (indeed, almost certainly not) what would be designed if policymakers were now starting from scratch. Furthermore, different parts of the system have different aims, so it is not possible to identify one aim, and it is even arguable what the main aim of the system is. With these reservations in mind, Box 1.1 lists some of the possible objectives of social security.

Within these general aims, systems are also usually designed to achieve the following:

Box 1.1

Possible Aims of Social Security

- Insuring against the risks of particular events in life, such as unemployment
- Relieving poverty or low income
- Redistributing resources across people's life-cycles
- Redistributing resources from rich to poor
- 'Compensating' for some types of extra cost (such as children and disability)
- Providing financial support when 'traditional' families break down

- To maintain incentives for self-provision (such as through earning and saving)
- To keep the non-take-up of benefits low
- To counteract possible fraud
- To ensure that administrative costs are low.

Before discussing each of the general aims of social security, it is worth mentioning that the aims of the British system have traditionally been more limited than those of systems in Europe, if wider than in some parts of the rest of the English-speaking world. The International Labour Office (1984) has stated that 'The fundamental aim of social security is to give individuals and families the confidence that their level of living and quality of life will not, in so far as possible, be greatly eroded by any social or economic eventuality.' While international bodies may mention ideas of ensuring that risk is reduced, or of maintaining equality, the alleviation of poverty in Britain has traditionally been a particularly significant objective of social security policy (Walker with Ashworth, 1994), although by no means the only objective.

This difference between Britain and continental Europe is manifest in several different ways. First, the British system typically involves benefits paid at a *flat-rate level*, compared with benefit levels usually related to former earnings in continental European systems. In other words, when people are unemployed in Britain, their benefit will be a particular amount of money each week regardless of how much they earned before. In the systems in many other countries, benefit payments will be some proportion of people's previous earnings (as high as 90 per cent in Denmark and Sweden). This is not to suggest that either system is inherently superior to the other, just that they are different and that these differences are likely to reflect alternative underlying motives. The British approach to unemployment benefits seems to be that of warding off poverty by providing a minimum level of income regardless of previous earnings; the continental system that links benefit payments to prior earnings is concerned with avoiding disruption to a person's accustomed lifestyle (see Chapter 2 for further international comparisons).

The importance of relieving poverty in the British system also explains the considerable reliance on *means-testing* in Britain. The receipt of means-tested benefits depends on a person or family having resources (typically income, and perhaps savings) below a certain level in order to receive benefits. Means-testing is also common in America, New Zealand and Australia but much less common elsewhere, especially in continental Europe, where it also tends to be less centralised.

We will now discuss the aims of social security to explore the extent to which each plays a role in the British system.

Insuring against risk

The clearest root for the current social security system lies in the Beveridge model published in the early 1940s, although insurance-based and other benefits had been introduced well before this time (see Chapter 3). At the heart of the Beveridge approach – of 'social insurance' – is the idea that people face a range of risks that might lead to severe reductions in living standard. These include the risk of unemployment, or being incapacitated and unable to work, or retiring and losing the main income-earner in a family. Some risks such as widowhood are rather uncommon and relatively unrelated to economic circumstances. Others, such as retirement, are much more widespread and predictable.

The main issues that arise with social insurance include:

● Why should the state, rather than private insurance, provide this service? What relationship should there then be between state and private insurance?
● What risks should be covered?
● On what basis should contributions be made or be deemed to be made?

Practical choices must also be made about the level of coverage and which groups are to be covered. In the Beveridge system, the main risks to be covered were unemployment, sickness, widowhood and retirement. In Britain, the level of coverage was set to cover subsistence needs rather than guaranteeing the maintenance of previous living standards. Those covered were typically employees who had made contributions to the National Insurance fund, typically by paying a fixed sum of money each week in the early days, but this had become an almost entirely earnings-related system by 1975.

State versus private insurance

Social insurance parallels the functions of private insurance schemes. In practice, there have been important differences between them, even if these need not reflect the state–private divide. In a system of social insurance, as typically implemented, the level of individuals' contributions does not reflect the risk of a particular event happening to them. In contrast, in most private systems, the level of payment into the scheme will be based on identifying those with higher or lower risks of making a claim (Burchardt and Hills, 1997). For example, the cost of home contents insurance will reflect geographical location (as a proxy for the risk of being burgled), and life insurance will depend in part on occupation (as a proxy for life expectancy). However, social insurance against the risk of unemployment will usually require all participants to pay the same amount (or the same proportion of income) even though some groups are at greater or lesser risk of having to make a claim. To some extent, therefore, social insurance involves the redistribution of income from low-risk individuals to those with greater risks.

The second main difference, at least for most current systems if not in principle, is that private insurance systems rely on accumulating money in a fund before paying out entitlements. Social insurance, however, is usually based on paying money to those entitled using the current contributions of those paying into the system. For example, today's state retirement pensions are paid from the contributions of today's workers, unlike private pensions, which link individuals' final pensions to their own previous contributions, along with the capital growth accumulated during a person's years of contributing.

A third difference is that social insurance tends to be compulsory, while private insurance is usually voluntary. Again, this difference reflects common practice as much as any difference in principle. It is possible to opt out of some types of state insurance (earnings-related pensions), whereas it is also possible for the state to compel people to take out private insurance without being involved in its provision, as occurs with compulsory third-party insurance cover for all car drivers. In some areas, social insurance exists alongside private insurance, and the state system may also incorporate various features that are common in the private sector. For example, in the area of pensions, the state system contains both a basic and an earnings-related element. Alongside state pensions, private pension schemes also exist provided both by employers ('occupational pensions') and by insurance companies ('personal pensions'). Indeed, Beveridge recommended flat-rate social benefits precisely because he wished to leave intact incentives to make additional provision.

There are several reasons why the state might want to implement a social insurance system rather than relying on the private sector (Creedy and Disney, 1985). Some of these reasons are concerned with economic efficiency (Barr, 1993) and the inability of the private sector correctly to identify the risks that individuals actually face. Social insurance has also sometimes been a response to a concern about high administrative costs in the private sector (now resurfacing in debates about personal pensions) and probably reflects a great deal of 'paternalism' in state decision-making.

What risks to cover?

While means-tested benefits will generally pay out if people have low incomes, whatever the reason, social insurance benefits are designed to meet one of a list of particular eventualities. Benefit is usually received for just one of those reasons: a person may receive a social insurance benefit for being sick, retired, or unemployed – but not for more than one of these eventualities. While Beveridge envisaged that each would attract the same level of benefit, there are now important differences in the levels of payment to each group.

The main risks covered within the British social security system today are retirement, long-term sickness among those of working age, widowhood and short-term unemployment. There are a wide range of other risks that could, at least in principle, be covered by an insurance-based system, for example the risk of separation among couples (which Beveridge investigated). The guiding principles seem to be that the risk should be largely outside the control of the individual, and either small and spread across a large proportion of the population (such as widowhood) or predictable, with a strong degree of certainty (such as retirement). In other areas, the state is content for people to take out private insurance if they wish. Home contents insurance is one example. With third-party car insurance, the state requires people to take out a minimum level of cover, but they may choose between a range of competing private sector providers. In areas such as pensions, a very strong private sector has developed to allow people to take out additional insurance, sometimes with state tax-breaks to do so. For example, people may effectively transfer the contributions that would have gone towards a state-provided second pension (via the State Earnings-Related Pension Scheme – SERPS) into their own personal or occupational pension.

There are clearly several options open to government about the areas in which it should insure and those which may be either compulsory or left as voluntary. That does not mean that each has the same effects on those in the system. As mentioned above, a distinctive feature of social insurance, in Britain at least, is that contributions are not related to risk. It is known that the risk of unemployment is higher in some industries and occupations than in others (McKay *et al.*, 1997), but people in such jobs are not charged higher rates of contribution. This contrasts with private insurance, where, in car insurance, those with the most accident-prone records end up paying more to be insured than do those with better (or more fortunate) driving histories. Other groups do better or worse for factors that they are unable to affect, such as the young paying more than the old because they are in a generally higher-risk category.

The basis of contributions

Another factor in a social insurance system is that of who is covered. A private system will clearly include those paying the relevant premiums, but, with social insurance, matters can be rather more complex. More details are provided in Chapter 4, but, broadly speaking, employees pay contributions from their earnings that give entitlement to a range of insurance benefits. The self-employed pay a fixed contribution that gives entitlement only to the basic retirement pension and some benefits related to sickness (Brown, 1994: Chapter 5).

It should be clear that only those in paid work would be covered if this were the limit of social insurance. To protect the rights of people when they are actually on benefits, a system of 'credits' has been established. Hence, while unemployed or off sick, people do not actually pay National Insurance but are instead credited with having done so. It has long been recognised that these provisions mean that those not in paid work and not receiving a contributory benefit are thereby excluded from cover. This traditionally included women bringing up children or looking after disabled relatives. Since 1978, their rights to state pensions have (to an extent) been safeguarded under a system known as Home Responsibility Protection, but years of caring before then are effectively 'gaps' in contribution records that may reduce a person's pension.

Employees or employers?

Who should actually pay insurance contributions – employees or employers? This question is often presented as implying some real choice about who really pays, but, according to economists, there is no such difference in the long run (Kay and King, 1978). This is because the question of 'formal incidence' is often quite separate from that of who is really affected ('effective incidence') when we are talking about tax-like policies. This can be explained simply in the following way: if employees pay the contributions directly out of their own wages, their take-home wages will obviously be reduced; if employers pay the contributions directly, they will have less money to pay in wages, so employees' wages will, indirectly, be reduced. It therefore makes little effective difference in the long term whether it is the employer or the employee who formally pays.

Alleviating poverty

Another means of structuring social security is to pay benefits to those with a current need. Instead of having an insurance-based approach, it is possible simply to pay out benefits to those identified as having a current need for assistance. Social assistance is generally taken to mean meeting the needs of those below a certain level of resources. Such benefits are usually paid out of general tax revenues (either locally or, as in Britain, through central funds).

Countries differ a great deal in the extent of this type of provision. In Australia and New Zealand, almost all benefits include an element of 'means-testing'. This does not mean that only the poorest may receive benefits – in some instances, the aim is to exclude the richest rather than to include only the poorest. In Britain, social assistance is almost synonymous with the benefit Income Support and the income-based part of Jobseeker's Allowance for unemployed people (see Chapter 5). These benefits are paid to those whose income and savings are below defined levels, taking into account the size and type of the family. Additional conditions are often attached to receiving social assistance. People of working age without sole responsibility for caring for children or disabled adults must be able to work, be available for work and be actively seeking work. In the past, they may have had to enter a workhouse to qualify (see Chapter 3).

In much of Northern Europe, social assistance plays a much smaller role, picking up those not covered by the main social insurance system (see Chapter 2). In addition, it is often administered locally, local organisations having some discretion about the precise rules of entitlement.

The aim of Income Support in Britain is, therefore, to alleviate poverty by providing a safety net, yet it seems that those on Income Support may not be receiving enough money to save them from poverty. The concept of poverty is a highly emotive one and has received considerable attention from researchers who have tried to define and measure it (see Abel-Smith and Townsend, 1965; Holman, 1978; Townsend, 1979; Piachaud, 1987). Other books go into much greater detail on this subject (Alcock, 1987; Roll, 1992; Spicker, 1993), but it is worth briefly discussing the main issues.

Defining poverty

If the system aims to reduce (or alleviate or prevent) poverty, it is important to have some idea of what poverty actually is. Discussions about defining poverty usually begin by making a distinction between absolute and relative poverty. Absolute poverty is said to exist where people lack sufficient resources to maintain their physical subsistence. People clearly need a minimum amount of food, warmth and shelter in order to survive; absolute poverty would exist where people could not afford this minimum. This definition makes no allowances for lifestyles and cultural expectations. People can physically survive without an indoor toilet or a bath or a fairly varied diet, but we would generally consider these to be fairly basic requirements, and if people could not afford them, we would probably consider them to be poor.

Another problem with the concept of absolute poverty is its lack of a time perspective. If people lack sufficient resources to provide a minimum amount of food for one day, does this constitute poverty? Also, at its extreme, the definition suggests that there will be no-one actually living in poverty because they will have all starved to death (or be in the process of doing so). Of course, some poor people may starve or may die of cold or cold-related diseases because they cannot afford to heat their homes. Generally, however, we do not usually consider death to be a necessary outcome and therefore the sole proof of poverty.

These problems with the concept of absolute poverty lead many authors to prefer the concept of relative poverty, which is generally derived not by calculating minimum needs but by considering the general standard of living in society as a whole. For example, it might be argued that people are in poverty where their income is lower than two-thirds of the average wage, or half the average household income, or some other threshold. Mack and Lansley (1985) used a different approach – asking members of the general public what they consider to be necessities and then asking people whether or not they can afford these necessities. If people cannot afford things that the majority of the public consider to be a necessity, they might be said to be living in relative poverty.

Relative poverty is not just a measure of inequality. As long as some people are better off than others, there will always be some who are worse off than others. However, they will only be described as (relatively) poor if they are seen to lack the necessities for proper participation in society. It is certainly true that, as expectations rise, what we consider to be necessities will change: is someone poor if he cannot afford a video recorder? In recent years, the debate has moved away from a focus on poverty to a discussion about social exclusion and social integration (Jordan, 1996: Chapter 3).

The term 'social exclusion' may be used in rather different ways, each to some extent indicating its origin in European discussion. For some, it is simply a term that is interchangeable with poverty, one that was, helpfully, deemed politically acceptable to Conservative governments in the 1980s and 90s, who did not recognise the existence of widespread poverty. For others, 'social exclusion' is a wider term that incorporates all manner of deprivation that the definition of poverty, which is very often operationalised into a particular income level, does not readily capture. Yet another perspective is that the word 'poverty' is more appropriate for individuals, while 'social exclusion' is something that is experienced by whole communities. This tends to reflect French academic use (Room, 1995).

There are a number of points to make about social security benefits and poverty. First, there are many both implicit and explicit objectives of social security that do not relate to providing assistance to the poor. As we have just seen, providing for the poor is just one of the possible aims of social security. The introduction of social security in some countries, for example by Bismarck in Germany and (arguably) within Britain, was more about yielding to strongly felt desires for social revolution that, if refused, might have led to concerns about political revolution. Another very important objective is that of redistributing incomes across the life-cycle. In many other countries, the maintenance of living standards for those of all income levels has been given a higher priority. Finally, another aim of the system is to encourage people to work – or at least not to put too much of a financial barrier to working in their way.

Alleviating poverty depends on setting benefit levels at a level that can achieve that aim, but there is considerable disagreement about what that level should be. Chapter 4 discusses benefit levels and their adequacy in greater detail.

The dynamics of poverty, low income and benefit receipt

A key issue in measuring and understanding poverty is that of how long people stay poor. The idea of an underclass suggests that people are likely to stay poor and on benefit for a very long time. However, others have argued that people leave poverty all the time, and at quite a fast rate of change.

At a first glance, there does seem to be something of a contradiction in the research findings. Some sources seem to suggest that there is a large number of long-term poor. In many surveys, a lot of the poor people have been in that state for a long time. We saw earlier in this chapter that the proportion of people spending long periods on Income Support has increased substantially over the 1980s and 90s. However, studies of unemployment (an important cause of poverty) show a high degree of movement between unemployment and employment.

This apparent contradiction in research evidence arises from the fact that most people who *become* poor (or start to claim Income Support) stay in that situation for relatively little time. However, the majority of those who *are* poor (on Income Support) have been in that situation for a rather longer time. Bane and Ellwood (1986) have argued that an emphasis on data over time radically changes the way in which policy-makers should look at poverty. It is quite clear that there is no simple distinction between the poor and the non-poor.

Figures for poverty in Germany tend to show that about 10 per cent of the population have incomes below half the average at any point in time. Panel data from a recent period covering 9 years, however, show that three times that proportion were poor (Leibfried and Leisering, 1995). Hence poverty affects a greater number of people than some research would suggest, and it affects them often for only a short time.

Poverty may have very different effects depending on how long it lasts. However, most policy is based on limited evidence about the length of time that different groups spend in poverty and the effect of this on the experience of deprivation. For example, in 1988, resources were moved from pensioners to families with children, since there seemed to be more families with children in poverty, but there was no information on how long that poverty lasted. It could be the case that pensioner poverty is worse because it is likely to continue indefinitely, whereas poverty among families with children is more likely to be short lived. On the other hand, those who face indefinite poverty can perhaps adjust to it better than those who hope for an upturn in their economic situation.

The importance of dynamic considerations is such that broad esti-mates of income changes are now published with official estimates of the number of families on below-average incomes.

Other objectives of social security benefits

The preceding sections have investigated social insurance, which aims to insure people against particular risks, and social assistance, which aims to alleviate poverty. These two motives are central to the British system, but they do not cover all of the objectives that states have in mind when designing or reforming benefits: there are other aims that some benefits try to achieve or functions that benefits appear to carry out.

Redistribution

It is sometimes thought that the social security system performs a 'Robin Hood' function by redistributing resources from the rich (through taxation) to the poor (through social security benefits), but an alternative interpretation of social security benefits, particularly social insurance pensions, is that they equate to a form of redistribution over the life-cycle. This is, in effect, a form of 'forced saving', although the term has more negative connotations.

Some policies do aim to redistribute income from rich to poor, but most redistribution takes money from people when they are of working age and then gives it back to the same people in times of unemployment and finally in retirement. This 'savings bank' concept of the welfare state functions such that as much as two-thirds of social security spending concerns shifting money to and from the same people over the course of their lifetime (Falkingham and Hills, 1995). Critics might question how far the state needs to become involved in what may be portrayed as mostly 'paternalist' behaviour.

Compensation for extra costs

In the British social security system, some benefits recognise that certain groups of people face extra costs that the state will share. The clearest example is benefits for dependent children. Child Benefit is paid to parents who have responsibility for children. There is no test of contributions, and the family's level of income is not (at the present time) taken into consideration. There are, however, certain tests of residence that must be satisfied. Disability benefits provide another example, in which some elements are purely contingent and reflect neither means nor previous contributions (see Chapter 4 for a more detailed description of disability benefits).

Social security systems clearly do not seek to support all of the extra costs that people might take on (pets, for example). Paying benefits to meet particular extra costs or responsibilities requires a political judgement about which should attract financial support. The role of the state in supporting children, for example, varies across both time and different countries (Harding, 1996). Should children be the subject of considerable universal state support, or should people, once they 'decide' to have children, bear the financial costs if they are able to do so? In the USA, there is no universal benefit for families with children, and some states do not increase benefits if a mother has more children while on 'welfare' (the 'family cap'). Many countries start to remove benefits for children if their parents' income reaches a certain level. In contrast, Scandinavian countries are identified with high levels of universal support, both financial and through services.

Providing financial support when 'traditional' families break down

Another objective might include that of 'stepping in where the family fails' (Hills, 1993: 15), as a method of paying women (in particular) who are left without independent resources following divorce or separation. Some benefits have been specifically designed for lone parents (such as the lone-parent premium on Income Support and One Parent Benefit). However, One Parent Benefit has now been abolished (no new claims will be accepted), and there is a view that simply providing support when traditional two-parent families break down may actually enable or even encourage such couples to separate (see Chapter 8).

A mixed economy of social security?

As well as discussing the aims of social security, it is also important to consider how these aims might be met. There are, in fact, various ways in which these aims could be achieved, involving different mixes of provision by the state, family, private sector and voluntary bodies. Social policy commentators identify a 'mixed economy of welfare' (Glennerster, 1992), meaning that different sectors may play a role in providing different types of welfare. According to Titmuss (1958: 53), 'social welfare... represents only the more visible part of the real world of welfare'. Thus, in the area of welfare related to maintaining income, there are different means by which this may be achieved. Of foremost importance is the private sector, for example earnings from employment and profits from self-employment being the chief source of income for most people of working age.

Alongside earnings and profits, there are various other benefits accruing from being employed, or what has been called occupational welfare. The most important of these are probably occupational pensions, covering close to half of the population in employment. Employers often pay large amounts into the occupational pensions of employees, and some occupational pensions are even non-contributory, especially in the financial services and public sectors. Employers may also provide benefits for sickness or for pregnant women that exceed statutory provisions. In particularly favourable employment conditions, employees might benefit from reduced-cost health insurance, company cars, cheap mortgages – albeit that some of these will attract extra tax liability. It may be argued that occupational benefits such as pensions mean a reduction in other benefits, or lower pay, in which case they would not necessarily be of advantage to employees. However, it seems that this possibility is somewhat exaggerated. Such benefits, however, are clearly not available to all employees and are obviously unavailable to those without paid work.

Earnings are received by individuals, but a great deal of money also moves between people living together. Indeed, the rules of most means-tested benefits assume that these flows take place and define low income as a feature of couples rather than individuals (Roll, 1991). This point is discussed further in Chapter 4. There are also flows of income within the *extended* family; for example, grandparents may give their grown-up children financial help, particularly when there are grandchildren involved (Kempson *et al.*, 1994).

A third area of non-state welfare is that of charities, or the 'informal' or voluntary sector of the economy. Charities may provide direct assistance to families on low incomes or with high-level needs of some kind (such as having disabled children). Charitable support was particularly important in the ninteenth century before the state system developed. It has been argued that we are witnessing a return to charities, as public support has proved inadequate in some areas (Institute for Public Policy Research, 1993: 11). In some cases, charities may assist by providing particular items rather than cash.

There are also good examples of organisations that illustrate the 'mixed economy' of welfare provision and the differences between administering benefits and financing them. For example, the Family Fund Trust is a charity that was run by the Joseph Rowntree Foundation until becoming an independent trust in 1996 (Family Fund Trust, 1996). It administers and distributes money that is provided directly by the government (the money being paid to families with disabled children). Similarly, the Independent Living Fund was established in 1993 to distribute government money to adults with substantial care needs, but it was largely administered by representatives from disability organisations (Kestenbaum, 1993).

Benefits in cash and in kind

In most cases, the aims of the social security system are achieved by paying out cash benefits. However, this need not be the case. Benefits could be provided 'in kind', through providing either services or vouchers that may only be spent on certain types of good. In the USA, an important method of providing for poor families is through the Food

Stamps programme. This pays out vouchers that must be exchanged for food. In Britain, the receipt of Income Support and some other benefits carries with it rights to some services at no charge, such as dental treatment, eye examinations and legal aid.

As we shall see in Chapter 3, the British system developed along two lines: the national social security system generally provided cash benefits to cover some needs such as those for food, clothes and money for bills, whereas other needs, such as the need for social care, were covered by local social services departments, who provided in-kind services.

A related issue concerns the interaction between what is paid for by social security and what might be provided through other areas of social policy. Should weekly benefits include the cost of vital utilities (such as water), or should benefits meet the direct costs of such services?

An important example is the cost of Housing Benefit. Local government is involved in providing housing to (increasingly) low-income families. In the past, the levels of such rents were kept well below market levels. This clearly had an indirect cost as councils could have charged more rent and therefore gained higher revenues. The removal of such 'bricks and mortar' subsidies has meant faster rising costs for Housing Benefit, which have arguably led to various changes in policy to curtail the rising spending. These questions are examined in greater detail in Chapter 6.

The treatment of care for disabled and older people forms a particularly crucial area in terms of differences between cash and in-kind provision (Becker, 1997). In the 1980s, Income Support paid for the costs of residential care for older people and became the fastest growing area of social security spending. There were also concerns that, since entitlement depended on receiving Income Support, houses had to be sold and other assets used up for those whose financial savings were above the Income Support threshold.

The Department of Social Security used to have a direct role in some housing and care provision for the single homeless through Resettlement Units, formerly run by the Resettlement Agency. These Units, which date back to the Poor Law concept of 'indoor relief', have now been closed, and direct management has been replaced by grant aid to achieve similar objectives.

Other areas of government policy affecting income maintenance

The function of social security is not the same as that of the Department of Social Security (DSS), even if the role of that organisation provides a convenient outline of the areas in which discussion most often takes place. There are several ways in which other areas of government become involved in the wider issue of income maintenance. This section outlines some of the most important of these areas.

The tax system

Increasing the spending power of families may be achieved through either direct cash benefits or tax concessions. There are a number of examples that may illustrate this point. Within the tax system, and particularly through VAT, the cost of certain types of good may be made artificially higher or lower. Children's clothing, books and many food items have no VAT charged on them, and fuel has a special lower VAT rate, making these items cheaper than would be the case if VAT were levied at the same rate on all goods.

Similarly, the income tax system contains allowances for certain dependants, for example children. These types of tax concession, where the tax system gives special advantages to certain groups of people or types of spending, are sometimes known as 'tax expenditures' (McDaniel and Surrey, 1985). The most recent, is the Working Families Tax Credit, which replaces the benefit Family Credit in October 1999, with a transfer of responsibilities from the DSS to the Inland Revenue. There may be further scope for replacing benefits, particularly those for people in work, with tax credits, or for the use of the tax system as a means of collecting child support from workers.

Before Child Benefit was introduced as a cash benefit, there was instead a dual system in which money in the form of a 'family allowance' was paid directly to mothers, and an allowance for children was made additionally within the income tax system. Tax expenditures remain an important part of government policy, although the value of some of them has been reduced in the past 10 years. Other examples include: those paying a mortgage enjoy tax relief on some of the interest paid; those contributing to non-state pensions pay lower contributions because of tax relief; and married couples pay less tax than cohabiting couples as a result of the married couples tax allowance.

Two areas in the field of housing are of particular interest. First, it is worth noting that tenants have their rents met by benefits if they are in households with low overall incomes. In contrast, all families paying a mortgage enjoy tax relief that keeps their housing costs lower. Thus mortgage interest tax relief covers everyone with a mortgage, but its costs are much less visible than those of Housing Benefit paid to tenants on a low income.

There are a number of rather technical questions about the relative efficiency of tax-based provision compared with direct provision. Social policy researchers have, however, often been more interested in the different treatments of these areas within government budgets and in the different types of discussion that each area of provision generates (the two being linked). It is easy to portray benefits as a 'burden', while tax concessions promote 'incentives'. The government's system of accounts records the amount spent on different cash benefits, but information on the costs of tax-breaks is more difficult to come by, and the correct means of costing the latter is more controversial.

Employment policy and employers

As we show in Chapters 3 and 9, the New Labour government has placed great emphasis on its various Welfare-to-Work programmes because it is regarded as preferable for people to gain their income from the labour market rather than social security. There are also other ways in which labour market policies interact with social security. The first is the introduction of a national minimum wage. Restrictions on how little employers may offer workers have long been a feature in Britain. During most of the twentieth century, Wages Councils and their predecessors drew up legally binding wage agreements (and by no means just minima) for selected industries that were most likely to include lower-waged workers.

Some social security benefits, particularly Family Credit (to be replaced in October 1999 by Working Families Tax Credit) effectively 'top up' earnings that are considered too low for families to live on. Critics of in-work benefits claim they thereby act as a means of subsidising employers who pay the lowest wages.

At a wider level, the rate of employment maintained in an economy will contribute to the degree of reliance on benefits for those who do not have jobs. Governments have recently tended to downplay their ability to control employment levels, but certain policies do aim to create jobs. For example, some schemes provide employers with government funding to subsidise the wages of employers so that more workers can be taken on.

The balance of responsibility between employers and the state may also change over time. Workers experiencing short periods of illness could have their incomes paid direct from the state, or, alternatively, employers could be mandated to provide such cover. And, indeed, Statutory Sick Pay is now paid by employers whereas it was formerly effectively paid for by the government.

2

The International Context

Introduction

Social security systems are a central feature of most modern, industrialised countries, but even countries at a similar level of economic development adopt quite different approaches to their social security policies. In the course of this chapter, we focus on a number of these differences. According to Hirsch (1997), social security systems in Europe differ from those in the UK such that:

- Social security is designed to include everyone, not just a poor minority
- Contributions to National Insurance are viewed differently from taxation
- Social security is about 'solidarity'.

While some of these features have echoes in the UK, it is argued that, in Europe, they form a strong part of the social security system.

This chapter looks at the UK social security system in an international context and has two main aims. First, it seeks to demonstrate the importance of taking a comparative viewpoint when looking at social security issues and at social policy more generally. Second, it distinguishes between different types of comparative study and presents some of the main findings from some recent studies of social security.

Why look at other countries?

Historically, the study of social policy has been strongly influenced in many countries by the 'social administration' tradition. The social administration approach (Mishra, 1977) puts a strong emphasis on pragmatism and problem-solving within a framework of gradual reform. There is generally much less of an interest in theory, and little support for considering results from other countries. In 1971, Robert Pinker argued that:

> As a discipline, the study of comparative social administration scarcely exists... In many ways the discipline has remained stubbornly resistant to comparative treatment. (Pinker, 1971: 48)

This lack of a well-developed comparative component to social policy is in marked contrast to disciplines such as sociology or political science. Even the founding fathers of sociology, such as Durkheim and Marx, had a central concern with applying theories and searching for empirical evidence across countries.

In more recent years, the study of social security, and social policy more generally, has embraced a more comparative approach. This has partly reflected a greater theoretical emphasis. Other factors, such as the growing influence that supranational bodies such as the European Union have on policy-making (referred to below), may have been just as important. Whatever the reason, social security researchers within social policy now increasingly turn to comparative research. Indeed, for John Clarke, justification must now be given for approaches that restrict themselves to only one country: *The future?*

> it is perhaps no longer necessary to make the case for a comparative approach to the study of social policy... it may now be single-country studies that need to be justified. (Clarke, 1993: 1)

However, a relatively weak form of comparative method is often implied in the arguments made by those writing in the area of social policy. A number of studies appear to concentrate on describing the systems in different countries, with perhaps one chapter for each country. Attempts to compare and contrast different systems and draw pertinent conclusions are often limited.

For Jones (1985), the comparative method is important because it can provide both more policy ideas and an improved understanding of the home social policy environment. The first of these reasons is often summed up in the phrase 'lessons from abroad' and may be a particular interest of policy-makers within social security (see below).

Another clear advantage of looking to comparative research is to understand better the home experience. It might not occur to a British commentator to describe benefits as 'flat rate', but this would strike many foreign observers as a most distinctive feature. The growth of

means-testing might be commented upon in a narrowly British context, but it is only through comparisons with elsewhere that one would iden- tify the particular emphasis given to means tests in Britain and a few other countries.

However, while these types of justification may contribute towards greater theorising, this would be an additional advantage rather than the central reason for such studies.

UK / India

Lessons from abroad?

It is often difficult to test out new ideas in one country, so the experi- ence of other countries (or fairly autonomous states within them; Wald- fogel, 1997: p. 14) may provide a useful testing ground for which types of system seem to work and which do not. It is sometimes possible to discern particular policies that seem to have been copied from experi- ence elsewhere, not always successfully. Taking a comparative approach to the study of social policy is, therefore, likely to include the attempt to 'learn lessons' from abroad, and perhaps to indicate where lessons might have been learned but were not. Millar and Whiteford (1993) imply that this happened with the UK's attempt to borrow from the Australian model of child support for separated parents. For example, Britain chose to locate child support within the DSS rather than (as in Australia) the main tax-collecting body. The policy quickly became associated with seeking to recover benefit-spending rather than encouraging mutual obligations to support children, for the benefit of children. More recent proposals for simplifying the formula used to calculate child support (Department of Social Security, 1998a) seem to emulate the approach of several American states. It remains to be seen how far it is the details of policy, rather than perhaps different cultures, that affect the success of child support – 'aggressive child support enforcement in the United States has had little effect in raising the percentage of lone mother families receiving the child support that they are owed' (Waldfogel, 1997: 12).

British governments of the 1980s and 90s often looked abroad for help with policy formulation, particularly to the USA (or particular states). With the apparent similarity of views between President Clinton and Prime Minister Blair, there are few reasons why British policy- makers should not continue to look at American reform for particular ideas – policies concerning 'Welfare-to-Work' seem to have involved many British analysts travelling to Wisconsin to investigate their approach ('Wisconsin Works'), or to Australia. Moreover, the emphasis on a more active welfare state is in line with similar developments in the rest of Europe.

However, welfare systems in other European countries are often very different from those in Britain. The emphasis on social insurance is much greater on the continent and the role of means-tested social assistance often much reduced. The particular contexts facing each country are often rather different and make the learning of lessons rather more difficult. For example, the idea of 'workfare' is often suggested as a means of assisting the unemployed into work and perhaps of further checking their eligibility. Arguably, the experience with workfare in other countries could provide a way of determining its probable effectiveness. It is important to note that workfare in the USA is concerned only with lone parents and not with the unemployed. The European experience of workfare may be more useful in that it concerns the unemployed, but benefits tend to be rather different – sometimes directly involving trades unions (as in Denmark). European labour markets are also much more regulated, and many have long experience with national minimum wages and compulsory training provision.

These points emphasise the difficulties of learning lessons from the social policy experience of different countries (the next section looking at further problems). However, in the absence of a straightforward method of testing policies in a particular country in advance of full implementation, this may be the best or only option. The move from in-work benefits to tax credits does seem to have built on lessons learned from both the USA and Canada (Walker and Wiseman, 1997; Mendelson, 1998), and proposals for the national minimum wage have been developed in the light of experience of some other countries (Low Pay Commission, 1998).

Problems of comparative social security research

All comparative studies face a range of methodological problems (for detailed studies of comparative research methods, see Przeworski and Teune, 1970; Warwick and Osherson, 1973; Dogan and Kazancigil, 1994). These range from practical difficulties of language to the choice of countries (should they be 'similar' or 'different'?), to inconsistency in data and to theoretical problems.

Limiting the inquiry to social security raises problems of its own. First, it should be remembered that social security benefits are just one means of redistributing income within society. An area often neglected is how the tax system may be used to achieve similar ends. The value of tax expenditures seems to vary widely across OECD countries (Greve, 1994; Wood, 1988) and often benefits better-off families (Dewson, 1995). In a similar way, some functions of social security (such as employees' sick pay) may be routinely undertaken by the market or even imposed on the private sector by government. Comparisons across countries should also recognise that there may be one or more benefits or different types of benefit for particular groups; to give an example, lone parents might be catered for within social insurance (as is the case for widows in the UK), advanced child maintenance systems, general social assistance (means-tested) schemes or categorical benefits aimed specifically at lone parents.

Social security and the European Union

While the European Union was principally conceived as a union based on economic principles, its effects on social policies have become more important. Differences in social security provision and employment protection measures may affect labour costs; a generous welfare state may, therefore, place a country at a competitive disadvantage. For similar reasons, health and safety regulations are supposed to be equalised across countries within the European Union to prevent unfair competition. The emphasis has moved from harmonisation of social protection policies towards some degree of policy convergence (Hantrais, 1995: Chapter 2), and this has occurred particularly since the aim of establishing a single market has taken higher priority (Gold and Mayes, 1993).

So far, the main effects of European Union law on the UK has been through the implementation of equal treatment regulations and directives designed to equalise the treatment of men and women. Pensions have been particularly affected. Luckhaus and Moffat (1996) have documented various changes that have both improved and worsened pensions policy from the point of view of those directly affected. Changes include the equalisation of state pension ages between men and women, the extension of occupational pension membership to part-time workers, and improved rights for those moving between countries when working or choosing to settle in another country after retirement. From a UK perspective, the possibilities of convergence give greater emphasis to simply learning what systems apply in the rest of

Europe. As a result, the DSS has funded various (largely descriptive) studies of differences in social security provision, some of which are summarised below.

Results from comparative and related studies

In this section, we consider the different types of comparative study that may be carried out. Various attempts have been made to classify different types of comparative study (Rose, 1991; Hauser, 1993; Bradshaw, 1994), although none seems to have found widespread application. One of the criteria that may be used to classify research studies is whether the investigation is designed to look at particular policies or instead at the outcomes of those policies. To give an example, one could examine the different rules and administration of social assistance benefits in a range of countries (*policy*) or instead look at how many people are in poverty in each country (*outcome*). There is likely to be *some* relationship between the two, but they represent rather different studies: a country might have a very 'good' benefits system but have to deal with marked inequality of earned incomes. Alternatively, a country with a high level of employment might have few poor people despite having a rather rudimentary system of social assistance. Some research projects may seek specifically to link outcomes with policy.

In addition to the difference between outcomes and policies, one might be interested in looking either at whole systems or at particular 'parts' of systems. Some noted authors have attempted to classify whole countries on the basis of their 'welfare regime'. A less ambitious approach would mean looking at, for example, just the system of support for income among old-age pensioners.

We use these rather *ad hoc* two elements to help analyse studies under five headings:

- Studies seeking to chart the development of welfare as a response to industrialisation and other historical forces
- Classifications of the mix of benefits in different countries
- Research based upon whole countries or designed to identify particular welfare regimes
- Studies of the different policies within particular elements of social security

● Studies concerned with particular outcomes of relevance to social
   security policy.

Historical-comparative studies

In different parts of this chapter, we examine the degree of diversity and
similarity between different welfare states. Different countries appear to
spend (very) broadly similar amounts on social security and often seek
to insure people against the same sorts of risk. One of the questions
asked by various commentators is how far the development of the
welfare state responds to some universal economic and modernising
trends, and how far individual countries are able to follow different
paths dictated by their history, institutions and political systems.

The development of Western Europe and North America has
involved a number of common features. People have moved from agri-
culture to manufacturing and then services, and have in the process
become more likely to live in urban communities. Mass production has
helped to ensure high standards of living. Is it likely that these features
imply common concerns that might be addressed by common welfare
systems (Hill, 1996: 18–24)? For Marshall (1950), the development is
of one of social rights, following the earlier development of civil and
then political rights.

Investigators who stress commonalities may be found in both func-
tionalist (Wilensky, 1975) and critical (Gough, 1979) perspectives, and it
is difficult not to attribute a major role in the development of welfare
states to the process of industrialisation. This created forms of wage and
interpersonal dependence not seen in a stable agricultural context.
Greater insecurity could have led to pressure for the forms of risk-
sharing inherent in social insurance systems. Alternatively, rulers may
need such a system to ensure that workers do not become a revolutionary
force (also see Offe, 1984). Once one country has developed a working
social security system, irrespective of any 'underlying logic' a process of
copying could ensure the diffusion of welfare state ideas and practice.

Determinism, however, is an unpopular academic stance. A compro-
mise viewpoint has been put forward by Heidenheimer *et al.* (1990:
224), who suggest that:

> Industrialization, and its accompanying social changes, set in motion the neces-
> sary preconditions for contemporary income maintenance policies. However the
> timing and content of those policies remain heavily influenced by political
> processes.

There is not the space to consider these arguments in any great detail, and there remain unanswered questions. For example, why did the emergence of welfare states, principally a twentieth-century phenomenon, take so long after most of industrialisation had taken place? The argument also turns, in part, on the degree of difference that people recognise in existing welfare state systems and how far those differences are more real or apparent.

Comparisons of benefits in different countries

One means of locating the UK system in a comparative context is to show differences in the coverage of different benefits, using the typology of different benefits from Chapter 4. Table 2.1 is one attempt to illustrate some of the ways in which different countries provide social security benefits. The last row of the table concerns significant benefits provided by the private sector, particularly by employers.

Table 2.1   International comparisons of the mix of different types of benefit

Benefit type	Britain	Denmark	Germany	USA
Contingent	Children Disability	Children ⌀ Pension Sickness Maternity	Children	
Contributory or social insurance	⌀Pension Unemployment Invalidity	Unemployment	Unemployment ⌀Pension Maternity	Old age Sickness Disability Unemployment
Means-tested or social assistance	Income support Family credit	Social assistance	Social assistance	TANF (children) Supplemental social security
Private or occupational	⌀ Pension Sickness Maternity		⌀ Pension Sickness	⌀Pension Sickness Maternity

TANF = Temporary Assistance for Needy Families

Source: Commission on Social Justice Paper No. 2 (IPPR 1993:17)

This table shows that different countries have different mixes of benefits, and, in fact, the non-UK countries shown have been selected as exemplars of different types of system (as we discuss in the next section). In Denmark, means-testing and contributory benefits play a minor role. Most of the important benefits are based on various contingencies, and there is very little role played by the private sector. In Germany, in contrast, the system is largely based on the insurance principle. In both countries, however, there is a 'safety net' benefit that provides income to those who would otherwise have none. This safety net feature is common to the majority of European Union countries (exceptions being described below). In the USA, and indeed also the UK, social assistance is often the first port of call rather than being the last resort as is true in continental Europe.

In the USA, it is means-tested benefits (or 'welfare') that provide most assistance to low-income families with children. The main benefit – Temporary Assistance for Needy Families (TANF) – goes overwhelmingly to lone parents, and couples were in the past almost completely excluded from eligibility. There is no system of universal benefits for children of the types commonly found in Europe. In the USA, a contributory system (known as 'social security') is available to provide for retirement, and insurance benefits also cover disability and short-term unemployment.

It might be worth speculating about some of the reasons for these differences. While more rigorous analysis is possible (see below), there are clear differences between the individualist and collectivist traditions in some of these countries. It should come as no surprise to see a large role for the private sector in the USA, for example. Scandinavian countries have tended to be rather more positive about the role that the state may play.

The above table looks at each country in turn. In beginning the study of comparative social security, it is often helpful to look at specific studies or summaries of the situation in different countries. Such information is quite readily available (examples include Bryson, 1992: Chapter 3; Spicker, 1993: Chapter 9; Eardley *et al.*, 1996a). The next step is, arguably, to attempt to classify the systems of different countries into various types. There are various ways of trying to classify the systems of different countries into groups. These rely on a mixture of theoretical and empirical insights, and are discussed within this chapter. Such classifications may be helpful in seeking to understand the system of any given country – if the categories are well designed, we may learn something about each country from knowledge of the group to which it belongs (Mitchell, 1991). A relatively simple division of the systems of different countries has been proposed by the European Commission (1995: 34). It divides the then 15 members of the European Union into four 'geo-social' clusters:

- *Scandinavia*, where there is universal coverage seen as a citizen's right, and most financing is through general taxation.
- *The UK and Ireland*, which have universal coverage but with benefits at much lower cash levels than in Scandinavia. Insurance contributions also play an important role in the entitlement to benefits.
- The 'Bismarckian' systems, of *Germany, France, Austria, Belgium, the Netherlands and Luxembourg*, which have benefits based on a strong insurance principle, often with different rules for different occupations. Social assistance plugs any gaps in insured coverage.
- *Italy, Spain, Portugal and Greece*, where there is some evidence of 'Bismarckian' schemes, including generous pension schemes, but no minimum income schemes and large gaps in scheme coverage.

Not surprisingly, spending on social security therefore varies in importance across different countries (see Figure 2.1, which also includes public spending on health systems). It is worth noting that, although British governments often draw attention to the large scale of spending on social security (around £100 billion), this is, when expressed as a proportion of Gross Domestic Product (GDP), below that typically found in other countries of the European Union.

Social protection spending increased in importance in most countries in the 1980s. Spending on health and social security was more than one-quarter of GDP in 8 of the 19 countries shown above. Spending was lowest in Japan, the USA and Australia.

Studies of 'whole systems'

Perhaps the most ambitious comparative studies are those which attempt to look at entire welfare systems, which often means looking wider than simply social security systems. It is common to identify an important difference in the way in which different social security systems have developed, particularly in terms of the coverage and financing of social security systems. Many European countries bear the

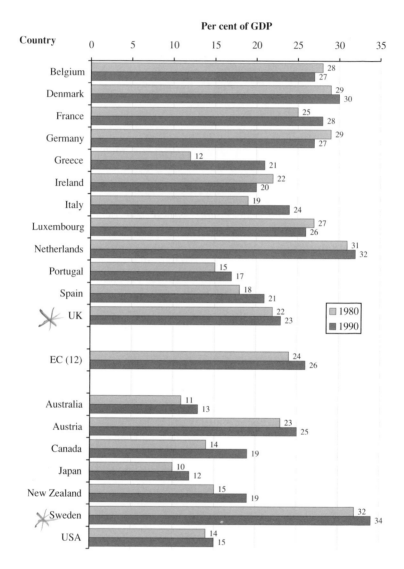

Per cent of GDP

Figure 2.1 Social protection expenditure as a percentage of Gross Domestic Product (Department of Social Security, 1993a)

hallmarks of whether their lines of development are based on the ideas and approaches of either Bismarck (the German Chancellor in the late nineteenth century) or Beveridge (a liberal writer in Britain in the early and mid-twentieth century). The '*Bismarckian*' model, or 'welfare regime', relies heavily on social insurance. Contributions and benefits are linked to earnings, and there are often separate schemes for different groups of employees in different occupations. The '*Beveridgean*' model is based on flat-rate benefits and is universal across all groups in society. Benefits are often met from tax revenue.

Neither system is found in such a pure form, but many systems lean towards one rather than the other. The former model dominated in continental Europe. It has broadened out to embrace more universal coverage (such as for family allowances and to reduce gaps in coverage) and reduced the degree of occupational differentiation between social insurance systems. Social assistance schemes, not based on contributions, do play a small role but involve a higher degree of discretion and often function rather separately from the social insurance schemes.

The universalist Beveridge model is common to Britain and Scandinavia, although its subsequent development has been rather different in the two places. In Scandinavia, the universalist emphasis has become bound up with notions of citizenship and rights. Earnings-related supplements to many benefits have also developed. In the English-speaking countries, earnings-related benefits are rare or are instead left to the private sector to provide. Universality is tempered by a much greater degree of means-testing than elsewhere. It is 'need', rather than citizenship, that provides a strong motive for social security.

Elements of this view are articulated and built upon in Esping-Andersen's (1990) analysis of welfare state regimes, perhaps the most influential study seeking to classify welfare states into different types. In a study of 18 countries, he describes three clusters of welfare regime type, which he distinguishes by 'the quality of social rights, social stratification, and the relationship between state, market, and family' (1990: 29).

The first cluster he terms the *liberal welfare state* (1990: 26–7):

> in which means-tested assistance, modest universal transfers, or modest social insurance plans predominate... entitlement rules are therefore strict and often associated with stigma... the state encourages the market, either passively – by guaranteeing only a minimum – or actively – by subsidising private welfare schemes.

The best examples of this model, he states, are the USA, Canada and Australia. Later, he puts the UK into this category. The second regime type Esping-Andersen identifies as conservative or strongly corporatist. These states do not share the concerns with market efficiency that are common in liberal welfare states. The regimes show the influence of the Church, and there are strong pressures to preserve a particular model of family life. Their main social security systems are based on social insurance:

> What predominated was the preservation of status differentials; rights, therefore, were attached to class and status... a state edifice perfectly ready to displace the market as a provider of welfare... the state will only interfere when the family's capacity to service its members is exhausted. (1990: 27)

The countries chosen as an illustration are Austria, France, Germany and Italy. The third type of welfare regime is the social democratic:

> a welfare state that would promote an equality of the highest standards, not an equality of minimal needs... all strata are incorporated under one universal insurance system, yet benefits are graduated according to accustomed earnings. This model crowds out the market... The principle is not to wait until the family's capacity to aid is exhausted, but to preemptively socialise the costs of family-hood. (1990: 27–8)

Social democratic states, or their nearest representation, are to be found in Scandinavia. They also rely on achieving high levels of employment, which the state attempts to guarantee.

There have been other attempts to classify welfare states, or philosophies of social policy, both before and after Esping-Andersen. Titmuss (1974: 30–1) also made a division that was based essentially on the extent to which welfare policy was distanced from the market. He identified a 'residual model' (in which social security operated temporarily should the market or family fail); an 'industrial achievement-performance model' (in which social security was linked to merit in the form of work performance); and an 'institutional redistributive model' (where the welfare state operated mostly outside the private market). The first group was characteristic of the USA, the UK was a mix of the first two, and Scandinavian countries were of the last type.

A later work by Furniss and Tilton (1977) identified three types of welfare state, again based on how the state dealt with problems that arose from the operation of the free market. The 'positive state' was concerned to minimise work disincentives, the 'social security state' went beyond this to guarantee a minimum level of support, whereas 'social welfare states' put social goals before economic goals through the state.

Kvist and Ploug argue more simply. They claim that 'there are three bases for the provision of social security: need, merit and citizenship' (1996: 7). Systems based on need pay benefits to a poor minority and require means tests. Systems based on merit incorporate wage-earners. An approach based on citizenship does not have such a selective base but instead covers the whole population (and probably adopts a tax-financed, flat-rate approach to benefits). How far this approach may be generalised to entire welfare states, rather than simply individual benefits, remains unclear.

A criticism of each of these classifications, although not the four-fold division proposed by the European Commission (1995) and listed above, is that they tend to leave out the 'Latin rim' of Southern European countries (Leibfried, 1993), who do, nevertheless, show elements found in each type of system. There have also been criticisms about the particular allocation of countries to the three clusters (Mitchell, 1991; Sainsbury, 1996). Thus the UK sits rather unconvincingly with the highly residual USA, and Australia may form a rather different type of welfare state or even regime (Mitchell, 1991). However, it should also be recognised that such a classification will always create 'border problems', where some countries fit the welfare regime rather well, while others appear to incorporate elements from more than one system and are thus difficult to position correctly. Experts on any one country are bound to see differences between it and one of the overall models.

A more fundamental (feminist) criticism has been put forward which has argued that Esping-Andersen's approach (and by implication that of other authors) has focused so heavily on the conditions affecting paid work, and the operation of the employment market, that the role of women in conducting unpaid work in the home has been ignored (Lewis, 1992). Lewis has argued that a division of welfare states focusing on the extent to which the 'family wage' and male breadwinner model predominates would produce an alternative clustering of countries.

Specific elements of social security systems

Some studies have looked at particular policies in a range of countries. Recent research that has included work on a range of countries includes that on:

- Housing allowances (Kemp, 1997)
- Benefits for children (Bradshaw *et al.*, 1993)
- Social assistance (Eardley *et al.*, 1996b)
- The treatment of carers (Glendinning and McLaughlin, 1993)
- The delivery of social security benefits (Bolderson and Mabbett, 1997)
- Benefits for the unemployed (Morris, with Llewellyn, 1991; Kvist and Ploug, 1996)
- Policies to assist disabled people in returning to work (Thornton *et al.*, 1997).

These studies have varied considerably in the range of countries surveyed, the methods used and the extent to which the research has sought to apply an analytical framework to the analysis and data collection. The main findings from these and other studies are reported in Chapters 5 and 6, where benefits for particular groups are discussed. However, it is worth describing some of the main methods used in some of these studies. We also summarise some results concerning social assistance schemes across a range of countries.

The two studies coordinated at York University (Bradshaw *et al.*, 1993; Eardley *et al.*, 1996b) used very similar methods, followed to some extent by Kemp (1997). These studies aimed to collect information about the different forms of benefit (and other forms of support) available in each of a wide range of countries. Naturally, a great deal of interest has been expressed in their conclusions about the relative generosity of different countries. The studies were based on creating a number of 'model families' whose entitlement to benefits could be calculated by experts in each of the countries included in the study. These model families were chosen by the researchers to reflect diverse characteristics.

The earlier study discussed the reason for this choice of method. Approaches based on administrative data on total spending were rejected, largely because of the difficulty of making comparisons with existing national accounts and the problems of valuing (non-cash) services. A second method would have been to look at the forms of benefit received by actual families. This was rejected for similar reasons – a lack of available data and the problems of valuing non-cash assistance.

There are several disadvantages, however, of looking at results based on hypothetical families. The first is that they describe the system as it 'should' be rather than as it actually works. Some countries may have provision that is available but rarely used, and which may, therefore, give a misleading picture of provision when the support for 'model' families is calculated. A second limitation concerns the choice of hypothetical examples. No set of choices can be representative across the countries in the study. Some countries may also seek to favour particular family types, which may not be adequately captured in the range of model families selected in the research. These studies provide a detailed description of the types of benefit available in each country. In some cases, they also incorporate differences in the level of services provided and variations in treatment by the tax system. Having collected such data, it then becomes possible to begin to put the countries into various groups or to theorise about links between benefit provision and the social, economic and political differences between countries.

The study of social assistance found huge diversity in its importance across different countries. In some countries, all or most benefits could, under the definition used (which was close to means-testing), be described as social assistance. Elsewhere, social assistance was a trivial component of the benefit system. The study recorded that 100 per cent of benefit-spending in New Zealand was in the form of social assistance, compared with 33 per cent in the UK, 12 per cent in Germany and 5 per cent in Austria (Eardley *et al.*, 1996b: 166; Figure 2.2). It is remarkable that the English-speaking countries (except bilingual Canada) dominate the list of countries spending the largest proportion of social security benefit through means-tested social assistance. Compared with Britain, spending on means-tested benefits is rather higher in Ireland and the USA, and much higher in Australia and New Zealand. Aside from this group, spending on social assistance, as a proportion of all social security spending, is much lower in Canada than in the UK, and even lower in the remainder of OECD countries.

The differences in the proportion of the population receiving means-tested benefits were just as pronounced and tended to follow the pattern above. Figure 2.3 shows the varying proportions covered by social assistance in 1992. This figure also indicates the different levels of low income found in these countries.

Across the 24 countries studied, levels of benefit for a couple with two children in the UK were 15th highest before housing costs and 8th after housing costs. Among the other features of social assistance investigated in detail were administrative aspects, groups included and excluded from support, the treatment of housing costs, meeting exceptional needs, non-take-up, work incentives and adequacy.

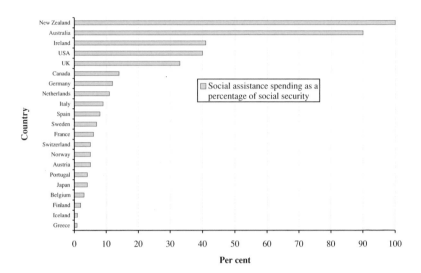

Figure 2.2   Social assistance spending relative to social security
(Eardley *et al.*, 1996b: Table 8.1)

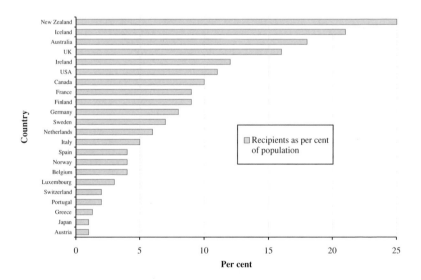

Figure 2.3   Social assistance recipients as a proportion of the total
population, 1992 (Eardley *et al.*, 1996b: Table 8.1)

The researchers classified the systems they found in two different ways. First, countries were placed by reference to the two dimensions of the extent of coverage of benefits (high and low) and the level of benefit actually paid. Thus, Australia had wide coverage and high benefits, the UK wide coverage and low benefits, Southern Europe low coverage and low benefits and so on. The authors suggested that seven different types of system could be identified. However, they did not aim to *explain* the types of variation that they found.

The study of support for children, which covered 15 countries, tried to relate the amount of benefit paid to families with the demographic, social, political and economic characteristics of the countries included. A range of possible hypotheses was suggested – perhaps left-of-centre governments would pay more generous benefits, or countries with low fertility would pay higher benefits to encourage people to have children. This analysis was not particularly successful in identifying the level of the package paid to children, although the number of countries included makes a detailed analysis of this type rather difficult.

The results collected by this study were very detailed and hard to summarise. It is possible to look at different types of family and people on different levels of earning. The results may also be presented in various ways – are we interested in the amounts of money paid to families, or the amounts over and above those paid to people without children? If the latter, should we look at money amounts or the percentage increase in income? In Figure 2.4, results are based on a couple with two children with the man on average earnings, and before housing costs. The presence of the UK around the middle of these countries in terms of level of generosity is confirmed across different types of family and levels of earning. The UK does slightly 'better' if comparisons are made after housing costs because it is unusual in sometimes meeting 100 per cent of people's housing costs (see Chapter 6).

Studies of particular outcomes

Instead of looking at the characteristics of social security benefits, we could instead examine outcomes of particular interest to social security policy. Researchers and others have traditionally been particularly concerned with the extent of poverty. Two key questions are how far poverty varies across different countries, and what role social security plays in affecting the level of poverty. In recent years, there has also been interest in the role that benefits may play in affecting incentives to

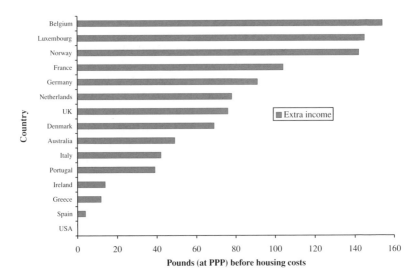

PPP = Purchasing Power Parity, a type of exchange rate between currencies adjusting for differences in the cost of living in each country

Figure 2.4   Additional disposable income of a couple with two children over a childless couple (at average male earnings) (Bradshaw *et al.*, 1993: 60)

work among populations highly reliant on social security benefits, particularly lone parents (Perry, 1993).

Studies of income distribution or poverty in different countries require detailed financial data on large samples collected in each country. The main database that has been assembled to fill this role is the Luxembourg Income Study, which has been used on several occasions to investigate poverty and the effects of state transfers (Mitchell, 1991; Atkinson *et al.*, 1995; Bradshaw and Chen, 1997). Studies have also been based on standard definitions, even if the data sets used in each country have not been fully comparable.

Studies of poverty must deal with a range of conceptual questions. The analyst must then solve a range of research problems, including:

● Should the analysis be based on income or spending?
● Should income be taken for individuals, families or households?
● How should households of different sizes be treated?
● What time period should be used for income?

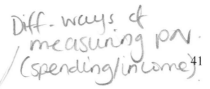

Diff. ways of measuring pov. (spending/income)

The answers to these questions will depend on what data are available and the motives for calculating the number with low resources. European poverty studies have typically identified as poor those with household *spending* less than half of the national average. Improved sources of data should enable newer estimates to be based instead on income. Eurostat (1994) has provided figures for the late 1980s.

The poverty definition used was specific to each country – the poor in, for example, Germany, would not all be counted as poor in Portugal, and some of the non-poor in Greece might be poor in Denmark. It, therefore, indicates people's position compared with that of people around them rather than across Europe as a whole.

On the basis of these figures, poverty was lowest in Denmark (3.9 per cent of people), Belgium (7.4 per cent) and the Netherlands (4.8 per cent), and highest in Portugal (24.5 per cent), Italy (21.1 per cent) and Greece (18.7 per cent). The figures for the different countries varied a great deal. The UK had more poor children than might have been expected.

A study by Bradshaw and Chen (1997) was able to use the third stage of the Luxembourg Income Study to calculate the proportion of people with below half of the average income in the participating countries. The third stage of the Luxembourg Income Study relates to a year of data from around 1990. This data set provides a rather different approach from that of Eurostat because spending tends to be more equally distributed than income. Some of their results are illustrated in Figure 2.5.

The figure shows the proportion of people on a low income both before and after government transfers comprising taxes and social security benefits. One of the main effects of government transfers is to reduce the proportion of people on a low income, although the extent to which this happens varies across the countries. Overall, the proportion on a low income is actually quite consistent across the countries, figures between 30 and 40 per cent being very common. However, the picture after transfers have taken place is much more varied. Living on a low income is almost eliminated in the Czech Republic and in Spain. In contrast, the effect of state transfers is rather small in Russia, and also in Taiwan, which has among the lowest number in poverty before government intervention. The UK appears close to the foot of the figure, representing, according to the authors of the analysis, 'reason for dismay' (Bradshaw and Chen, 1997: 17).

These results for the UK, based on different methods, are not entirely consistent. If we use spending as our yardstick, the UK's level of

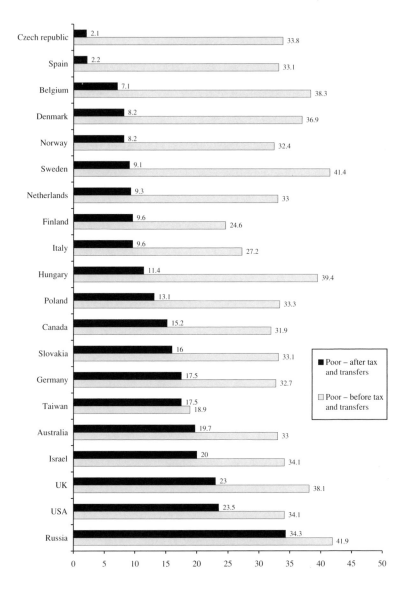

Figure 2.5   Low incomes pre- and post-transfer, and direct tax
(Bradshaw and Chen's 1997 analysis of the third wave of the
Luxembourg Income Study)

poverty appears comparable to that of many other European countries. If we use income, the UK seems to sink towards the bottom of the international poverty league. Does this tell us much about the efficiency of social security? Hausman (1993), using different data, has found, perhaps surprisingly, that the social security systems of each country perform similar roles in reducing the extent of poverty. We are clearly still some way from the definitive comparative study of poverty and the effectiveness of social security policy in reducing the prevalence of low incomes.

3

The Historical Context

Introduction

Some people have a fascination for history for its own sake – they are simply interested in how things were in the past. But history is also important in enabling us to understand the present. This is particularly true in relation to the social security system. If policy-makers today could begin with a blank sheet of paper and design a social security system to meet current social and economic needs, it is unlikely that their newly designed system would resemble the one we have today. Attempts are made, of course, to update the system and adapt it to social and economic change, but the system generally lags behind such change because major reforms affect the lives of virtually all citizens – because they are either benefit recipients or tax-payers (or both). Such major reforms are thus rare except in unusual circumstances such as the aftermath of the Second World War. The system we have is, therefore, heavily based, and inevitably so, on the structures and assumptions inherited from the past.

The aim of this chapter is to increase our understanding of the current social security system by placing it in its historical context. As always with such a task, it is difficult to know how far back in history to explore. This chapter starts at the beginning of the seventeenth century with the Elizabethan Poor Law and traces the impact of industrialisation on the system of welfare, but the main roots of our current system can be found in developments during the twentieth century – with the reforms of the Liberal governments at the very beginning and then the reforms of the Labour government in the middle of the century. The lack of major reform since the 1940s suggests that the system is ripe for an overhaul, given the substantial social and economic change that has occurred between then and now. The Labour government, elected in 1997, has certainly talked about the need for major reform, for example with its 1998 Green Paper (Department of

Social Security, 1998c), but whether such rhetoric turns into reality is, at the time of writing this book, yet to be seen.

The Poor Law and industrialisation

The Elizabethan Poor Law

The development of social welfare is closely linked to changes in the economy and society. For example, the long and complex transition from feudalism to capitalism led to important shifts in the economic and social obligations between the rich and poor. As a result of these shifts, and in fear of social disorder following a series of bad harvests, the Elizabethan Poor Relief Act was introduced in 1601. Fraser (1973) has argued that this Act, and the policies behind it, 'abandoned mere repression in favour of a logical solution soundly administered'. Under this Act, relief for the poor was provided by the local parish with the Justice of the Peace (JP) as the prime figure in its administration. The main principle underlying the Act was local relief, administered and funded locally for local people. Another important principle was the *liability of dependants*, which meant that parents were responsible for the well-being of their children and vice versa. The underlying aim of the Act was to provide a minimum level of poor relief to prevent social unrest.

Geographical mobility in the seventeenth century meant that some poor people moved from poor parishes to rich parishes and sometimes sought to claim relief in their new location. To deal with this perceived problem – of people taking advantage of more generous treatment in richer areas – the Act of Settlement was passed in 1662. This Act gave JPs the right to return people to their original parish (the parish of their birth, marriage or apprenticeship) within 40 days of their arrival in a new parish if the JP believed that the migrant might become a 'burden' on the parish at a later date. In practice, however, the law did little to prevent social mobility from rural to urban areas in the eighteenth century.

At the end of the eighteenth century, bad harvests led to fears that a revolution similar to the recent one in France might be repeated this side of the channel. Partly as a response to these fears, Berkshire JPs in Speenhamland in 1795 decided to supplement the wages of poor labourers to ensure that they could afford to buy bread in an inflationary economic environment. The 'Speenhamland System' was, however, relatively short lived and localised. Critics argued that it kept wages artificially low because employers knew that wages would be increased by other means. Similar criticisms are levied today against wage-supplementation schemes, in particular that they subsidise bad employers at the expense of firms paying higher wages. At the time of the Speenhamland System, there were also difficulties in funding such a scheme, given large downward pressures on wages and high price inflation.

By 1830, there were 14 million people in England, living within 15,000 parishes. The growth of industrialisation had begun to transform the country from an agrarian society to an urban one, with migration occurring from the countryside to the towns. Although the prevailing political philosophy of *laissez-faire* made governments wary of interfering in social and economic development, memories of the French Revolution and concern about widespread agitation for the right to vote led the British élite to consider how they might keep control of the masses. Thus, social reform was often motivated more through fear of the crowd than any purely paternalistic desire to improve their situation. Expenditure on poor relief began to increase after the financial crisis of 1826, reaching £7 million in 1831 – or 10 shillings per head (Fraser, 1973). Despite this expense, however, the Swing riots of 1830 had demonstrated that the Poor Law failed to relieve distress and prevent unrest.

The Poor Law Amendment Act

In 1832, the Royal Commission for Inquiring into the Administration and Practical Operation of the Poor Laws was set up. The Commission's 13,000 page report found that the principle of local help for local people was inadequate because of the concentration of poverty – poor parishes had large numbers of poor people so could not afford to look after them. Poverty and destitution led to discontent in the new urban areas. Following this report, the Poor Law Amendment Act of 1834 was introduced. This Act incorporated three main principles, as shown in Box 3.1. Those responsible for the Act hoped that people seeking help would be regarded as moral failures, thus employing shame and stigma to deter people from applying for help. In many ways, the Act was an attempt to maintain the basic principles of the Elizabethan Poor Law, while modifying the system in the light of economic and social change.

As well as facing shame and stigma, those who entered the workhouse were often separated from their families because men, women and children were usually divided. The worst effects of the Poor Law Amendment Act may have been lessened by the fact that some parishes could not afford to build workhouses so maintained more outdoor relief than in other areas. The experience of the Poor Law therefore varied by locality (Rose, 1972).

The Act appeared at first to be successful in cutting costs – in the mid-1840s, poor rates fell nationally to about £5 million compared with £7 million in 1826 (Fraser, 1973), but these low rates probably owed as much to good harvests and a high demand for labour on the newly emerging railway system. Indeed, the measures in the Act proved ineffective in the light of serious economic distress in the middle of the ninteenth century. Additional Poor Law Amendment Acts in 1847, 1848 and 1871 reformed the system still further. The last of these provided for the unification of the administration of the Poor Law under local government boards.

The Poor Law is often criticised for causing humiliation, degradation and stigmatisation to those who sought assistance. Such criticisms are understandable in light of a twentieth-century system that has moved towards claimants' rights, but, at the time of its implementation, the Poor Law provided some relief for those suffering the worst consequences of industrialisation. Rather than being too harsh, perhaps the system can be criticised for being too helpful and thus maintaining the inequalities of a newly emerging capitalist state rather than leading to revolution or radical reforms of the system.

Box 3.1

Poor Law Amendment Act 1834

Basic Principles

Less eligibility – those who received help from the Poor Law had to be worse off than the lowest-paid labourer. A *workhouse test* was applied (to see if people were prepared to move into workhouses), and outdoor relief (help given outside the workhouse) was abolished for non-disabled people

Deterrence – conditions within the workhouse were harsh, and this was intended to act as a deterrent to those who might otherwise seek help

Central administrative control – three Commissioners were appointed, along with a number of inspectors. Money was still collected locally, but services were administered centrally with the help of the inspectors.

During the nineteenth century, it was widely thought that people without paid work were either idle or unwilling to sell their labour. Hill (1990) states that the concept of 'unemployment' was meaningless to the founders of the Poor Law in 1834 as it only entered into political vocabulary in the late nineteenth century. By this time, regular fluctuations in the business cycle led to cyclical unemployment and also to an understanding that unemployment could not be seen as (merely) the result of individual idleness. As we shall see, this increasing understanding of economic processes was partly responsible for changes in poor relief in the early part of the twentieth century.

The role of voluntary and charitable help

The late eighteenth century saw a rapid growth in voluntary and charitable help. For example, the Charity Organisation Society for the Relief of Mendicity and Prevention of Crime coordinated much charitable help while keeping careful records about applicants, which it divided into 'deserving' and 'undeserving'.

Alongside charities, a variety of voluntary and self-help groups sprang up, including friendly societies, building societies and trade unions. These aimed to work for the collective good of the individuals (usually all men) who belonged to them. Many of these groups were dominated by the newly emerging 'respectable' working class, who were skilled manual workers with a culture of hard work and thrift. Located within the working class but with some economic power at their disposal (primarily through their unions), this group provided a potential threat to the middle- and upper-class élite. However, with their aspirations to a better (or more middle-class) life, skilled workers also provided a means by which the élite could divide and rule the poor. Policies that were relatively inexpensive and might incorporate the 'respectable working class', such as state-run insurance-based benefits, were, therefore, most likely to be introduced, and such schemes could also build on the existing voluntary insurance schemes. Thane (1982) has estimated that about six million people were covered by voluntary insurance schemes in 1904. Policies towards the urban masses were seen as less urgent as long as voluntary and charitable help could keep this poorer and politically weak group relatively quiet.

Social research

The development of social security in Britain has been influenced by the findings of social research since the late nineteenth century. At this time, pioneering social researchers began to investigate the extent and causes of poverty. In 1886, Charles Booth estimated that about one-third of those in the East End of London were living in poverty (Booth, 1889). He found that unemployment was the major cause of poverty but that low-paid work was also an important factor.

Another pioneering study was carried out in York in 1899 by Seebohm Rowntree. Rowntree (1901) made a distinction between *primary poverty* – where income was inadequate for the basic necessities of life – and *secondary poverty* – where income was adequate to meet basic needs but deprivation was caused because some money was being spent on non-essential items. Rowntree found that about 10 per cent of the population in York were experiencing primary poverty and a further 18 per cent secondary poverty. In his study, low pay was found to be a more important cause of poverty than unemployment.

Social research into poverty in the late nineteenth century was used to argue that poverty was not necessarily a result of fecklessness but of conditions outside the control of the individual. Furthermore, poverty could not be tackled on a small scale or at a local level but needed much greater attention and central state administration.

Early twentieth-century reforms

At the very end of the nineteenth century, the Boer War highlighted the poor health of the nation's men. In 1899, 8,000 of the 12,000 volunteers were rejected, and only 1,200 were considered fully fit (Smith, 1972). For a nation that prided itself on its military strength, such weakness in its potential reserves caused great concern, and a Parliamentary Select Committee was set up to investigate the matter. The committee pointed to the extent of poverty, deprivation, malnutrition and ill-health among a large section of the population, and its report contributed to calls for social reform.

The Royal Commission on the Poor Laws

From 1905–9, the Royal Commission on the Poor Laws and the Relief of Distress looked into ways of relieving poverty from unemployment. Two reports emanated from this Commission. The Majority Report was produced by supporters of the Poor Law, who argued that the Poor Law should be retained but that greater use should be made of charities, together with specialised public institutions for children, older people and sick or disabled people. The Poor Law supporters wished to retain the original principles of the Poor Law while improving some of its administrative machinery by passing on responsibility to county councils and county borough councils, which had been introduced 20 years before. They also argued for renaming the Poor Law 'public assistance'.

The Minority Report was produced by those such as Beatrice Webb and Charles Booth who wished to see the Poor Law abolished. They argued that there should be a move away from stigmatising the poor in favour of an emphasis on *preventing* poverty. More specifically, they called for the abolition of the Poor Law in favour of a number of specific reforms such as the improved care of children (including the provision of childcare services) and the protection of adults from the risks of poverty that would result from sickness, disablement and unemployment. Both the Majority and Minority Reports agreed that public labour exchanges should be set up to reduce unemployment.

Although no radical changes were implemented immediately following the Commission's reports, many of the ideas, particularly those in the Minority Report, influenced the reforms of the Liberal government before the First World War and formed the basis for later changes in the social security system.

Reforms of the Liberal governments from 1906

The Liberal government elected in 1906 introduced a number of important measures that formed the foundations on which Beveridge then constructed the main social security system of the twentieth century. In 1908, the Old Age Pensions Act was the first *non*-contributory pensions Act. Pensions were available to those over 70 years of age who were on low incomes and had not been in prison during the previous 10 years. Thane (1982) states that the pension was designed for 'the very poor, the very respectable and the very old'. The use of a simple means test to measure eligibility to a pension signalled a move away from the pure discretion of the Poor Law towards more rational ways of measuring entitlement. Thus, we see the start of people having rights to benefits. However, we also see the continuing theme of concern over cost – which led to the introduction of a pension age of 70 rather than 65.

In 1909, Labour Exchanges were established under the Board of Trade, replacing the 61 private Labour Exchanges that had previously existed. By 1913, there were 430 Labour Exchanges throughout the country (Smith, 1972). Also in 1909, Trade Boards were established to ensure that certain minimum wage levels applied to particular trades, for example the largely non-unionised 'sweated' industries in which many women worked. These were regarded as essential to ensure that bad employers did not drive out good employers, and they were the forerunner of Wages Councils, which existed in particular industries until very recently.

One of the major and most innovative reforms was the National Insurance Act of 1911. This reform covered health insurance as well as unemployment insurance. Unemployment insurance was based on the premise that individuals would pay premiums when they were young and then draw out benefits when they were older. It was also assumed that unemployment would be relatively rare. This was the first time that the insurance principle had been introduced in the state system in Britain. It was similar in some respects to the German system, which had insurance schemes against sickness, accident and old age based on contributions from employer, employee and the state. However, it was also leaning heavily on British traditions of self-help and self-provision.

Contributions were made in the form of stamps that were bought every week and stuck on to a card as a record of payments made. This system survived for decades but was replaced in the 1970s by a system of direct debits paid by employers from their employees' gross income. Nevertheless, the idea of stamps is still prominent in many people's minds, and the terminology remains today even if the practice has long since disappeared. The emphasis on contributions shows that the system built heavily on the principles of voluntary insurance schemes, so it can be viewed as a form of state support for self-help. Alongside the contributions of employees, employers also made contributions to the system. This made the system very popular, and it was charac-terised by the slogan '9d for 4d', which meant that for every 4 old pence contributed by the employee, the employer would add another 5 old pence, making 9 old pence in total.

The scheme was initially confined to three trades – ship-building, engineering and building – as these were thought to be particularly vulnerable to fluctuations in the business cycle. Partly as a result of confining the scheme to a limited number of trades (mostly those employing men), Gilbert (1966) has estimated that only 2.25 million workers in seven industries were covered initially. This was in sharp contrast to the more widespread membership of voluntary schemes (which covered 8 million people in 1904 according to Thane, 1982). The 1911 Act also provided for insurance against sickness that was also based on contributions but covered manual workers in all industries.

The introduction of National Insurance for workers in mainly skilled manual industries demonstrates once again the desire of the state to win over the support of the most respectable working classes. As Gilbert (1970) argued: 'National insurance was the Liberal response to the threat of socialism.'

The inter-war years

The end of the First World War brought increasing calls for welfare reform as the returning soldiers made demands for some reward for their sacrifices and those of their lost comrades-in-arms. Once again, the British government was prompted to carry out social reform to stave off revolution (this time it was the spectre of the Russian rather than the French Revolution that frightened the middle and upper classes). A new benefit, labelled the 'dole', was brought in to provide temporary help to ex-servicemen who were looking for work. Unemployment cover was then extended to all workers in 1920. Rising unemployment in the early 1920s led the government to find ways of curtailing expenditure, so several measures to 'control' the unemployed, such as checking that they were genuinely seeking a job, were introduced (Deacon, 1976).

In 1925, the Widows, Orphans and Old Age Contributory Pensions Act extended the benefits of the 1911 National Insurance Act to widows and orphans. This Act also extended the contributory principle to old-age pensions. By 1937, a large proportion of the population was covered by National Insurance (Smith, 1972).

The shadow of the workhouse still haunted many, but various progressive social movements tried to reduce its role. In east London, the Poplar Board of Guardians provided generous outdoor relief and thereby came into conflict with central government. In 1929, central government struck back by abolishing the Poor Law Boards of Guardians and transferring their functions to local councils. In many ways, 'progressive' ideas triumphed – Poor Law institutions such as workhouses were transformed into hospitals, maternity centres and such like. The term 'public assistance' replaced that of 'Poor Law'.

The depression of the 1930s led to great difficulties for the unemployment insurance fund as it was insufficient to cover the number of claims made on it. National funds were used from 1931, and, in 1934, the Unemployment Assistance Board was established as a central means of administering relief. As argued above, centralisation was, in part, a means whereby central government could maintain greater control over the system, and over expenditure; it was not merely an attempt to rationalise the system. Appeals tribunals were also established during this time. In 1941, the liability of dependants, whereby extended family members were expected to support each other financially, was removed. This had been a key feature of the Poor Law since 1601 and was thought to have caused families to drift apart so that they could avoid the crippling financial responsibility for each other. After 1941, only the resources of the claimant, the claimant's spouse and their dependent children were taken into account when assessing household resources.

Thus, by the early 1940s, many aspects of the Poor Law had disappeared, and people knew roughly what level of benefit to expect under Unemployment Assistance. However, the means test still existed, albeit on a nuclear family level rather than an extended family level. The insurance principle had been introduced, but many people were still not covered by insurance, and the heavy demand on the system because of the high level of unemployment in the 1930s revealed the inadequacy of the system to deal with such levels of need. The needs of children had not been addressed, nor had the needs of those disabled or injured while at work. The system had grown incrementally without any fundamental consideration of its underlying principles or administrative procedures.

Box 3.2 summarises the main social security reforms from the Poor Relief Act in 1601 to the establishment of the Unemployment Assistance Board in 1934.

Box 3.2

Social Security Reforms up to Second World War

1601 Poor Relief Act

1834 Poor Law (Amendment) Act

1847 Poor Law (Amendment) Act

1848 Poor Law (Amendment) Act

1871 Poor Law (Amendment) Act

1908 Old Age Pensions Act

1911 National Insurance Act

1920 Unemployment insurance extended to all

1925 Widows, Orphans and Old Age Contributory Pensions Act

1929 Poor Law Boards of Guardians abolished

1934 Unemployment Assistance Board set up

Beveridge, full employment and the post-war consensus

While the Second World War was still being fought, the British government was already working on ways of reforming the social security system. Such preparations meant that the post-war Labour government already had the basis for major reforms to the system.

The Beveridge Report

In 1942, Sir William Beveridge headed a Committee on Social Insurance and Allied Services that reviewed the existing schemes of social insurance. The Committee had a relatively limited mandate, so when Beveridge went well beyond his remit, the other members of the committee left, the review thus becoming Beveridge's sole responsibility. The Beveridge Report argued that there were 'five giants' that were stalking the land and that should be tackled: want, disease, ignorance, squalor and idleness. Beveridge was most concerned with tackling 'want', his Report finding that between three-quarters and five-sixths of all want was due to a reduction in earnings (Smith, 1972), the remainder being mainly the result of difficulties faced by large families in trying to make ends meet.

The Report noted that social security should only be one part of a comprehensive social policy that would deal with all social evils. Wider social policies, such as the maintenance of full employment and the creation of a free National Health Service, were seen as essential.

It was argued that the existing insurance 'system' to deal with want had evolved piecemeal and thus left out certain groups of people and certain situations. One of the main principles behind reform was that there should be co-operation between the state and the individual – the state should not stifle individual initiative such as thrift and hard work. There was to be no general project of redistribution from rich to poor through social security. The Report recommended some redistribution of income through social insurance, but the bulk of redistribution would be of two main types. First, redistribution would be from one part of the individual's life-cycle to another, such as from working age years to retirement, in effect through 'forced saving'. Second, there would be some redistribution to groups with high risks of unemployment, and away from groups with low risks of unemployment.

The proposed insurance scheme involved individuals paying into a fund on which they could then draw in the event of certain contingencies, such as unemployment, sickness, widowhood and old age. For those who were not covered by insurance, non-contributory, means-tested assistance was planned, but it was believed that this would rarely be used. The administration of the scheme would be undertaken by a Ministry of Social Security. There would be flat-rate benefits with additions for dependants, mainly wives and children. These benefits would be paid to those meeting the contribution and entitlement conditions, at a level suitable for subsistence but without a direct test of need. Baldwin (1990: 117) identifies the key features of the proposed system as follows: 'Benefits were to be universal, flat-rate, subsistence and not conditional on need.' (Box 3.3).

There were also proposals for higher benefits for those who were injured or became ill during the course of paid employment. Maternity Grants and Widows' Benefits were also proposed based on husbands' contributions. New Maternity Benefits would be based on women's own contributions, and, finally, there would also be a system of Death Grants. This widespread coverage encourages the use of the epithet that the welfare state provides support 'from the cradle to the grave'.

Box 3.3

Key Features of Beveridge's Insurance System

- *Universal* – covering all groups
- *Flat rate* – paying the same level of benefit to everyone for the same level of contributions
- *Subsistence* – aiming to meet only basic needs
- *Not conditional on need* – not requiring a means test

Beveridge recognised that an insurance system would, on its own, not be sufficient to eliminate want because some people would not have made sufficient contributions to qualify or would be in a situation that did not qualify. Hence, he suggested that a system of social or National Assistance should be provided as a safety net for those who would not be covered through insurance.

The Beveridge Report was based on a number of key requirements, without which the new social insurance system could not be expected to work. First, there would have to be full employment and economic prosperity. Thus, the scheme would be financially viable as there would be many contributors and few benefit recipients, typically being on benefit during short periods of unemployment. Second, the two-parent family would have to remain the norm, with a male breadwinner and a female housewife. Third, there would have to be a comprehensive health and rehabilitation service. Fourth, there would have to be a Family Allowance to help larger families, and these would be paid to all families irrespective of work status, so that they would not affect incentives to work.

There was widespread hope that reform of the system, along with Keynesian economic policies to achieve full employment, would ensure that the depression and hardship of the 1930s would never return. Far from attacking the foundations of capitalist economic relations, the Beveridge plan proposed a way of enabling better-off workers to insure themselves against certain risks while at the same time preventing and alleviating the worst problems faced by the poorest individuals. The plan was therefore liberal rather than socialist, and reformist rather than revolutionary. It sought to maintain the capitalist system and forestall any calls for redistribution of income and wealth from one social class to another.

Compared with meeting the costs of social security from general taxation, the proposed insurance system was regressive rather than progressive. The system was regressive because the flat-rate contribution meant that the poorest workers were paying a larger proportion of their income than were better-off workers. However, benefit payments were also flat rate, which meant that richer groups would be likely to take out private provision on top of the state system – a situation that persists today and is most obvious in the area of pensions (as Chapter 5 shows).

Although many reformers, including many social security academics, have hoped that the social security system would play a role in reducing inequality and preventing poverty, those who have implemented policy have rarely pursued such a goal. Policy has always been geared more towards maintaining the position of better-off workers and providing a basic safety net for the poorest groups in order to reduce any challenges to the *status quo*.

There was strong popular support for the plans in the Beveridge Report, but, despite its endorsement by the wartime coalition government, there were some reservations about it in the Conservative Party and among some civil servants. Contrary to Beveridge's hopes, a decision was made not to implement the plan until after the war, when the new Labour government, elected with a landslide majority in 1945, introduced the main provisions of the welfare state.

It has often been argued that social insurance received widespread popular support because people felt that they, and others, had a right to receive benefits if they had contributed towards them. While it is certainly true that the insurance principle was widely supported, this could be largely because it was being compared with the degrading and stigmatising system of assistance that had previously existed. We do not know whether a different type of system, for example one based on general taxation, would have been equally supported.

Although the Beveridge Report is seen as the foundation stone of the current social security system, it built heavily on the reforms introduced by the Liberal government before the First World War (when Beveridge had, in fact, been a civil servant in central government). The existing insurance principle was the basis of the plan, and public provision was seen as a complement rather than an alternative to private provision. Social insurance formed the backbone of the new system, with National Assistance (means-tested support) as a back-up and voluntary private insurance still being seen as the best means of providing a decent standard of living in times of need.

Beveridge's proposals were almost implemented in full, but the government rejected the idea that retirement pensions should be introduced gradually. This meant that the scheme did not have time to mature as a true insurance scheme, so contributions went straight to pensioners rather than being invested. One of the consequences was that benefit levels were kept lower than they might otherwise have been. The government also rejected Beveridge's idea to have no time limit on entitlement to Unemployment Benefit. It was felt that this would be too costly, so the maximum period of entitlement was to be 1 year. The only other significant proposal that was not adopted was the idea that there should be only one agency to run the scheme. Most of the legislation built heavily on previous Acts, the only original Act being the Family Allowances Act of 1945. The main legislation is discussed below.

Family Allowances Act 1945

This Act covered the family as a unit and did not aim solely to help children. Benefit was paid after the birth of a second child, and extra money was paid for subsequent children. The family was eligible for children up to the age of 15, or 16 for certain disabled children, or 19 for those in education or apprenticeships. Eligibility and the amount of benefit did not depend on the income of the family or on National Insurance contributions. Hence, this was a universal or contingent benefit (see Chapter 4 for discussion of the different types of benefit).

National Insurance Act 1946

The aim of this Act was to provide a scheme of National Insurance that would eventually cover almost everyone in Britain. The Act extended National Insurance to cover Unemployment Benefit, Retirement Pensions, Widows' Benefits, Guardians' Allowances and Death Grants. All those of working age (15–65 for men and 15–60 for women) were compulsorily insured. Flat-rate contributions were paid, and both the state and, in most cases, the employer also paid into the scheme. The individual could then draw out a standard rate of benefit in time of need. Employed women who were married were usually covered by their husbands' contributions so did not have to make their own contributions. This separate 'married women's option' was open to women until legislation that came into effect as recently as 1978. This Act built heavily on previous legislation, firmly establishing the contributory principle.

National Insurance (Industrial Injuries Act) 1946

Prior to this Act, any employee who suffered an injury at work had to take his or her employer to court for compensation; the Act transferred liability from the employer to the state (Smith, 1978). Both employees and employers had to pay into a central fund, which then provided benefit in the case of injury, disablement or death caused by accidents arising out of a person's employment. This benefit could be paid on top of Sickness Benefit, the amount of benefit depending on the extent of the individual's impairment. The benefit would also be paid on top of any earnings, so someone receiving the benefit could, potentially, work full time and still receive it. However, the government retained the ability to claw back benefits paid from any lump-sum settlements that a firm made to injured workers.

National Assistance Act 1948

The main thrust of the legislation inspired by Beveridge had been based on the insurance principle, but it was recognised that there might be some people who would not be covered by insurance. These included unmarried mothers, women who had separated from their husbands and the long-term unemployed. This Act repealed the old Poor Law and replaced it with assistance provided by the National Assistance Board and local authorities. Whereas the Poor Law had dealt with the financial and non-financial welfare of those in need, this Act divided these up: financial welfare was to be dealt with by the National Assistance Board, whereas it was now the responsibility of local authorities to deal with the non-financial welfare of disabled people, older people and others. Thus, the system developed a sharp separation between cash and in-kind assistance. Social security was to be about the provision of cash, subject to national rules. The social services were to operate locally and apply a much greater degree of discretion in their day-to-day work. This split is not typically found in continental Europe, where local social workers are often also involved in the payment of cash benefits.

A means test was carried out to determine need, but this was only at the level of the individual or his or her partner – members of the extended family were not directly included in the test. Assistance was normally paid in cash to those out of work, and the principle of less eligibility remained – assistance was kept at a lower level than the person would receive if in full-time employment. Unlike the insurance scheme, there was to be no automatic right to assistance, so elements of the humiliation and stigmatisation associated with the Poor Law remained with the new system. This was reinforced by the fact that National Assistance Board officers used their discretionary judgement (Hill, 1969) to decide on whether or not a particular case was deserving of assistance.

Problems with the Beveridge system

Beveridge hoped that National Insurance would be the main instrument in the elimination of want, but this would necessitate levels of benefit being set at a rate higher than National Assistance. This would have been simple to achieve in theory, but in practice the 'problem of rent' complicated the issue. Rent levels varied greatly across the country, and Beveridge found that many recipients of National Insurance benefits needed supplements of National Assistance, which was available to help cover the cost of rent. There were thus far more people dependent on National Assistance than had previously been expected.

Even without the famous rent problem, the emphasis on paying benefits at a subsistence level was likely to lead to problems. If social insurance is set at such a level, how should the level of means-tested social assistance be set? To set National Assistance at below subsistence would appear perverse, but there would otherwise seem to be little benefit in claiming the insured variant benefit. Without a significant financial benefit of social insurance over social assistance, the 'point' of a contributory system appears hard to fathom and tends to undermine support for the deserving nature of contributory benefits – why bother making contributions if those (feckless?) people who do not contribute receive a similar level of income. This is one of the problems facing the current basic State Retirement Pension in Britain.

Another problem with the Beveridge scheme was its assumptions about the relationships between men and women, and between women and the labour market. Beveridge assumed that married women were dependent on their husbands' wages so men would make the insurance contributions and claim benefit on behalf of themselves and their wives in times of need. He based this assumption on census data from 1931, which showed that about seven-eighths of all married women were not in paid employment (Hill, 1990), but these data excluded certain types of less formal work that women were more likely to do. Also, the labour market situation of the late 1940s was rather different from that of 1931. Although we might see some justification for his assumptions at that time, the Beveridge system meant that even married women who were working paid lower contributions or no contributions at all. Beveridge justified this by arguing that married women worked for only small amounts of money that were not central to the family's income. Beveridge's view about the relationship between men and women was that couples worked as an 'equal but different' bread-winning/home-making team. Although this might on the surface sound egalitarian, it masks the fact that married women often had no option about staying in the home as they faced strong cultural and social norms that encouraged them to do so, as well as being explicitly barred from some forms of employment, particularly public employment. The idea of a 'team' also suggests that both members of the couple shared certain things, such as income and decision-making, which was not necessarily the case. Whether or not Beveridge's idea of marriage and employment patterns fitted the situation of the 1940s, changes since then have certainly undermined its applicability in subsequent decades.

Another issue that should be raised with regard to the Beveridge system is the 'myth of the insurance principle'. Beveridge emphasised the centrality of insurance to his whole system but, because of concerns for the benefits of the new system to come into effect as soon as possible, there was no time to set up a self-financing insurance scheme. Benefit payments were, therefore, financed from current contributions rather than from invested funds so there was a 'pay-as-you-go' system, and the notion of 'insurance' was more myth than reality.

The 1950s and 60s: the rediscovery of poverty

In the second election in 1951, the Labour government was defeated, this ushering in a 13-year period of Conservative Party rule. In the late 1940s, there had been a broad political consensus over the introduction of the welfare state, and the new government generally believed that most of the main provisions of modern social security were now in place. The system was very much geared towards providing a safety net in times of need. The insurance principle was firmly established, with flat-rate contributions and standard payments. It was believed that such a system would lead to little reliance on means-tested assistance.

In 1959, following concerns about the inadequacies and cost of the pensions scheme, the National Insurance Act attempted to alter one of the underlying principles of the system to date. Rather than have flat-rate contributions and standard payments, this Act introduced an (albeit very limited) earnings-related state Retirement Pension. Those on higher earnings paid more into their pension in return for higher benefits after they retired. Rather than just providing a safety net, such a scheme of 'graduated' pensions sought to maintain, after retirement, the differences in income that occurred during working life. The National Insurance Act of 1965 extended a similar scheme to unemployment, sickness and industrial injuries.

These Acts were influenced by a growing belief that flat-rate benefits, which aimed to remove absolute poverty, were not appropriate given the increase in affluence since the Second World War. There was an argument for wage-related contributions and benefits for retirement, unemployment and sickness. These benefits would have the advantage of lifting claimants off means-tested assistance benefits as the basic level of insurance benefits were often lower once rent had been taken into account. Discontent with the number of people reliant on National Assistance was widespread among Abel-Smith and his academic colleagues at the London School of Economics, including Titmuss, McKenzie and Townsend. These academic researchers also drew attention to the poverty suffered by people who were living below the state's semi-official poverty line – the level of National Assistance benefits (Abel-Smith and Townsend, 1965). Among this group were people in low-paid jobs, particularly those with children.

Thus, poverty persisted alongside affluence, and the 'rediscovery of poverty' called into question the extent to which the Beveridge reforms had eliminated want (Coates and Silburn, 1970). A number of issues were raised at this time such as:

- The desirability of earnings-related contributions and benefits in replacing flat-rate contributions and benefits
- The existence of poverty among people in paid work
- The lack of provision for children in the social security system
- The operation of means tests and the continued existence of the stigma attached to claiming benefit

● The continuing 'problem of rent', which Beveridge had acknowledged but failed to solve.

When the Labour Party returned to power in 1964, their plans for
reforming the system, which included an increased role for earnings-
related benefits, were scaled down because of their desire to return the
economy to the levels of growth witnessed in the 1950s. They were
reluctant to improve the system unless the economic base could support
it. However, they did reform the system in 1966, when the National
Assistance Board and the Ministry of Pensions and National Insurance
combined to form a new Ministry – the Ministry of Social Security.
Rather than introducing new systems and rules, the Ministry of Social
Security Act of 1966 had more subtle aims – to change the 'culture' of
benefit-claiming. The Act replaced the term 'National Assistance' with
that of 'Supplementary Benefit', and administration was undertaken by
a Supplementary Benefits Commission. Whereas under the National
Assistance Act of 1948, people 'applied' for assistance, they were now
entitled to claim benefit. Benefit now became a legal right to be
claimed rather than a charitable gift to be asked for. Supplementary
allowances and pensions replaced National Assistance to sick and
disabled people, the unemployed, widows, mothers with young children and pensioners. Earnings-related supplements were extended to
the first 6 months of unemployment, sickness or maternity, but they
were not extended to pensions (which had to await a thorough-going
reform in 1975).

In the 1960s, the stigma attached to applying for National Assistance
had been reduced with the introduction of Supplementary Benefit and
the emphasis on rights to benefit. However, the newly emerging
'poverty lobby', consisting of the Child Poverty Action Group, local
voluntary organisations and other pressure groups, aimed to extend the
'rights culture' by staging take-up campaigns to make sure that all those
eligible to benefit were receiving their full entitlement. The lobby also
closely scrutinised the Supplementary Benefits Commission and criticised the amount of discretion in the system: decisions were being made
by officers based on secret internal guidelines, and the lobby called for
more openness in decision-making. However, as Titmuss (1971) pointed
out, a call for clearer rules could result in clearer but harsher rules, so
the poverty lobby was in somewhat of a dilemma. Another dilemma for
the poverty lobby was whether to argue for a return to the insurance
principles of Beveridge or to accept the growth of means-tested benefits
and call for an improvement in the system of means-testing.

The 1970s and 80s: the end of consensus

The 1970s and 80s saw considerable social change: the elderly population was growing in size and the 'dependency ratio' (the ratio of older people to those of working age) was moving in a direction that began to make the payment of benefits to older people relatively more costly than before. Women, married women in particular, were increasingly part of the labour market, and there was a rise in the number of lone-parent families, mainly as a result of an increase in the number of separations and divorces.

Reforms in the 1970s

The 1966 Act had dealt with a number of issues raised by the rediscovery of poverty, but the issues about support for children and the working poor, which were in many cases interlinked, had not been tackled. The 1945 Family Allowances Act had aimed to deal with the issue of child poverty, but benefits for children were not routinely increased annually, leaving them to fall far behind inflation or wages. National Insurance and National Assistance both gave additional benefit depending on the number of children in the family. Wages, however, do not take account of family size, so it was quite possible for a family, particularly a large family, to be better off on benefit than in work. For some commentators, this demonstrated that benefit levels were too high, but for others, including those from the Child Poverty Action Group, there was a need to improve levels of Family Allowance. This benefit was payable to people whether or not they were in work and so increases in Family Allowance would improve the incomes of working families.

    The government had other ideas and considered the introduction of tax credits (sometimes called a 'negative income tax'; see Chapter 9) to improve the situation of low-paid workers with children. A system of tax credits would pay money to people whose earnings fell below a certain level. However, such a scheme would have entailed a rather radical departure from the principles of the system at the time, so, as a supposedly temporary measure, Family Income Supplement was introduced in 1971. This benefit topped up the earnings of full-time, low-paid workers with children. The amount of benefit depended on, among other things, the level of income and the number and ages of children in the family. The benefit, therefore, worked on a principle similar to that of the Speenhamland System of 1795, and similar criticisms were made about how the benefit was merely supporting low-paying employers. A further attempt to help children resulted in the introduction of benefits for free school meals and clothing.

The 1960s had also failed to address the 'problem of rent', and, in 1972, the Housing Finance Act introduced a system of rent rebates. Until this point, the provision of local authority housing had grown considerably since the Second World War. Rents had been kept low, and National Assistance or Supplementary Benefit had paid rent where necessary. In 1972, central government required rents to be increased towards more economic levels and also extended a system of rent rebates whereby central government paid some money directly to local government to cover the rents of those who, following a means test, were entitled to help with their housing costs. A system of rent allowance was also introduced to cover private rent, with the cash paid directly to the tenants. A similar criticism was made of this scheme as was made with Family Income Supplement because of concern that the government would be subsidising private landlords who were charging high rents.

The 1970s saw an expansion of means-tested benefits, in terms of both increasing reliance on current benefits and the introduction of new benefits. Some new non-means-tested benefits were also introduced. In 1975, the campaign to strengthen Family Allowance resulted in some success with the introduction of Child Benefit. This benefit replaced Family Allowance and child tax allowances. It was extended to the first child in the family, and it was agreed that the benefit would be regularly increased with inflation. The State Earnings-Related Pension Scheme (SERPS) was also introduced as a new earnings-related pension scheme. However, like previous pension schemes, SERPS was not a funded scheme. It worked on a pay-as-you-go basis, current contributions from workers being used to pay for the pensions of those who were retired. New benefits for disabled people and their full-time carers, for example Non-contributory Invalidity Pension, Attendance Allowance, Mobility Allowance and Invalid Care Allowance, were also introduced.

The 1960s and 70s had resulted in an expansion of the social security system, with increasing reliance on the main benefits and the introduction of new benefits. The existing principles and system of Beveridge were consolidated, but new principles were also established with the introduction of Child Benefit (replacing the Family Allowance and child tax allowances), Family Income Supplement and earnings-related benefits. The strengthening of the notion of 'rights' to means-tested benefits grew, as did a reliance on these benefits. But once again, the incrementalist development of the system led, by the mid-1970s, to calls for review and reform to take into account the widespread role of assistance, which had not originally been forecast in Beveridge's plan. A Department of Health and Social Security (DHSS) review in the late 1970s also argued that the increasing complexity of the rules could be dealt with by a move away from discretion by local officials towards more standardised rights to benefit (Walker, 1983).

Retrenchment in the 1980s

In the late 1970s, unemployment grew beyond the level at which Beveridge had argued that poverty could be eliminated, and, in 1979, economic recession and the election of a Conservative government led to a breakdown in political consensus over welfare. Previous governments, both Labour and Conservative, had felt constrained by perceived economic necessities to take a cautious approach to reforming the system. However, even without economic constraints, the new government, fired by ideology, would have aimed to 'roll back the frontiers of the state'.

Efforts were made to reduce public expenditure on social security, for example by increasing pensions in line with inflation every year rather than earnings. This meant that pensioners became increasingly worse off in relation to the working population. Cuts were also made in most National Insurance benefit rates, and earnings-related additions to unemployment and sickness benefits were abolished. Despite these attempts to curb costs, however, the recession of the early 1980s led to increasing unemployment and hence increasing public spending. Another source of growing expenditure was in rent rebates. This was due to a change in government policy from subsidising bricks and mortar (through low council rents) to subsidising renters (through higher council rents and means-tested rent rebate), even though the overall level of support for housing costs remained largely unchanged.

In 1982, changes were made to Sickness Benefit, effectively leading to a degree of privatisation of the benefit, with responsibility shifting from the state to the employer. Entitlement to benefit was cut, and employers were obliged to pay at least a minimum level of sick pay. In 1986, a similar reform occurred with Maternity Benefit, which was replaced by Statutory Maternity Pay. The introduction of Housing Benefit, to replace rent and rate rebate, also shifted responsibility away from the centre of the state – this time to local authorities.

The Fowler Review

In the early 1980s, the level of Child Benefit was frozen, and Unemployment Benefit was cut. Cuts and reforms like these were producing some savings for the Exchequer, but, in the mid-1980s, the social security budget of £40 billion was still considered to be a mammoth drain on the tax-payer; thus, a review of the system was begun. Four areas of provision were considered: Supplementary Benefit, benefits for children and young people, Housing Benefit and pensions. The ensuing Green Paper then led to the 1986 Social Security Act. The Green Paper, and the Act that followed it, marked a departure from Beveridge, with its new acknowledgement and emphasis on means-tested benefits as a key component of the system. Rather than seeing this as a regrettable but inevitable reflection of the lack of full employment, the Conservatives were openly supportive of a return to selectivity, or 'targeting' as it was more usually called. The focus on means-testing was slightly paradoxical for the Conservative government because means-testing requires heavy administrative machinery, and the government was also committed to reducing the number of civil servants. Hence, efforts were made to find ways of simplifying means-testing through other methods of 'targeting' benefits.

The reforms at this time also attempted to streamline and rationalise a system that had become complex and unwieldy. Thus, rather than pursuing radical reform of the entire system, the Fowler Review represented little more than a systematic (if overdue) tidying up of a system that had grown in complexity over the 1970s and 80s. Certainly, the remit of the review was to be 'cost-neutral', so additional resources committed to one area had to be matched by reductions in others. One of the aims of the review had been to direct greater resources towards low-income families with children, and, to some extent, reductions in pension provision provided the resources to achieve this. Put simply, after the Fowler Review, it was apparent that means-tested benefits acted as the framework for much of the rest of the social security system. They could no longer be regarded as acting as a fill-in for the gaps in coverage of the insurance system.

The main changes introduced by the Fowler Review were as follows:

- *Income Support* replaced Supplementary Benefit, and all means-tested benefits were aligned so that they were based on the same basic rules. Within Income Support, premiums for particular groups replaced a patchwork of additions.
- *Family Credit* replaced Family Income Supplement as a means-tested benefit for working families with children. The hours rule was changed such that all recipients could now be working for as little as 24 hours a week rather than 30 hours, as was previously the case. However, the major change, which often receives less attention, was that assessment for benefit was now based on net income rather than gross income (Minford *et al.*, 1983). This was an attempt to increase incentives to work because, under the previous assessment rules, some people could actually have been worse off had their earnings increased, as their benefit payment could have been reduced by more than their wage rise. The new assessment rules generally prevented such a situation occurring, although tax and benefit deduction rates were high across a wide range of earnings.
- The fiendishly confusing system of housing benefits was rationalised into the more moderately complex system of Housing Benefit, and (even before the introduction of the Community Charge/Poll Tax) householders were required to pay at least 20 per cent of their domestic rates bill. Previously, 100 per cent rebates had been available.
- Initially, there had been moves to abolish SERPS, but these were thwarted by major criticism, and the government settled for *reducing* SERPS (by about half) and increasing the incentives for individuals to take out personal or occupational pensions.
- Finally, the 1986 Act abolished entitlements to single payments under the Supplementary Benefit scheme, except in the cases of maternity needs and funerals. Single payments were now replaced by a new discretionary Social Fund, which mostly provided loans (for reasons of crisis and difficulties in budgeting) but also paid out some grants (known as 'community care grants', designed to assist people to remain within the community).

Another change at this time, one inspired by the Department of Employment rather than the Fowler Review, was that most 16–17-year-olds were now almost entirely removed from eligibility to Income Support, being expected to enter education or the labour market, or undertake vocational training (Maidment *et al.*, 1997).

Reforming disability benefits

One area that had not formed any part of the Fowler Review was that of disability benefits. These were subsequently the focus of a second review, published as *The Way Ahead* (Department of Social Security, 1990). Following this Report, two new social security benefits for disabled people – Disability Living Allowance and Disability Working Allowance – were introduced in 1992 (the former replacing Attendance Allowance for those under 65 and Mobility Allowance). Disability Living Allowance was designed to help disabled people to meet the extra living costs that they faced; Disability Working Allowance was a benefit for disabled people in employment to top up low pay, on a very similar basis to that of Family Credit. Applications for Disability Living Allowance came flooding in, and applicants had to wait excessive amounts of time before hearing whether or not their claim had been successful. This attracted highly negative publicity, not least when some of those who had applied for Disability Living Allowance died before their claim had been decided. In contrast, applications for Disability Working Allowance barely trickled in (Rowlingson and Berthoud, 1996).

The 1990s: towards a new consensus?

With the replacement of Prime Minister Thatcher by John Major in November 1990 and the development of New Labour, first under John Smith and then under Tony Blair, ideological strife in the political arena generally declined. This also occurred in social security, despite the fact that Peter Lilley, a strongly right-wing ideologue, was the Secretary of State for Social Security from 1992 to 1997. Although Peter Lilley appeared to take a hard line on welfare, his time at the DSS saw the end of attempts for root-and-branch reform of the system and a new attempt to make sector-by-sector improvements. Although the Conservatives were still committed to reducing the costs of social security, they planned to do this by 'targeting' benefits more precisely or, in effect, restricting entitlement rather than cutting the level of benefits. Government figures (Department of Social Security, 1993b) showed that, despite attempts to curb costs, spending on social security had risen at 3.7 per cent above the rate of inflation, and the future appeared to hold more of the same.

Various incrementalist reforms took place to reduce costs. In 1995, Incapacity Benefit replaced Invalidity Benefit. The new benefit was taxable, restricted the maximum age for recipients of the benefit and had stricter medical eligibility tests. It has led to a reduction in the number on benefit but perhaps not to the extent originally envisaged by the policy-makers. In 1996, Jobseeker's Allowance replaced Unemployment Benefit and Income Support for unemployed people. The contributory element of the benefit was reduced from 12 months to 6 months, and ever-more stringent checks on job-seeking were applied. A range of new initiatives was also introduced to provide further financial incentives to work. In 1995, the government announced, in line with European equal opportunities legislation, that the retirement age for women would be raised from 60 to 65 over the period 2010 to 2020. Finally, the government restricted help towards paying for mortgages during times of low income such as unemployment. From 1995, those taking out a mortgage were expected to make their own private provision and were thus no longer eligible for Income Support payments to cover their mortgage interest.

The 1990s saw a renewed emphasis on tackling fraud. In 1995, the DSS embarked on a Five Year Security Strategy to combat fraud. This involved a number of initiatives using new technology designed largely to make the system more secure so that fraud would be more difficult to commit. For example, it was planned that plastic cards like credit cards would replace benefit order books, which were relatively easy to forge or steal and use. There was also a move towards 'deterring' people from committing fraud, and a freephone hotline was introduced to encourage people to report fraudsters.

New Labour and social security policy

The end of ideological strife was not only brought about by changes within the Conservative Party: the Labour Party was also undergoing major change, which resulted in the creation of New Labour. Prior to the 1997 election, Labour promised the voters that they would not increase taxes, so they had to find ways to limit spending. Top of the agenda for Harriet Harman, the Secretary of State for Social Security in the New Labour government from 1997, was Welfare-to-Work – a scheme designed to reduce the spending bill by moving people from social security into paid work. Such a policy could conceivably have been introduced by the Conservatives, albeit in a slightly different form. The new government also retained the previous government's plans to phase out One Parent Benefit and the lone-parent premium in

Income Support for new lone parents, and they also maintained a tough stance against fraud.

So the Labour government that took power after 18 years of Conservative rule had much in common with the previous government and had few concrete radical plans to overhaul the social security system. However, more than 50 years after Beveridge, British society had altered dramatically, and the social security system no longer seemed to fit in with the new society's employment and family structures. The two-parent family, with a male breadwinner in a well-paid, full-time, permanent job, a female housewife and children is far less common now than it was in the late 1940s. The labour market has changed so that women, particularly those with children, are much more likely than before to be in paid work. Related to this, there has been a growth in part-time, low-paid work, often in the service sector. Traditionally male employment in heavy industry has seen a dramatic decline. Permanent jobs appear to be becoming less common, and self-employment is much more prevalent.

These changes in employment have occurred alongside changes in family structure and relationships. Cohabitation has increased; marriage and child-rearing occur at later ages than before (and sometimes do not occur at all). Separation and divorce have increased, leading to the growth of lone-parent families, step-families and people living on their own (McRae, 1999). The world of secure employment and stable families, upon which Beveridge based his social security system, no longer exists – and perhaps never existed to the extent necessary for a fully successful system. In 1961, 38 per cent of all households comprised a married couple with dependent children. In 1994–95, this figure had declined to 25 per cent because of the growth in single-person and lone-parent households (Central Statistical Office, 1997).

Another important change has occurred in the demographic structure of the country, as Britain has an ageing population. For example, in 1961, 12 per cent of the UK population were aged 65 or over, the figure in 1994 being 16 per cent (Central Statistical Office, 1997). Additionally, there has been a particularly sharp rise in the number of people who are very elderly (over the age of 80). The extent of a 'demographic timebomb' is often exaggerated, and Britain certainly faces less of a problem than many of its European neighbours, but there are still important challenges to be faced as a result of this change (Disney, 1996). We will return to some of these issues, and the challenges that face the current system, in Chapter 9. The next chapter provides an overview of the British system today.

4

The British System Today

Introduction

The current social security system has grown up in a piecemeal fashion, and any attempt to provide an overview of the system may give a false impression of some generally agreed principles or overarching structures that form its foundations. It is therefore important to bear in mind that a labyrinth of complexity exists underneath any simple description of social security today. As Roll has noted (1991: 21), 'almost any generalisation about it can be refuted'. It is also important to note that the social security system 'today' is likely to be different 'tomorrow' as governments are continually engaged in a process of reforming it. The description of the system in this chapter aims to be general, but the precise names of benefits and rules are based on information available up to August 1998.

The chapter begins by discussing the different types of benefit that exist in today's system. It then focuses on key issues such as expenditure and the number of people on benefit. It also covers benefit levels and the questions of poverty, inequality and adequacy. Finally, we discuss the benefit unit and the labels used to describe people who receive social security benefits.

Different types of benefit

There are various ways of classifying the different benefits in the UK system. If we use the rules of entitlement as our yardstick, the benefits within the social security system can be divided into three main groups as follows.

Contributory benefits

These are social insurance benefits where entitlement is based on having paid National Insurance contributions and being subject to a risk covered by these benefits (such as unemployment or retirement). These benefits are individualised in that entitlement is not generally affected by the earnings of a partner. The main benefit in this group is the state Retirement Pension. Other benefits are the contributory parts of Incapacity Benefit and Jobseeker's Allowance.

Means-tested benefits

Entitlement to means-tested benefits depends on the level of 'family' resources, particularly income and savings. The four main examples in the British system are Income Support, Family Credit (until October 1999), Housing Benefit and Council Tax Benefit.

Contingent benefits

These are sometimes referred to as categorical benefits, as non-means-tested and non-contributory, or sometimes as 'demogrants'. Entitlement depends on the existence of certain circumstances (or contingencies) such as having a child (Child Benefit), being disabled (Disability Living Allowance, Severe Disablement Allowance) or, at least until recent changes, being a lone parent (One Parent Benefit).

It is worth emphasising that this division into three groups is something of a simplification of the differences between benefits. Means-tested benefits not only depend on financial resources, but also tend to rely on some combination of being in a particular situation or a particular family type. For example, able-bodied single people may only claim Income Support if they meet conditions relating to being unemployed. Also, it is possible for certain sources of income to affect contributory benefits; for example Jobseeker's Allowance (which is contribution based) can be reduced if a person receives income from a personal or occupational pension.

This section discusses each of these different types of benefit in more detail.

Contributory benefits ('social insurance')

Contributory benefits are financed from the National Insurance fund, which is made up of social security contributions from employees, their employers, the self-employed and other people who choose to pay them. Money has also been paid into the fund in times of need by the Treasury, although the fund now aims to be self-financing. There are five classes of contribution (Box 4.1).

Employees paying *class 1* contributions do not pay National Insurance on all their earnings but only on earnings between certain amounts – known as the lower and upper earnings limits. In 1997–98, the lower earnings limit was £62 a week and the upper earnings limit £465 a week. In 1998–99, these were raised to £64 and £485 respectively. Employees pay 10 per cent on earnings between these two levels. However, the 1998 budget, following recommendations from Martin Taylor (1998), announced major changes that involved a considerable simplification of employer rates of payment. For employees, the two clearest changes were a significant increase in the lower earnings limit – to £81 – and the abolition of an 'entry fee' that was paid on amounts below the lower earnings level for those earning above it.

The existence of the upper earnings limit means that the system is regressive, that is, those on high earnings (above the upper earnings limit) will be paying a smaller percentage of their total earnings than will

Box 4.1

Classes of National Insurance Contributions

Class of contribution	Paid by
Class 1	Employees and their employers (related to earnings)
Class 1A	Employers where employees have company cars
Class 2	Self-employed earners (flat rate)
Class 3	Voluntary contributors (non-earners who wish to make contributions)
Class 4	Self-employed workers and levied against profits or gains

those on lower earnings. The existence of the lower earnings limit means that some people on very low earnings, particularly those working part time, do not pay any National Insurance contributions at all.

Not all contributions count equally towards benefit entitlement. In particular, *class 2* contributions paid by the self-employed may be used to gain entitlement to the Retirement Pension, but do not count towards the contribution-based Jobseeker's Allowance.

Some people pay no National Insurance contributions because they are not in employment, but many of these people are nevertheless 'credited' with contributions. This means that the government effectively pays money on their behalf, and this will be counted towards their contribution record when they claim contributory benefits. Credits are paid in a number of circumstances such as while unemployed or sick, while caring for a sick relative and receiving Invalid Care Allowance, while in certain types of education or training, while on jury service or while on maternity leave. These credits do not entitle people to benefit in precisely the same manner as full contributions do, and cannot in themselves confer entitlement, but they go a long way towards making up gaps in contributions records. Such credits, however, further separate the workings of social insurance from systems of private insurance – as people are not paying for themselves but are being 'rewarded' for what may be seen as socially beneficial activities (such as caring for children or adults). A system of Home Responsibilities Protection also exists, in effect, to credit people (usually women) who stay at home to look after children or disabled relatives and is designed to make the qualification conditions for the Retirement Pension easier to pass.

Entitlement to National Insurance benefits is dependent on the contributions record of the applicant (or, in the case of a widow, her husband). The rules about the necessary contributions record are, like much of the social security system, rather complex and, therefore, not described here. For details of this, along with any other specific details about the intricate workings of the system, the best guides are produced by the Child Poverty Action Group (1997a, 1997b, 1997c; these are updated each year). Broadly speaking, entitlement to the Retirement Pension depends on contributions throughout a person's working life, while benefits for those of working age (such as Jobseeker's Allowance) depend on contributions made in the previous 2 years.

By calling it a National Insurance 'fund', the impression is given that individual contributions into the fund are invested somewhere and then withdrawn by the individual at some point in the future when needed, but the National Insurance scheme has never been 'funded' in this way. Payments made to recipients in the year are drawn from the total amount of contributions made in that year. The fund only aims to be self-financing on a year-by-year basis.

Means-tested benefits ('social assistance')

As discussed in Chapter 1, the role of means-tested benefits is rather different from the insurance role of contributory benefits. Means-tested benefits are designed to provide a minimum income, or safety net, for people without sufficient resources from employment or elsewhere (although the idea of means-testing at higher income levels, or 'affluence-testing', has more recently been mooted; see Chapter 9).

Means-tested benefits do not depend on a person's past National Insurance contributions record: they depend instead on a test of the person's current means. 'Means' covers income from virtually any source, including income from earnings, self-employment and child maintenance as well as any money received from lodgers and any return received from investments. 'Means' also includes capital such as money in savings accounts, shares, property and land. The treatment of income and capital varies depending on which benefits are being claimed. All benefits have income and capital 'disregards' whereby a certain amount of income or capital will not affect the entitlement to benefit. For example, in 1998–99 within Income Support, single recipients can earn £5 a week without it affecting their entitlement to benefit, a level that has not changed since 1988. Any income above this is deducted, pound for pound, from their benefit. This is the basic earnings disregard, but there are different levels of disregard for different types of claimant. For example, the earnings disregard for couples in 1998–99 was £10 a week and for lone parents £15 a week. These low levels of disregard, dating back to the 1988 reforms, discourage all but the shortest of part-time jobs (Weale *et al.*, 1984). From October 1996, some recipients have been able to take advantage of the Back to Work Bonus, which stores up half of any income earned over the disregard, paying it if a person moves off benefit and into work.

The rules about capital for Income Support are that any capital under £3,000, will be disregarded, but if claimants have more than £8,000, they will not be entitled to any benefit. Those with capital between these amounts will be paid a reduced amount of benefit on a sliding scale depending on the amount that they have.

When applying for a means-tested benefit, it is not just the applicant's income and capital that are assessed. The unit of assessment is the family, which in this case means any partner and any dependent children. With the rise in divorce on the one hand and cohabitation on the other, it is no longer possible to use marital status as a way of judging whether people are living on their own or in a couple. The social security system, unlike the tax system, treats unmarried, cohabiting couples in the same way as married couples who are living together, but this begs the question of how to classify an unmarried couple as cohabiting. In many cases, it is clear when two people are 'living together as husband and wife', but some relationships are more ambiguous, so guidelines are needed in order to determine the nature of the relationship. The social security system asks the following questions when deciding whether to classify two people as a couple:

- Are they members of the opposite sex?
- Are they members of the same household?
- Are they in a stable relationship?
- Do they share joint financial arrangements?
- Do they share responsibilities for the care of a child?
- Do they have a sexual relationship?
- Are they 'publicly acknowledged' to be in a couple?

No single factor in this list is taken as conclusive proof that cohabitation is taking pace – each aspect of the relationship has to be weighed up before a final decision can be reached. Similarly, the fact that a couple may not satisfy any of these criteria does not prove that they are not cohabiting (although the first criterion listed *must* be met – gay and lesbian couples are not recognised by the social security system as couples).

With the growth of divorce and cohabitation, the boundaries between living as a couple and living on one's own are becoming increasingly difficult to define. With the growth of lone parenthood, absent parenthood and step-families, it is also increasingly difficult to define when a child is 'dependent'. For benefit purposes, applicants for benefit will be considered to have dependent children if they are 'responsible' for any children. They do not have to be the biological or adoptive parent of the child. The child must be under 16 or under 19 and in full-time education. For most means-tested benefits, the child must 'normally' live with the parent, so where the care of a child is split between two parents, a decision must be made about whom the child normally lives with; the child must be assigned to one or other parent for benefit purposes, although child support legislation allows for greater flexibility in allowing for shared childcare arrangements (Child Poverty Action Group, 1997d).

Thus, whereas an individual with a sufficient contributions record can receive a National Insurance benefit even if his or her partner is a millionaire, means-tested benefits are not individual based but take into account the family status of the applicant.

Contingent benefits

It is easier to explain what contingent benefits are not rather than what they are. They do not depend on an individual's National Insurance contributions record, nor do they depend on a family-based means test: they depend on an individual's circumstances. For example, Child Benefit is paid to people (usually women) who have children, regardless of contributions or means. Thus, even the wife of a millionaire who has never had a paid job will be eligible for Child Benefit. To take another example, the Disability Living Allowance is paid to all those who can demonstrate a need for help with care or mobility because of an impairment. If they can demonstrate such a need, they will be entitled to benefit even if they have no contributions record and they are on a high income.

Contingent benefits, therefore, exist as a recognition of the extra costs of certain circumstances – such as having children or being disabled. They are also, to some extent, a recognition that society values people who undertake particular tasks, for example bringing up children. It is often argued that they are expensive because of their universal, non-contributory, non-means-tested nature. In their defence, it is said that they are cheap to administer and non-stigmatising, but such features are not necessarily inherent in the nature of contingent benefits. For example, the Disability Living Allowance is administered postally at national centres rather than through local benefit offices and it is probably this factor, rather than the contingent nature of the benefit, which makes it relatively cheap to administer. And while claimants of Disability Living Allowance are not asked any intrusive and potentially degrading questions about family income, they may find it stigmatising to fill in a detailed form about their physical and mental condition, with the possibility of a medical examination to follow this up. So while contingent benefits may have some advantages over other types of benefit, these advantages should not be exaggerated.

We might also classify tax allowances, such as the married couples' tax allowance, as being similar to contingent benefits as they are not means-tested as such (although they do depend on the level of income). Child Benefit (which is usually paid to mothers) subsumed both child tax allowance (which was usually paid to fathers) and the Family Allowance that went to larger families. Thus, there was a shift from 'subsidising the wallet' to 'subsidising the purse'. Tax relief on mortgage interest payments is a benefit that goes to all those with a mortgage regardless of their means, although the value of this tax relief has been significantly cut in recent years.

The shift from contributory to means-tested benefits

As argued in Chapter 3, the Beveridge system placed contributory benefits (National Insurance benefits) at the heart of the social security system, which aimed to help people to insure themselves against unemployment, sickness and retirement. It was believed that the role of means-tested benefits (National Assistance) both should and would be minimal. In the decades following the Second World War, however, the importance of means-tested benefits grew as a result of a number of socio-economic changes, such as the growth in structural and long-term unemployment, the growth of lone parenthood and the lack of pension provision for those retiring. The increasing importance of means-tested benefits also reflected the lack of financial advantage of insurance benefits over means-tested National Assistance.

In recent years, many observers have perceived a deliberate policy shift towards means-tested benefits as successive governments argued that this was the best way to target resources to those most in need. The main motive for the shift, however, has often been to save money, as contributory benefits have generally been paid at higher rates than the corresponding means-tested benefits. (For example, Unemployment Benefit was paid at a higher rate than Income Support to unemployed people.) By tightening up the rules of entitlement to contributory benefits, people could be shifted on to cheaper, means-tested benefits, and some of these people would not be entitled to any means-tested benefit if they had a partner with a sufficiently high income.

The shift from contributory to means-tested benefits might save government money, but there are many problems with means-tested benefits. For example, they are especially prone to 'non-take-up', where those who are eligible do not claim them. They may also have effects on incentives to work, particularly in a couple where benefit may be lost if one person finds a job (see Chapter 8 for a fuller discussion of this). Administering means-tested benefits is also much more expensive than administering other types of benefit. While it is true that contributory benefits may be paid to people with working partners, who may not be considered 'poor', they have the advantage of higher take-up (eligible groups tending to claim and to receive them), lower administrative costs and fewer effects on changing incentives to work.

Contributory benefits are also more participatory in a general sense, rewarding those who have made contributions in the past. In the USA, there is much more of a distinction in public consciousness between means-tested benefits (called 'welfare') and benefits based on prior contributions (called 'social security'). Social security is viewed much more as a right than is welfare, which is viewed very negatively. Whereas recipients of social security feel entitled to claim, there is a great deal of stigma attached to receiving welfare. In much of continental Europe, benefits paid on an insurance basis tend to lie within a centralised system with fixed rules, whereas means-tested benefits (social assistance) may be discretionary and administered locally, often by those who would in Britain be described as social workers.

Thus, in many ways, contributory benefits are viewed much more positively than means-tested benefits, but there are also a number of drawbacks with contributory benefits, one of the main ones being that a significant proportion of the population does not make enough contributions to claim contributory benefits. This includes school-leavers, the long-term unemployed and young mothers in particular, as well as women in general. As we saw in Chapter 3, under Beveridge's system, married women who had paid jobs were allowed to opt for reduced contributions, which affected their individual entitlement to National Insurance benefits. The idea behind this was that they would receive benefit through their husband if he became unemployed, but this was of little help to women who separated from their partners or outlived them. Today, the rules for contributions are the same for all workers regardless of gender. Women (and indeed men) who are out of the labour market as a result of childcare and caring responsibilities are credited with some contributions through Home Responsibilities Protection. Only by 2020 will women be retiring with an average of 90 per cent of the full basic state pension (Government Actuary's Department, 1995).

Box 4.2

Features of Different Types of Benefit

	Main advantages	*Main disadvantages*
Contributory benefits	Encourage and reward participation in paid work Based on rights to claim, so not stigmatising	Certain groups are excluded or only partially covered by the insurance system
Means-tested benefits	Target resources on those in greatest need	Expensive to run Low take-up Affect work incentives May stigmatise recipients
Contingent benefits	Often cheap to run Not stigmatising Simple to understand Limited effect on work incentives	Not well targeted, so expensive through being universal

The relative advantages and disadvantages of each type of benefit are shown in Box 4.2.

Other methods of classifying social security benefits

The threefold classification of benefits into whether entitlement is contributory, means-tested or contingent is only one possible way of distinguishing between the many different social security benefits that exist. For example, in a pamphlet for the Institute for Public Policy Research (1993), Alcock makes a distinction between five different benefit types: contributory, means-tested, categorical, occupational and discretionary. This categorisation is the same as that used here, plus the addition of two further types of benefit: occupational and discretionary.

Occupational benefits (see Chapter 1) – such as occupational pension schemes – are not generally considered to be part of the state social security system because they are provided at the discretion of the employer. However, employees with an appropriate employment contract are legally entitled to Statutory Sick Pay and Statutory Maternity Pay, neither of which are contributions based or means-tested. They undeniably affect differences in living standards between those who do and do not benefit from them.

The main discretionary benefit is the Social Fund, established in 1988 (see Chapter 6). Payments from the Social Fund take the form of either grants or loans and are means-tested. We would, therefore, categorise the Social Fund as a means-tested benefit, but, unlike current means-tested benefits, there is no legal entitlement to loans from the Social Fund. Grants are, however, a legal entitlement for those meeting the qualifying conditions. Claimants have to pass the means test but are then, in most cases, subject to the discretion of the official dealing with their application.

Another way of classifying benefits is through their function. Some exist to relieve poverty (or low income), others to replace earnings, others to meet extra costs. We have already shown how there is some link between the rules of entitlement and the function of benefits, contributory benefits acting as insurance against certain risks, and means-tested benefits acting as a safety net to ensure a minimum level of income. In Britain, people may receive only one earnings-replacement benefit at a time, it being deemed, for example, that people cannot be both unemployed and a carer.

Box 4.3 shows the main social security benefits and where they fit into two classificatory systems: entitlement rules and functions of the benefit.

It is interesting to look at the relationship between different classifications of benefit and how they contribute to the overall aims of the social security system. In Chapter 1, we saw that the social security system has a number of aims, some of which compete with each other. For example, the system aims to alleviate poverty at the least cost, which means trying to focus expenditure on those who need it most. The system also tries to ensure that everyone who is entitled to benefit will claim and receive it, and this will keep non-take-up to a minimum. Additionally, the system aims to maintain people's incentives to provide for themselves through increasing earnings and/or savings. Finally, successive governments have attempted to keep the costs of administering the system as low as possible. Box 4.4 shows a broad evaluation of how the different types of benefit measure up against these criteria. It shows that means-tested benefits generally alleviate poverty at a low overall cost (as there will be relatively few claimants compared with universal benefits), but the administrative cost per claimant may be high, and means tests may reduce incentives for self-

Box 4.3

Different Types of Benefit by Function and Rules of Entitlement

		Rules of entitlement	
Function	*Contributory*	*Means-tested*	*Contingent*
Earnings-replacement	Jobseeker's Allowance Sickness Benefit Incapacity Benefit Retirement Pension Widow's Benefit		Severe Disablement Allowance Invalid Care Allowance Industrial Injuries Benefit Statutory Maternity Pay Statutory Sick Pay
Safety net		Income Support Family Credit/ Working Families Tax Credit	
Meeting extra costs		Housing Benefit Social Fund	Child Benefit Disability Living Allowance

provision while at the same time discouraging some people from applying for the benefit.

Yet another way of classifying benefits is through the types of people who receive them: pensioners, disabled people, families with children and unemployed people. The next chapter will look in detail at each of these groups.

When classifying benefits, the term 'universal' is often used to distinguish some benefits from those which are either 'selective' or 'targeted'. For example, the contingent benefit Child Benefit is universal for those who have children, and the contributory benefit state Retirement Pension is universal for those who are over a certain age and have made sufficient contributions. Thus, 'universal' generally refers to non-means-tested benefits, and it is often appropriate to make a simple division between universal and means-tested benefits. Equally,

Box 4.4

Comparison of Universal and Selective Approaches to Social Security Benefits

	Universal (non-means-tested)	Means-tested
Cost of alleviating all poverty	High	Low
Effect on reducing work incentives	Low	High
Administrative cost	Low, unless contribution conditions complex	High, particularly if benefits change with circumstances
Probable take-up	High	Medium

a simple division is sometimes made between contributory and non-contributory benefits. Our threefold classification enables such divisions to be made.

Expenditure and number of people on different benefits

As we saw in Chapter 1, spending on benefits has reached approximately £100 billion and has risen steadily in the past decade despite attempts by governments to curb this rise. The social security system that operated in 1949–50 would cost £12 billion at today's prices, indicating the long-term growth in this area of spending. However, the economy tends to grow faster than changes in price level, so this may exaggerate the extent of growth. Even so, the proportion of GDP that social security represents has risen from 5 per cent in 1949–50 to 13 per cent in the mid-1990s. Over the same period, the number of pensioners has risen from 4 to 11 million. As we saw in Chapter 1, social security expenditure was one-third of all government spending in 1996–97, or as much as spending on the health, education and social services combined.

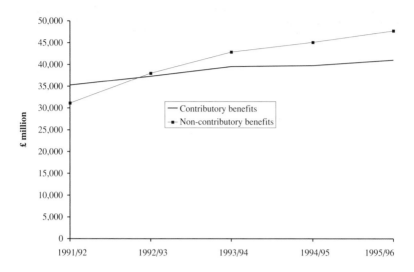

Figure 4.1   Expenditure on contributory and other benefits

As mentioned above, expenditure on contributory benefits has declined in relation to other benefits. Figure 4.1 shows that, despite socio-economic changes and deliberate government policy in favour of means-tested benefits, expenditure on non-contributory (mostly means-tested) benefits overtook expenditure on contributory benefits only quite recently, in 1992–93.

The gap between the two types of benefit then started to diverge in the following few years. However, in 1995–96, contributory benefits still accounted for 46 per cent of all benefit expenditure. The main reason for the continued importance of contributory benefits, despite government policies and socio-economic changes, is the prominent role played in the social security system by the state Retirement Pension. Despite a rise in the number of pensioners, the relative importance of the Retirement Pension has reduced because of the fast growth in other areas of social security spending, especially on families with children (particularly lone parents) and on sick and disabled people.

The number of people on benefits has also risen steadily. Since 1979–80, the expenditure on unemployed people has fluctuated quite dramatically as the economy has moved in and out of different recessions. Generally, however, spending on the unemployed has remained at a much lower level than outlay on other types of benefit. Spending

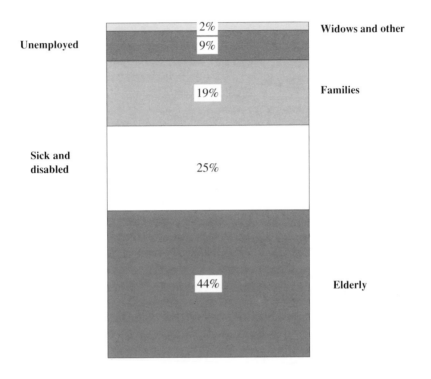

Figure 4.2   Spending on different groups
(Department of Social Security, 1997)

on the family has increased year on year, partly because of the increase in the number of lone-parent families. Spending on sick and disabled people has grown dramatically. Funding for pensioners has always taken up the largest proportion of social security spending and has also increased over the past decade and a half.

Figure 4.2 shows the current division of benefit expenditure by different groups. Elderly people accounted for 44 per cent of the expenditure in 1995–96, the next largest chunk of money going to sick and disabled people. Thus, while the main image of someone on social security is an unemployed person, and governments pay a great deal of attention to helping people move off benefit and into work, expenditure on unemployed benefit recipients accounts for only £1 in every £10 spent on social security.

Benefit levels and adequacy

As illustrated above, expenditure on benefits has risen in both absolute and real terms, but increasing expenditure on benefits has not been fuelled by rises in the real levels of benefit, and there is indeed widespread evidence that benefit levels are not adequate to meet people's basic requirements. Beveridge initially aimed to set benefits at subsistence levels according to budget studies in the 1930s, but there is disagreement about whether he achieved this. The existence of price inflation means that benefit levels have to be raised every year ('uprated') or they will be worth increasingly less in real terms. There is some evidence that both the initial levels of benefit and the uprating of prices in the 1940s were not performed correctly. In more recent years, some benefits have been frozen and others have been linked to price inflation rather than wage inflation (if it was higher). This means that benefit recipients have become increasingly worse off relative to workers. Moreover, since the early 1980s, more benefits have been brought within the scope of income tax – for example state Retirement Pension, Unemployment Benefit and Incapacity Benefit – and this has affected the relative generosity of these benefits.

To illustrate some of these points, let us take Income Support, the main safety net benefit. The Income Support rate varies depending on whether the claim is made on behalf of a single person or a couple. The rate also depends on the age of the adults and children who are being claimed for. Single people over the age of 24 are paid more than younger ones. The reasons could include the fact that wages for the younger group are generally lower than for older people, and there is concern to ensure that people will not be better off on benefit than in work. Couples without children are paid about twice the rate of an 18–24-year-old but much less than twice the rate for those over 25. The argument here is that two people living together can live more cheaply than if they were living separately, but if this assumption is incorrect, there may be a financial disincentive for two single people to live together.

People with children are entitled to more than just a basic rate of Income Support. Various extra amounts (known as premiums) also exist depending on whether the claim is made on behalf of a couple or a lone parent. Taking into account the premiums available, a couple with a 5-year-old child are paid about £23 a week more than a lone parent with a similar child, and there is a lively debate about whether this difference means that couples are relatively worse off compared with lone parents. Indeed, the government is currently phasing out lone-parent premium so that lone parents making a new claim no longer have such an apparent advantage over couples. Table 4.1 gives the rates of Income Support for different family types from 1998–99. There are also premiums available to disabled people, carers and some other groups to top up their Income Support entitlements.

Table 4.1   Weekly Income Support rates, 1998–99

	Single person aged 18–24	Single person aged 25+	Single person over 60	Couple both aged 18+	Couple with a 5-year-old	Couple with children aged 10 and 12
Allowances						
Basic rate for adults	£39.85	£50.35	£50.35	£79.00	£79.00	£79.00
Rate for younger child	–	–	–	–	£17.30	£17.30
Rate for older child	–	–	–	–	–	£25.35
Premiums						
Family premium	–	–	–	–	£11.05	£11.05
Pensioner premium	–	–	£20.10	–	–	–
Total benefit	£39.85	£50.35	£70.45	£79.00	£107.35	£132.70

These weekly amounts of benefit have to cover all outgoings apart from housing costs (for which Housing Benefit and some help towards mortgage payments may be available) and Council Tax (for which Council Tax Benefit may be available). Otherwise, all expenditure on food, gas, electricity, telephone, household goods, clothing, travel, furniture and so on must be financed from these benefit payments. This prompts the question 'Is it enough?' and how we should calculate 'How much is enough?' Various studies have carried out detailed interviews with people on benefit and found that trying to make ends meet on benefit is a full-time job at which it is almost impossible to succeed, particularly in the long term (see, for example, Kempson *et al.*, 1994;

Kempson, 1996). Other studies have approached the issue from the opposite direction, beginning with the question 'What level of income would be adequate?' in order to have a particular standard of living. These 'family budget' studies have used evidence about how people in the UK actually spend their money and what the public thinks about standards of need and adequacy to construct a 'basket of goods' containing items that more than two-thirds of the population consider to be necessities. The cost of this basket of goods therefore represents a minimum standard of living, and a study in 1993 found that families with young children needed incomes about a third higher than their Income Support rates to maintain such a standard of living (Oldfield and Yu, 1993). Single pensioners, however, seemed to have just about enough money on Income Support to maintain a minimum standard of living. Thus, some types of claimant may be better or worse off than others.

Benefit rates are designed to be low so that people do not choose to live on benefit rather than work. This is partly why there are premiums for pensioners and disabled people, who are not expected to be able to find paid employment. However, as we saw in Chapter 1, social security also aims to alleviate poverty, yet, as just mentioned, studies suggest that many benefit recipients live in considerable hardship (Kempson *et al.*, 1994; Kempson, 1996).

The benefit unit

As mentioned above, the benefit unit for means-tested benefits is the 'family'. For the purposes of Income Support, which is often a model case, a family comprises one of the following:

- A single person without children
- A couple without children
- A couple with dependent children
- A lone parent with dependent children.

This raises the question of when two people constitute a couple and when a child is considered to be dependent, which we discussed briefly above. Generally speaking, children must be under 16 or 18 years of age and in non-advanced, full-time education, and a couple must be one male and one female who are living together as husband and wife. The rules for other benefits may include a wider or narrower range of people, as discussed below.

Roll (1991) has identified different 'stages' of the process of making a claim for social security benefits. At each stage, the appropriate 'unit' for benefit purposes may vary. These stages are (Roll, 1991: 22):

The claim – who applies for the benefit?
Entitlement – which people are taken into account when calculating the benefit?
Coverage – who is the benefit supposed to pay for?
Payment – who receives the money?

If we take Housing Benefit as an example, one person will generally apply for the household, although some households (such as groups of unrelated young people living together) will make separate claims for each person. The entitlement will be based on *all* the people living in the dwelling rather than just the Income Support benefit unit (through the application of what are known as non-dependent deductions). The amount of payment will be expected to cover the rent for all those people. The payment itself may be made to the applicant, or it may, in some cases, be paid directly to the landlord (as was particularly seen when social housing was a larger part of the housing stock).

There are complex examples from various parts of the benefit system that illustrate the different rules for the appropriate unit of assessment for benefits. The value of the state Retirement Pension may be based on the contribution record of one's divorced, separated or deceased spouse. The receipt of Invalid Care Allowance depends on the benefits received by a person being cared for; conversely, entitlement to the severe disability premium in Income Support relies on there *not* being a carer receiving Invalid Care Allowance for that person, and that the person lives alone. The rules for Council Tax Benefit are very complex, but they permit deductions on the basis of the situation of any 'second adult' within the household, perhaps someone unrelated to the benefit applicant. In rare cases, a claim for widows' benefits may allow for people married to more than one partner.

The fundamental question concerns whether benefits should be based solely on the individual (like income tax, for example) rather than on couples and wider groups of people. The system is currently based on the assumption that couples share their income and that there are certain economies of scale from living as a couple. Neither of these assumptions is wholly valid. The victims of the current system are often women in couples, who may have limited access to their partner's income and yet may have the main burden of providing food and paying bills for the family.

A completely independent system of benefits would mean that someone who was out of work would be able to claim benefits regardless of a partner's income. Such a system might be more expensive than the current situation and could form the basis of a Citizen's Income (see Chapter 9). It is sometimes criticised as (needlessly) paying money to the spouses (usually wives) of the well-off who do not require financial support, but the overall distributional consequences of such a system are rather more complex than this example suggests (Esam and Berthoud, 1991). Additionally, there are many possible reforms that move the system towards a greater degree of individualisation without requiring a full Citizen's Income. An idea that has been seriously discussed recently is to split benefit payments within couples so that, for example in families with children, most benefit money would be paid to the woman. Splitting benefit payment is possible according to the rules of the current system, but it is rarely carried out in practice.

However, the treatment of joint costs, such as for housing and Council Tax (or other local taxes), will always create a problem for a wholly individualised basis of entitlement (Brittan and Webb, 1990).

5

Who Receives Benefits?

Introduction

In the previous chapter, we suggested that one way of classifying benefits is by considering the groups of people who receive them. This chapter looks at each of the different types of benefit recipient in the following order, arranged by the size of current social security spending on each group:

- Pensioners
- Disabled people (and their carers)
- Families with children
- The unemployed.

Some social security benefits can only be received by a particular group; for example, only disabled people can (or at least should) receive Incapacity Benefit. There are, however, some social security benefits that can be received by more than one group. In particular, Income Support could (at least in the past) be claimed by all of these groups, and Jobseeker's Allowance could be claimed by unemployed people with or without children. As well as describing the different types of benefit available to each group, we also discuss the reasons for providing particular benefits to particular groups and consider the types of people claiming and the main issues relating to them.

We begin with some basic figures on the importance of different benefits within the social security budget (Figure 5.1) and how that picture has altered since 1979. The general picture is that two of the large 'universal' benefits – the state Retirement Pension and Child Benefit – now account for much smaller proportions of overall social security spending, although the former remains the largest overall benefit in spending terms. Over the same period, there has been a strong rise in benefits for disability and sickness, which have grown at

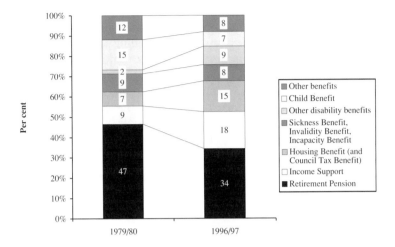

Figure 5.1 The changing composition of social security spending
(DSS Focus File 01, 1998b)

an annual rate of 14 per cent in the intervening period, and in the importance of means-tested benefits. Means-tested Income Support, Housing Benefit and Council Tax Benefit now account for around one-third of DSS spending, more than double the figure for 1979–80.

Pensioners

Pensioners form the largest group of recipients of benefits spending, accounting for about one-third of all social security spending in 1996–97.

The rationale for benefits in retirement

The perceived need for state Retirement Pensions was at the heart of the development of the social security system in this country during the first half of the twentieth century. The rationale for benefits in retirement rests heavily on the rationale behind the concept of retirement. The notion that people should cease work at a particular age is taken for granted today, but this idea has, in fact, developed only within the past century. The idea of a group of people retired for a substantial number of years is an even more recent phenomenon.

Retirement is often seen positively as providing a chance for older people to increase their leisure time after a long working life. However, it can also be viewed as a means of excluding older people from the labour market. Between 1931 and 1971, the proportion of men aged 65+ who were retired increased from under one-half to more than three-quarters. Walker has argued that older people have been used as a reserve army of labour that is tapped into when labour is in short supply and shed when the demand for labour falls:

> The advent of large scale unemployment in the 1930s was crucial in the institu-tionalisation of retirement, and its return in the early 1980s has resulted in the growth of early retirement. (Walker, 1986: 210)

Retirement can also be viewed as rather a male concept. You retire from paid work – whereas unpaid work that takes place within the home is, presumably, expected to continue (Walker, 1992). Retirement, there-fore, affects men and women differently, but this may change given higher female employment rates among younger population cohorts.

Current benefits available for pensioners in Britain

There are several different categories of basic Retirement Pension, along with SERPS, graduated pensions and additions for the over 80s as well as the more general means-tested benefits paid to this group. However, the basic state Retirement Pension accounts for around four-fifths of spending on those older than the state pension age. Alongside state pensions, there is also a strong non-state pension system. Occupa-tional and the more recently introduced personal pensions cover the majority of those now retiring.

The cost of the state Retirement Pension is high and has increased at a steady rate in recent years to more than £30 billion in 1996–97. It alone, therefore, amounts to about a third of all social security spending. There has also been a rise in the number of recipients of state Retirement Pension – from 8 million in 1979 to 10.4 million in 1996. Expenditure on Income Support for the elderly amounted to another £4 billion in 1996, covering about 1.8 million recipients.

Although men are more likely than women to receive contribution-based benefits for unemployed people of working age, most recipients of the basic Retirement Pension are women (6.6 million women compared with 3.7 million men in 1996). This is not because women are more likely to build up contributions to state Retirement Pension during their working lives but because men's contributions cover their wives, who tend to live longer than their husbands. In some ways, this aspect of the contributory system can be seen as redistributing wealth on gender lines from men to women, although it could also be argued that women's lower rates of contribution result from the undervaluing of the unpaid work that they do in the private sphere compared with the paid work that men do in the public sphere.

The level of the state Retirement Pension is lower than the rate of Income Support for pensioners, so those without any additional source of income or with low levels of contributions are usually entitled to a top-up from Income Support. Changes announced in July 1998 have recognised the low incomes of many pensioners and led to a guaranteed minimum income of £75 for single pensioners from April 1999, which is three times the increase expected under Income Support uprating rules (DSS Press Release, 1998, No. 209). It is also planned to use data-matching and personal advisers to improve the take-up of Income Support.

Those with occupational or personal pensions above the level of Income Support will not qualify for any top-up, and it has been argued that this causes a disincentive to contribute to an occupational pension – or leads to an unfairly low return for contributing to one. Recent changes can only worsen this feature in the long run.

As we saw in Chapter 3, the basis of the current state pension scheme was set in 1908, the first contributory pensions being paid from 1925 onwards. However, the most important reform was that following the Beveridge Report in 1942. This established the basis of pension provision – the receipt of a flat-rate pension. Also, full pensions were based on a considerable number of years of contributing to the scheme.

State Retirement Pension is, therefore, based on contributions made during an individual's working lifetime, which means that years out of the labour market reduce benefit. Thus, groups likely to be away from paid jobs, such as women and those persistently unemployed, do not have a full entitlement on entering retirement.

Prior to 1980, the state Retirement Pension was increased in line with rises in earnings, or in line with price changes if they were higher. However, in 1980, the break with earnings was made. From that point on, pensions have only been increased in line with price changes. In 1977, the state Retirement Pension was worth 20 per cent of average male earnings, but 20 years later, it was worth nearer to 15 per cent. In the longer term, the value compared with earnings will continue to decline to well below 10 per cent early in the next century. The effect of this is easily demonstrated. Had the earnings link been preserved from 1980 to 1993, the basic Retirement Pension in 1993 would have been worth £74.55 for a single person and £119.30 for a couple. However, because the earnings link was broken, the pension was actually worth only £56.10 and £89.90 respectively, and the gap continues to grow. The state Retirement Pension is, therefore, becoming increasingly insufficient as a long-term subsistence benefit.

In 1976, an additional earnings-related component, the State Earnings-Related Pension Scheme (SERPS), was introduced. However, it is possible to 'opt out' from this, and it is not as favourable as originally planned following changes in 1986 and 1995, in each case roughly halving the future benefits of SERPS membership. Reform in the late 1980s, however, stopped short of the complete abolition that the Green Paper had proposed. It has been suggested that pressure from employers' representatives, fearing a clamour for employer-provided replacement pensions, was the key factor in effecting this change in approach.

In 1993, the decision was made to equalise state pensions for men and women at the age of 65 (for a discussion, see Hutton *et al.*, 1995). This satisfies the needs of formal sex equality and also helps to keep expenditure lower than alternative equalisation options below the age of 65.

Private pension provision

As well as the basic Retirement Pension and Income Support, some pensioners may be receiving income from other sources, such as a private pension. The most important type is occupational pension provision. These are schemes set up and run by employers, individual employees often benefiting from their employer contributing to the scheme. There are, in addition, tax advantages to such a provision. Private personal pensions are also available. These are usually set up by individuals who take them out through private pension companies. They are usually not as favourable as occupational pensions but may offer a beneficial way of opting out of the earnings-related part of the state scheme (SERPS). The value of private pensions depends on the salary while contributing or on the amount paid into the scheme.

There was a very rapid growth in occupational pension provision in the 1950s and 60s. According to the surveys of the Government Actuary's Department, the number contributing towards these pensions doubled, from around 6 million in 1953 to 12 million in 1967. However, there has been no growth since then. Indeed, numbers are now below that level, although personal pensions have since taken off. Access to an occupational pension is of great importance to the final standard of living in retirement. Also, there are important differences in the potential access to these types of pension. They are characteristic of larger, rather than smaller, firms. They are more likely to be taken up by men, typically those in full-time work. They have also, at least in the past, tended to benefit those workers who stayed put in one firm rather than those who moved about from firm to firm (McKay *et al.*, 1999).

There has clearly been pressure to increase the role of private provision. We must always remember that the majority of pensioners are still highly dependent on state benefits. The level of private income is clearly increasing but currently forms the greater part of income for only a minority of pensioners. Around 50 per cent of current employees are members of occupational schemes. In 1992, about 28 per cent of male employees and 19 per cent of female employees had personal pension plans. However, the growth of part-time employment, and other forms of flexible working, may have important consequences for the pensions scene.

Pensioners and poverty

Many previous studies have found that older people are at a high – or a higher than average – risk of poverty. As early as 1899, Seebohm Rowntree, in his study of York, found a high risk of poverty in old age, which was part of a life course perspective: poverty was associated with childhood, bringing up dependent children and then older age (Rowntree, 1901). Studies by Townsend (1979) and Walker (1986) have confirmed this.

However, figures are often presented suggesting that pensioners are doing better now than in the past. These figures show the growing level of average (mean) income among older people and the declining importance of the basic state Retirement Pension. They also show that income from private sources, occupational pensions in particular, has been rising quite rapidly. At one time, advertisers and others believed that a new so-called 'grey economy' would be appearing. However, figures showing mean income are often skewed upward because of a few wealthy people. They, therefore, tell us nothing about the distribution of income among all pensioners, and it turns out to be important to look at the distribution of income among older age groups. Thus, although the state Retirement Pension represents only about half of all pensioner income, most pensioners rely on it for the overwhelming majority of their income.

For most pensioners, any income from occupational pensions or savings will be quite trivial. Moreover, the income from such sources will often be of little or no benefit to the recipient. This is because means-tested social security benefits are reduced pound for pound for income from occupational pensions. Savings also reduce the entitlement to means-tested benefits.

Since 1979, inequality among pensioners has increased. The income of the top 40 per cent of pensioners has increased by two-thirds, whereas for the bottom fifth, real growth has been only 10 per cent. The Commission on Social Justice (1994) argued that one-third of pensioners were income tax-payers (and, therefore, relatively well off), one-third were at or below the poverty line, and the remaining one-third lay somewhere in between.

This inequality between pensioners is not surprising given that status in retirement is determined to a large extent by status during working life. For example, women often have to rely on their husband's record of contributions rather than qualifying in their own right. Years spent in unemployment, or in low-waged occupation, or in companies not providing pensions, or switching employers, will all tend to reduce the amount of income available to people when they cease employment.

It is true, however, that older people are more likely to have accumulated wealth than are people of younger ages (Rowlingson *et al.*, 1998). They have had time to save; they are likely to have long paid off any mortgage that they might have had. However, the ability to make use of a housing asset is limited. For those on lower incomes, is this an advantage? Owner-occupiers may have no weekly or monthly housing costs, but tenants will also have no housing costs because Housing Benefit will meet all their rent. Also, owner-occupiers will be faced with maintenance costs that may be particularly high if they have lived for many years in the same home. The main way of unlocking housing assets is to move to a smaller/cheaper home or to move to rented accommodation.

Retirement benefits in other countries

The basic state pension in Britain is based on a flat-rate benefit. The maturing of SERPS will introduce an earnings-related component over time, but basic state pensions are not directly linked to the level of contributions made during the course of an individual's working life. However, in most countries with well-developed social insurance systems, the state sector takes on the role of providing earnings-related pensions. The British state pension system, therefore, replaces a lower proportion of average and higher earnings than do the systems typically found in continental Europe. This, of course, explains why the private sector for pensions has become so prominent in the UK.

Comparative studies of pensions remain surprisingly rare. Ploug and Kvist's (1996) comparative research compared old-age pension systems in eight different countries from among the more developed Northern European welfare systems. They found that British state pensions tended to 'replace' a lower proportion of earnings than did those of most other welfare states. They calculated that state pension entitlements would replace about 44 per cent of the average blue-collar wage, compared with rather higher figures in the other countries studied (Figure 5.2). However, the UK system was closer to wage levels for those on lower earnings, reflecting the largely flat-rate nature of UK state pension provision. Ginn and Arber (1992) have documented the ways in which caring responsibilities are taken into account in differing pensions systems.

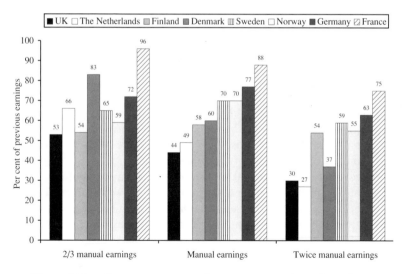

Figure 5.2 State statutory pensions as a proportion of previous earnings, by earnings level and country (Ploug and Kvist, 1996: 80, copyright Kluwer Law International)

Benefits for sickness and disability

The system of disability benefits is one of the more complex areas of the benefit system. Benefits exist to cover impairment or disability (Disability Living Allowance, Attendance Allowance, Industrial Injuries Disablement Benefit and War Pension), carers (Invalid Care Allowance and the carer's premium within Income Support) and incapacity to work (Incapacity Benefit, the disability premium on Income Support and Severe Disablement Allowance).

Rationale for disability benefits

Disabled people tend to be disadvantaged in three ways. First, they have a lower than average chance of getting a job, and, when they are in paid work, the level of pay they receive is often lower than that of a comparable person who is not disabled. Second, disabled people experience higher costs of everyday living than do other people. Certain conditions may require adaptations to be made to living quarters or greater amounts of heat to be provided (Berthoud *et al.*, 1993). Various attempts have been made to calculate these costs, for both adults (Berthoud, 1990; Large, 1990) and children (Baldwin, 1985; Dobson and Middleton, 1998), but the issue remains controversial. Third, there may be an effect on the people who live with, or support, disabled people. If a family is engaged in providing support, the employment prospects of those who provide care may be reduced; alternatively, family members may have to pay out for professional carers for part of the time.

This combination of reduced earnings and higher costs means that disabled people are likely to be rather worse off than other members of the population. In other words, they are rather more likely than average to be in need of social security (Berthoud, 1998).

However, it is also true that some other groups in society face similar types of disadvantage in the labour market but are not given separate benefits. Minority ethnic groups are one example. The explanation for this is partly historical as the insurance principle, which formed the basis of the modern social security system, made insurance against sickness or disability a key feature of the system. In addition, the very definition of disability within benefits has been to emphasise people's inability to work. Issues of disability discrimination, and promoting a return to work, have only recently reached the agenda. There also seem to be higher levels of public sympathy for disabled people: they tend to be viewed as part of the 'deserving poor'.

Each point partly explains why sick and disabled people receive separate benefits that are also relatively more generous than the corresponding benefits for non-disabled people. For example, the contributory element of Incapacity Benefit is currently not time limited (whereas the contributory element of Jobseeker's Allowance runs out after only 6 months), the level of money paid to the recipients of Incapacity Benefit is higher than the level paid to the recipients of the contributory element of Jobseeker's Allowance, and occupational pensions count as income against Jobseeker's Allowance but not Incapacity Benefit, although change has been proposed.

The government is currently reviewing the system of disability benefits (Berthoud, 1998). The extent of public support for this group means that any proposed cuts are likely to be strongly opposed, although adverse images about 'bad back' benefits may help those seeking to make cuts. Demonstrations by disabled people in December 1997 appear to have led to the direct involvement of the Prime Minister in reforming social security and to increased concern about the reform agenda.

The cost of disability benefits

The cost of almost all benefits for disabled people has increased in recent years. In 1983–84, total spending on this group was £7.3 billion. By 1993–94, spending had reached £17.1 billion (both figures being quoted in 1993–94 terms). This represents an increase of 9 per cent per year over and above the rate of inflation. The biggest increase affected benefits to help disabled people with meeting extra costs. Nevertheless, Invalidity Benefit (designed for those incapable of work) remained the largest benefit, accounting for £6.7 billion in 1993–94. Spending on all disability benefits has risen from 15 per cent of total social security spending in 1979–80 to 25 per cent in 1997–98.

This big increase in spending was not mainly the result of more generous benefits, even though it is true that there were increases in the rates of one or two disability benefits and that some new groups became entitled to claim. The main reason for the growth in disability benefit was the rising number of claims. About 500,000 people received Invalidity Benefit in 1975. By 1997, 1,750,000 were receiving Incapacity Benefit on a similar basis. This increase outstrips any

change in the proportion of people in surveys who report that they have
a limiting long-standing illness (Department of Social Security, 1998b,
Focus File 04). So why has such fast growth occurred?

For Invalidity Benefit, there is some evidence on the reasons for this
growth. Research among GPs showed that they were aware that
patients might be exaggerating the effects of their conditions, but GPs
were not prepared to question this too far in case they harmed the
doctor–patient relationship (Ritchie *et al.*, 1993). However, this qualitative work seems to be somewhat contradicted by certain other
evidence. It has been shown that the rise in the total number of Invalidity Benefit claims was not caused by more people claiming for the
first time. Instead, the main cause was the reduction in the number of
people *leaving* the register (Berthoud, 1993). People out of the labour
market had thus found it increasingly difficult to get back into work.
The increase was not caused by excessive ease of entry but instead by
difficulty of exit from the benefit case-load.

Current benefits available for disabled people in Britain

Within what is already a complicated system, disability benefits have a
reputation of being among the most difficult to grasp. Berthoud *et al.*
(1993) refers to a 'bewildering array of benefits'; in a historical study,
Brown (1984) declares that the benefits for this groups were 'a muddle
from the beginning'.

While the Beveridge Report was able to introduce a measure of
coherence in the arrangements for most groups (such as for pensioners
and the unemployed), strong diversity remained within the system for
disabled people. War Pensions have long been an important and relatively generous form of provision, having been introduced in their
current form in 1917. A separate Industrial Injuries Scheme was set up
for those who became disabled in the workplace. The insurance principle was very important in the development of disability benefits, but
it is clear that this principle cannot help those who are disabled from
birth or childhood and have, therefore, not had the opportunity to
contribute into the National Insurance scheme. There was thus a strong
distinction made between the different causes of disability rather than
the consequences of disability.

Berthoud *et al.* (1993) consider that benefits for disabled people are
based on five main principles: earnings-replacement, means-testing,
compensation, extra costs and benefits for carers. Box 5.1 divides the

main disability benefits into these five different types. The numbers in brackets show how many people were receiving these benefits in 1996–97.

Earnings-replacement benefits

Incapacity Benefit represents a key benefit in the insurance system. It was introduced in April 1995 as a replacement for Invalidity Benefit, and provides an income for people who are unable to work for long periods because of ill-health or disability and who had been paying National Insurance contributions before they left their previous employment. It is relatively similar in principle to benefits for unemployed people but has two main advantages over these. First, this benefit is not time limited: it may be received up to the point that the Retirement Pension takes over. Second, the amounts of money – although by no means generous in comparison with average wages – have always been rather higher than the amounts granted in Unemployment Benefit.

When Incapacity Benefit replaced Invalidity Benefit, three main changes occurred:

● Entitlement was now based on strictly medical criteria.
● Incapacity was now measured by a scoring system based on the answers to a questionnaire.
● Most of the responsibility for medical judgements was transferred from the claimant's own doctor to the 'official' doctors working for the Benefits Agency.

It is the first element of this that appears the most controversial – and new. A number of other measures are also included, most of them designed to reduce expenditure on the benefit:

● The abolition of entitlement after pension age
● Bringing the benefit into tax
● Abolishing the earnings-related additional pension for disabled people
● Limiting dependency additions to families with children.

The Office of Population Censuses and Surveys (OPCS) study of disabled people in 1985 showed that about half of the out-of-work disabled people below pensionable age received Invalidity Benefit (Martin *et al.*, 1988). It was paid at higher rates than some other social

Box 5.1

Principal Benefits for Disabled People and Carers
(Based on Berthoud *et al.*, 1993)

Earnings replacement benefits

Incapacity Benefit (1.8 million)

Severe Disablement Allowance

(350,000)

Means-tested benefits

Income Support to disabled

(790,000)

Housing Benefit/Council Tax

Benefit

(with disability premium

+ disabled child premium

+ severe disability premium

+ higher pensioner premium

+ carers premium)

Disability Working Allowance

(12,000)

Compensation benefits

War Pensions (330,000)

Industrial Injuries scheme (250,000)

(+ Constant Attendance Allowance

+ Exceptionally Severe

Disablement Allowance

+ Retirement Allowance)

Extra costs benefits

Disability Living Allowance

(1.9 million)

Attendance Allowance (1.2 million)

Carers' benefits

Invalid Care Allowance (360,000)

Latest recipient figures shown in brackets are taken from Department of Social Security (1997).

security benefits, so it was relatively successful at protecting claimants from the extremes of poverty. Only 9 per cent of Invalidity Benefit claimants had to top up their income with Income Support compared with 50 per cent of claimants of the similar – although non-contributory – Severe Disablement Allowance. By 1996–97, the proportion of those receiving Income Support was 12 per cent for recipients of Incapacity Benefit and 72 per cent for those receiving Severe Disablement Allowance. The insurance principle, of course, limited the coverage of Incapacity Benefit to people with a record of employment, so married women, and people who had been disabled since childhood, were unlikely to qualify.

As argued above, there are various reasons for having separate benefits for disabled people. If we confine ourselves to those without jobs, there are three main reasons why disabled people might be treated differently from non-disabled people. First, there may be a feeling that disabled people are a deserving group because they have not brought their own misfortune on themselves. The non-disabled unemployed, on the other hand, may be seen as causing their own suffering through idleness or laziness. This reflects the long-standing issue of the 'deserving poor' and the 'undeserving poor'. Disabled people may be taken to represent one part of the 'deserving poor'. Second, there is less of a concern about disincentives to work. As we shall see in Chapter 8, policy for the unemployed has sometimes been based on concerns about whether the unemployed give up looking for work if benefits are seen to be 'too generous'. Until recently, there were few such concerns regarding disabled people. This is partly because unemployment is a changeable social condition whereas disability is often seen as an unchanging physical condition. Third, and building on this point, it may be expected that disabled people will tend to stay on benefits for a long time. Their prospects of 'escape' are said to be less than those of other groups, so they need more money to cope with the difficulties of living long term on benefits.

It is possible, however, to take issue with all of these arguments. It is not necessarily true that disabled people's behaviour in response to the system is never a factor. Also, more conventionally, the unemployed often have few options if they are sacked in an area of high unemployment. The other issues relate to work incentives and prospects for moving off benefits. In fact, the chances of the long-term unemployed leaving unemployment are often rather low, so they might require additional benefit as much as disabled people do.

As well as Incapacity Benefit, Severe Disablement Allowance is a benefit designed particularly for disabled people of working age who are not in employment. It is a non-means-tested, non-contributory benefit that is contingent on a certain (and severe) level of impairment. The benefit is aimed *mainly* at severely disabled people who are disabled from birth so have not had time to build up sufficient contributions to be eligible for Incapacity Benefit. It pays a lower weekly level of money than does Incapacity Benefit.

Compensation

The system of compensation benefits for disabled people is a particularly complex and arcane area. As Berthoud *et al.* (1993: 120) put it:

> The social security system is a Russian doll of complexities. The system as a whole is complicated; benefits for disabled people are a complex subset of the whole; the industrial injuries scheme and war pensions introduce a new layer of complications even within disability benefits.

Pensions for those affected by wars were among the earliest types of benefit introduced in many countries. The War Pensions Agency has been responsible for handling applications for War Pensions since it was established as a separate (Next Steps) agency in 1994. Claims may be made by the person affected or by the widows of those whose death was hastened by service in the armed forces (Nove, with McKay, 1995). Those covered are members of the armed forces who were disabled or who died as a result of active service, members of certain support services and civilians who were injured in the course of the Second World War. It is worth noting that the term 'War' Pension is, therefore, something of a misnomer since it also covers members of the armed forces during peacetime. By 1996–97, the total spending on War Pensions was some £1.4 billion, paying benefits to 266,000 disabled people and 60,000 widows (giving an average payment of £83 per week per person on the case-load).

The Industrial Injuries Scheme includes both Industrial Death Benefit (for deaths before April 1988) and Industrial Injuries Disablement Benefit. Industrial Injuries Disablement Benefit is available from 90 days after an industrial accident, rates of payment varying with the degree of disability caused by the accident. In 1996–97, there were 245,000 pensions in payment, at a total expenditure of £661 million (an average of £52 per person per week). The maximum rate of payment is £104.70 (for those 100 per cent disabled) from April 1998, but there are also supplements available in the form of Constant Attendance Allowance (maximum £84 per week), Exceptionally Severe Disablement Allowance (maximum £42 per week) and Retirement Allowance (maximum £10.47 per week). For previous applications, there were supplements in the form of Unemployability Supplement and Reduced Earnings Allowance, which continue for pre-existing awards.

These benefits raise important issues of fairness. Why is it appropriate to pay £100 per week to someone who falls off a ladder at work but not to someone who falls off a ladder at home? A soldier who breaks his back in a swimming pool may receive twice as much benefit as a civilian who breaks his back in the same pool. Why should the *cause* of the impairment be an important consideration in determining benefit entitlement? In the case of Industrial Injuries benefits, it might be asked why the costs fall on the state rather than on employers, who could insure their workforce against injuries. The presence of such a scheme, with costs not falling on employers, provides no incentive for employers, other than through health and safety legislation and possible litigation claims, to run the safest possible workplaces.

However, as we saw in Chapter 3, before the introduction of these state benefits, employees had to take their employers to court to secure compensation, which was often difficult for them to do. The liability of employers, which was established with the 1897 Workmen's Compensation Act, was taken over by the state in 1946 (Smith, 1978).

Means-tested benefits

All of the benefits discussed so far are underpinned by a set of means-tested benefits, the main one being Income Support, that form a 'safety net'. However, not all means-tested benefits are aimed at people without other sources of income. For example, the introduction of Disability Working Allowance (modelled on Family Credit) was based on the assumption that disabled people might be able and want to work but might face financial disincentives. It aims to provide a top-up to the earnings of disabled workers, but, contrary to government hopes and expectations, it has encouraged relatively few disabled people to take a job and claim the benefit (Rowlingson and Berthoud, 1996). From 1999, Disability Working Allowance is replaced by higher rates of award under the Disabled Person's Tax Credit.

Benefits to meet the extra costs of disability

Disability Living Allowance was introduced in 1992 following evidence that disabled people faced extra costs of living – for example extra transport costs and costs to pay for care – compared with others (Berthoud *et al.*, 1993). Disability Living Allowance largely replaced Mobility Allowance and Attendance Allowance, which dated back to the early 1970s. The number of people applying for Disability Living Allowance increased rapidly and soon surpassed government expectations.

In 1997, there were 1.9 million recipients of Disability Living Allowance and 1.2 million receiving Attendance Allowance. Most Attendance Allowance recipients (70 per cent) were female, reflecting the longer life expectancy of women. These benefits for extra costs do not count as income against means-tested benefits, and indeed they provide a passport to particular premiums within Income Support. There are a considerable number of people on both benefits. In 1997:

- 37 per cent of Disability Living Allowance (care) recipients received Income Support
- 31 per cent of Disability Living Allowance (mobility) recipients received Income Support
- 40 per cent of Attendance Allowance recipients received Income Support.

Benefits for carers

Britain is relatively unusual in having a specific benefit for those providing informal care, in the form of Invalid Care Allowance (McLaughlin, 1991a), even if the amount being paid is relatively low (Glendinning and McLaughlin, 1993: 153). It has been a controversial benefit since its introduction in 1975, not least because it was denied to married women until a European Court ruling in 1986 (Glendinning, 1992: 172).

Invalid Care Allowance is available for those caring for at least 35 hours a week who earn less than £50 per week. The receipt of Invalid Care Allowance also provides a passport to receiving the carer's premium within means-tested benefits such as Income Support. Recipients of Invalid Care Allowance may benefit from National Insurance contribution credits, and their entitlement to the basic state Retirement Pension is looked after through Home Responsibilities Protection.

The 357,000 current awards cost a total of £768 million in 1996. Three-quarters (76 per cent) of recipients are women.

Disability benefits in other countries

There are few comprehensive comparative studies of the range of benefits for disabled people and their carers, despite the fact that benefits for industrial injury and sickness are often the first to be established in many countries (Ploug and Kvist, 1996: 14).

Lonsdale and Seddon (1994) identified common patterns of growth in the number receiving disability benefits in the UK, the USA, Sweden, Australia and the Netherlands. Their study, which was restricted to benefits for those of working age deemed less able to work, found that disability benefits usually entailed a large premium over benefits for people who were unemployed. All five countries had attempted to stem the rising tide of spending on these benefits. Thornton *et al.* (1997) reviewed benefits for partial capacity in seven different countries and noted the lack of a demand-side strategy in the UK. In other words, the UK had few policies aimed at creating jobs for disabled people, either directly or indirectly by encouraging employers to create such jobs.

Glendinning and McLaughlin (1993) looked at benefits for informal carers in a range of countries. Britain appears to have fairly distinctive individual rights to social security for carers, instead of their rights being derived from others (such as the person being cared for).

Families with children

In this section, we move on to consider families with dependent children. As mentioned in the previous chapter, the term 'dependent child' can have different meanings, but, for the purposes of social security in Britain, we mean all children aged up to 16 years and those aged 17–18 who are still in full-time education. In other countries, children may be thought to be dependent until they are much older (such as France and Germany) or possibly a little younger (for example, Portugal and Greece). Families with dependent children can be supported in many different ways – through cash benefits, through tax allowances or through provision in kind such as education, childcare, health and so on. Families will also be affected by more general measures of financial support such as unemployment benefits and housing benefits.

Spending on specific benefits for families with children has accounted for a fairly constant one-fifth of social security spending for the past 20 years. There has, however, been some upward pressure on spending from the rapid growth in the number of lone parents, many of whom rely on means-tested benefits. In 1996, it was estimated that there were 1.7 million lone parents, of whom 1 million were on Income Support and a further 300,000 on Family Credit – leaving just 400,000 on neither means-tested benefit. The introduction of the Working Families Tax Credit in October 1999 will increase still further the proportion of lone parents on income-related benefits (or 'credits'). In 1979, just 7 per cent of dependent children (0.9 million) were in families receiving Income Support; by 1996 this had risen to as many as one in four (3 million) children (Department of Social Security, 1998b, Focus File 07).

The rationale for and development of family benefits

It has been argued that family benefits are a little separate from the traditional systems and functions of social security. Social security is often analysed in terms of insurance- versus assistance-based approaches. Within a social assistance approach, the prime aim is to alleviate poverty. This need not require any separate system for families. Within social insurance approaches, families have received little explicit recognition partly because contributions are usually tied to paid work. However, in the UK and Germany, credits have been introduced to recognise caring responsibilities; Britain, for example, has Home Responsibilities Protection. Another issue is the definition of what counts as a 'social risk'. Generally speaking, the care of children, or of disabled or elderly relatives, has been excluded from the scope of such risks. Instead, this has often been viewed as a private matter – to be dealt with within families.

Pro-natalist factors have been very important in the development of family benefits in some countries. For example, at certain times, French politicians were particularly keen to increase the birth rate as their population dwindled in relation to that of their great rival, Germany. Such factors may become increasingly important as fertility in Europe remains rather low. There may also be a range of other objectives – relieving poverty experienced by children, covering the extra costs associated with children, providing equity between different family types, encouraging or discouraging births, encouraging or discouraging employment.

Bieback (1992) has argued that benefits for families developed in a number of stages. First came benefits for widows. Widows were often favourably treated under old systems of public assistance and were included very early within insurance schemes. Widows' Benefits were introduced as early as 1911 in Germany and 1926 in Britain. The relatively favourable treatment of widows – compared with the separated or the divorced – continues in many social security systems. Second, amounts for dependants were introduced in social assistance schemes, and, in the UK and some other countries, additions were included in social insurance benefits. Third, explicit benefits were introduced for the care of children, these often being paid directly to the carer (usually the mother). Fourth, and less well developed, are benefits specifically for carers. Childcare within the nuclear family is traditionally seen as a private matter – or one to be tackled through social services – so it is not usually covered within social insurance schemes.

Current family benefits available in Britain

If we turn now to the specific benefits available to families with children in Britain, Child Benefit is available to all those with children regardless of income or work status. The amount for the first or oldest child is now higher than for other children. This effectively means a slightly lower average payment per child for larger families.

In 1996, there were over 7 million families receiving Child Benefit on behalf of more than 12 million children. As we can see from Figure 5.3, the number of families receiving Child Benefit has remained fairly

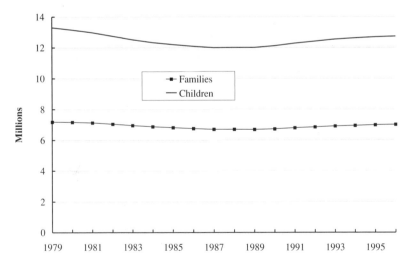

Figure 5.3   Numbers receiving Child Benefit (Social Security Statistics, various years)

constant, although there have been some fluctuations, reflecting some changes in the birth rate between 1979 and 1997. Similarly, spending on Child Benefit has risen in actual terms, but it has not grown to the same extent as for other benefits. In 1996–97, spending on Child Benefit amounted to £6.7 billion.

The 1998 budget announced the largest ever increase in Child Benefit – an extra £2.50 per week for the first child over and above normal inflation uprating. This increase was accompanied by raising the possibility of taxing Child Benefit for higher rate tax-payers and piloting changes for over-16s (announced in July 1998) to convert it into an education maintenance allowance.

Another £4.2 billion goes on Income Support for families with children. This is a means-tested benefit available to lone parents who work less than 16 hours a week and to couples where neither works 16 hours a week or more. Until October 1999, Family Credit also goes to families with children on a means-tested basis where there is someone working 16 hours a week or more. Working Families Tax Credit introduces a number of changes from that date onwards, principally to expand the size of the benefit/credit.

The hours requirement for Family Credit had been successively reduced over time, from 30 hours in 1971 when Family Income Supplement was introduced. This has been particularly to the advantage of lone parents, who usually work fewer hours than people in couples. The number of recipients of Family Credit has increased substantially over the past decade or so – and consequently so has the cost of the benefit. Figure 5.4 shows that there were just over 200,000 recipients of Family Income Supplement in 1986. This figure then doubled by 1992 and more than tripled, to nearly 700,000, by 1996 (almost half of these recipients being lone parents). Working Families Tax Credit is expected to reach an additional 400,000 families, from October 1999, and there are currently around 300,000 families who are entitled to claim Family Credit but who do not.

This growth in the Family Credit case-load is one of the most significant changes in social security policy over the late 1980s and 90s. It has changed the benefits landscape from one in which employment usually meant that few benefits were claimed, to one in which benefits play a key role in sustaining people in low-paid jobs. However, to some, Family Credit has become a victim of its own success. The costs of the benefit have risen from £180 million in 1986 to over £2 billion in 1996. Working Families Tax Credit is an expansion of Family Credit in a different guise, with an explicit role for taxation rather than benefits

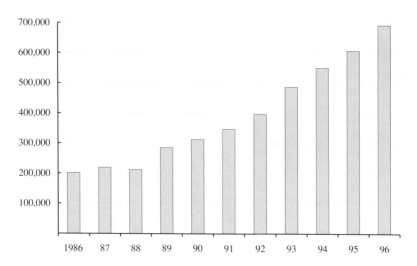

Figure 5.4   Family Credit (Family Income Supplement) recipients
(Department of Social Security, 1997)

as a means of delivering it, although it will only be paid through wage
packets from April 2000.

Benefits for lone parents

In 1996–97, the majority of all social security spending on families
with children went to lone parents (£10 billion out of a total of £18
billion; Department of Social Security, 1997). The main benefits
received by this group are the same as those received by couples with
children, namely Child Benefit, Income Support and Family
Credit/Working Families Tax Credit. However, until recently, lone
parents have also been entitled to One Parent Benefit and a lone parent
premium on Income Support. Until April 1997, all lone parents were
eligible for One Parent Benefit regardless of whether or not they were
working. Those out of work had their income from One Parent Benefit
taken into account when their entitlement to Income Support was
calculated, which meant that they were no better off than if they had
not been receiving One Parent Benefit. The main advantage of One
Parent Benefit was as a means of encouraging lone parents to find a
paid job as they could keep this benefit alongside their earnings. From

1997, however, entitlement to One Parent Benefit ended for new claimants. Lone-parent premium (in means-tested benefits) is also being phased out for new claimants.

The number of lone parents has risen from fewer than 600,000 in 1971 to around 1.7 million in 1996. At the same time, the proportion of lone parents relying on Income Support has risen, so that the cost of paying Income Support to this group has been increasing sharply over time. Most lone parents (90 per cent) are women. The proportion in paid work has dropped from almost half (48 per cent) in 1979 to 40 per cent today (Department of Social Security, 1998b, Focus File 03). This drop has been fuelled by the recent rapid growth in the number of single, never-married lone parents, more than 90 per cent of whom are on Income Support. This rise has also meant there are more lone parents with very young children, the group least likely to be in paid work.

The growth of social security spending on lone parents has prompted a great deal of research into their living standards (for survey evidence, see Bradshaw and Millar, 1991; McKay and Marsh, 1994; Ford et al., 1995, 1997; for a more detailed analysis, see the edited collection by Ford and Millar, 1998).

One way of reducing benefit expenditure on lone parents is to increase the proportion who have paid work, or increase their income from other sources. An obvious starting point is to increase the income they receive from the absent parents (usually absent fathers) in the form of maintenance. In 1991, the government introduced the Child Support Act. Before this, mothers who divorced from their partners usually had court settlements that were discretionary and often resulted in low maintenance payments, rarely uprated and with variable enforcement (Department of Social Security, 1991). For cases that did not go through the courts, a social security officer ('liable relative officer') might track down the father and make an agreement.

The Child Support Act introduced a set formula that would apply to all cases, including those which had previously gone through the courts. The Act produced widespread criticism (Clarke et al., 1994), with particular opposition from absent fathers who were being asked to pay more maintenance. The state, rather than the lone mothers and their children, usually received the extra amount in the form of reduced Income Support payments (Garnham and Knights, 1994) – albeit that this might mean lower taxes for the population as a whole. There was also criticism of the inflexible formula, and the Child Support Agency was accused of tackling first the easy targets – the fathers who were already paying something – rather than the apparent villains – the fathers who were paying nothing. The Act has subsequently been reformed on a number of occasions (Department of Social Security, 1995) in an attempt to allay many of these criticisms. A recent Green Paper (Department of Social Security, 1998a) has signalled many changes, including a heavily simplified formula and permitting recipients on Income Support to retain some of their maintenance payments.

Approaches to family benefits in different countries

Some comparative studies concerning family benefits were discussed in Chapter 2, and this illustrated clear differences in levels of provision for families across different countries and the balance between family forms.

There have also been studies that have looked at *family policy* in greater detail. An early study by Kamerman and Kahn (1978) identified the UK as lacking or even rejecting the notion of family policy, while France had a very comprehensive family policy, and there were significant (if more narrowly focused) approaches in countries such as Germany.

Whiteford and Bradshaw (1994) have pointed out that there is a correlation between the employment rates for lone mothers and for married mothers, which suggests that it is factors affecting all mothers that are likely to determine the labour market participation rates of lone mothers (see also Perry, 1993). However, there is also a group of countries (Spain, Italy and Germany) where lone mothers are more likely to be working than married mothers – sometimes substantially so.

The unemployed

Unemployed people are one of the main groups that come to mind when people think about social security recipients. However, as we saw earlier in this chapter, the unemployed account for only 10 per cent of all benefit expenditure. The amount spent on this group is highly sensitive to the state of the economy, so the level of spending fluctuates from year to year.

In studying unemployment, it is important to appreciate its dynamic character. Most people *becoming* unemployed can expect to find jobs quite quickly, but many of those currently unemployed have been out of work for much longer. This result emerges because the group of those remaining unemployed quickly sheds those with short-term spells of unemployment. Over the longer term, those with long spells of unemployment will cost the most in benefit payments. It is also important to distinguish the unemployed from other people who do not have jobs. The International Labour Office defines as unemployed those who are not in work but have looked for work in the previous 4 weeks and are ready to start a new job in the next 2 weeks. Others without jobs are generally called 'inactive' and include those in full-time education and those looking after home or family. This definition has a substantial overlap with the group of those on benefits, but the fit is far from exact. Both the International Labour Office definition and the number of those on unemployment-related benefits are used to construct statistics on the number and proportion of the workforce who are unemployed.

Who are the unemployed?

Information about the unemployed is readily available from recent surveys (Bottomley *et al.*, 1997; McKay *et al.*, 1997). Among those unemployed in 1995:

● 74 per cent were male
● The average age was 34.1 years
● 63 per cent were single (or divorced, separated or widowed)
● 46 per cent had no academic qualifications, while 36 per cent had A levels or higher qualifications
● One-third (34 per cent) had been unemployed for over a year
● 40 per cent were *not* in paid work prior to signing on as unemployed
● Among those becoming unemployed in 1995, half had left unemployment benefits within 14 weeks.

The age distribution of unemployed claimants is shown in Figure 5.5. A large proportion are relatively young: almost one-third of the male unemployed and more than one-quarter of the female unemployed were aged between 25 and 34.

The general characteristics of benefits for the unemployed

Expenditure on unemployment benefits may be relatively small, but nevertheless, as we saw in Chapter 3, one of the main principles upon

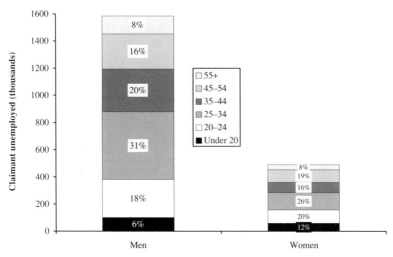

Figure 5.5   Age distribution of unemployment in 1996 (Department of Social Security, 1997)

which the social security system was based was insurance against the fluctuations of the labour market. Beveridge had assumed that the government would be willing and able to maintain full (male) employment so expected that workers would make substantial contributions to the National Insurance fund, rarely needing to draw from it or doing so for only short periods of time. Beveridge had proposed that the insurance element of Unemployment Benefit should continue indefinitely, in the same way as benefits for incapacity and retirement did, but this was overruled in favour of a time-limited system (Brown, 1990: 29).

Since the 1970s, full employment has often proved an elusive objective so social assistance (Supplementary Benefit, then Income Support and then the income-based element of Jobseeker's Allowance) has played more of a role in helping unemployed people who have no other means of supporting themselves. It has also provided support to those whose entitlement to contributory benefits has simply run out.

The main features of unemployment benefits in most countries are generally as follows:

- They, or at least a first tier, are financed by contributions.
- Entitlement depends on minimum periods of employment, so they often exclude the young and new entrants to the labour market.

- Abuse is controlled by rules excluding the 'voluntary' unemployed and administering tests to check that recipients are actively seeking and available for work. Ultimately, work may be created for those who have not found it by themselves, in what is known as 'workfare'.
- Benefit payments are usually related to previous earnings – the UK being a notable exception in paying out flat-rate benefits (although there were earnings-related additions between 1968 and 1982).
- Benefit payments are usually limited in duration, at least before people move on to alternative benefits.

A particular feature in many countries is the growth in irregular or 'flexible' employment patterns. Social insurance provision is tied to former earnings and to prolonged weeks of contribution. It thus tends to discriminate against employees who cannot meet the conditions of 'normal employment'. This will often include women (those working part time or seasonally), the self-employed (Brown, 1994) and workers in insecure forms of employment.

Benefits for unemployed people in Britain

Since October 1996, the main benefit for unemployed people has been Jobseeker's Allowance. Payments of Jobseeker's Allowance come from the DSS's budget, but the benefit is administered in job centres by the Employment Service, an agency of the Department for Education and Employment (DfEE). The most important conditions for the receipt of Jobseeker's Allowance are that recipients are *able* to work, *available* for work and *actively seeking* work. Recipients will have a New Jobseeker interview providing details of the assistance that job centres are able to provide and the sanctions available against those failing to maintain eligibility. At this interview, the newly unemployed will sign a Jobseeker's Agreement with an Employment Service officer, which details the steps they are expected to take to help move into paid work. Unemployed benefit recipients ('jobseekers') have to attend interviews at various stages during the time they spend unemployed. Interviews often take place at 13 weeks of unemployment, and then at 26 weeks and every 6 months thereafter.

From 1911 and until October 1996, the main benefit for unemployed people in Britain was Unemployment Benefit. This was a contributory (and therefore insurance-based) benefit lasting for 12 months if the claimant had paid sufficient contributions. After this, or if the claimant had paid insufficient contributions, claimants received the means-tested benefit Income Support if their family income was low enough for them to qualify. Jobseeker's Allowance has now replaced both Unemployment Benefit and Income Support for unemployed people. There are two components of Jobseeker's Allowance – a contributory component that, since April 1996, has lasted for 6 months (this previously being 12 months) and after this, or for those with insufficient contributions, a means-tested ('income-based') component.

Thus, although insurance against unemployment is still a key feature of the benefit system, the insurance-based aspect of benefits for the unemployed has been cut back, particularly in the years since 1979. The main group to be disadvantaged by the reduction in the contributory part of the benefit are those with employed partners. This is because a partner's income is not taken into account for the contributory component of Jobseeker's Allowance but is taken into account for the means-tested component.

The reduction in the contributory component of benefits for the unemployed can be seen in some ways as an attack on the basic principles of Beveridge's social security system. However, Beveridge himself believed that unemployment insurance should only be necessary to guard against *temporary* experiences of unemployment. He thought that the guarantee of full employment would mean that unemployment would only be a short-term phenomenon, and, indeed, it is still the case that most people who become unemployed find a job within a few months. Since the 1970s, however, the number of long-term unemployed has substantially increased. The social security system was never designed to cope with the increasing cost of such a group and, rather than raise taxes to fund the extra costs or intervene in the labour market to create demand and thus reduce the number of unemployed, Conservative governments in the 1980s and 90s undertook reform of the benefit system to cut costs. This reform included reducing the importance of the contributory component of benefits for unemployed people and also introducing new or stricter requirements to look for work or be available for work; young people aged 16 or 17 were removed almost completely from eligibility (Brown, 1990).

The costs of benefits related to unemployment have fluctuated over time. This is for a number of reasons, the most important one being that unemployment is cyclical, reflecting upturns and downswings in the economy. According to recently released DSS figures, spending on the unemployed in 1979–80 and 1996–97 represented around 8 per cent of benefit expenditure, but it reached 16 per cent in the mid-1980s

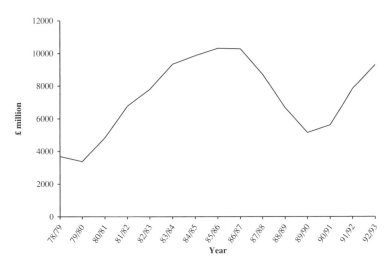

Figure 5.6   Real spending on the unemployed
(Department of Social Security, 1993b)

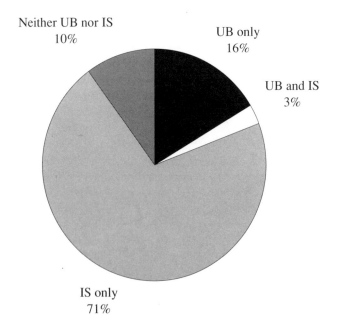

Figure 5.7   Benefits received by claimant unemployed in 1996
UB = Unemployment Benefit; IS = Income Support

(Department of Social Security, 1998b, Focus File 01). The changing level of real spending is shown in Figure 5.6 and closely mirrors the prevailing economic circumstances.

The economic recession of the early 1980s saw the cost of Unemployment Benefit rise to £1.5 billion, the recovery in the late 1980s causing a fall to £733 million in 1989–90. Costs then rose again to well over £1.5 billion in the recession of the early 1990s before falling off again. Reforms to the benefit, such as restricting access and limiting the contributory component, also cut costs at different times, but wider economic changes were far more influential. The number of unemployed recipients of either Unemployment Benefit or Income Support fell from over 3 million in the mid-1980s to fewer than 1.5 million in 1990, before rising to 2.75 million in 1993 and falling back down to just over 2 million in 1996 and towards 1.5 million in 1998.

Figure 5.7 shows clearly that the majority (over two-thirds) of the claimants unemployed in 1996 were receiving solely Income Support – the means-tested safety net benefit. Only a small proportion were receiving the contributory benefit for unemployed people. This is largely explained by the fact that a large proportion of unemployed benefit recipients have been out of work for long periods of time (Figure 5.8).

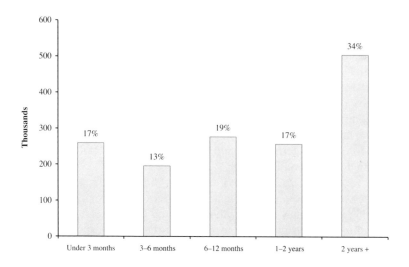

Figure 5.8 Claim duration of unemployed people receiving Income Support

Other ways of supporting the unemployed

Benefits that intend to replace or maintain income are only one means of supporting the unemployed. Other measures that are designed to try to get them back to work may be more beneficial. These may be divided into 'passive' and 'active' measures towards the unemployed. Generally speaking, passive measures (that is, measures within the benefit system) are rather more important than active measures in terms of expenditure. Despite their somewhat negative title, there are several positive labour market functions fulfilled by unemployment-related benefits. They permit people to get through short-term spells of unemployment and may, therefore, be useful in promoting mobility between different jobs. They may also encourage the unemployed to look for a good match between their skills and the available employment – although prolonging the duration of unemployment might also be seen as a negative consequence (see Chapter 8)

The benefit system also seeks to encourage people to take paid work through in-work benefits such as Working Families Tax Credit (the replacement for Family Credit as from October 1999), Disabled Person's Tax Credit (the replacement for Disability Working Allowance) and the benefit that is being piloted until April 2000 in eight locations – Earnings Top-Up.

The importance of 'active' labour market policies is on the increase, as welfare states move away from a primarily passive stance. The election of a Labour government in May 1997 put the idea of 'Welfare-to-Work' at the top of the policy agenda for social security. The New Deal for 18–24-year-olds was formally announced in the Chancellor's first budget in July 1997. Chapter 9 discusses in more detail the series of policies (each called a 'New Deal') that has created a model for providing advice and information that should promote people's entry into the labour market.

In more general terms, the main active labour market policies may be classified as follows:

- *A public employment service*: this decreases unemployment by facilitating job vacancy-filling with a minimum of delay and cost
- *Training*: which may help to break up the current spell of unemployment and add to skills that should increase the probability of leaving unemployment and reduce the probability of re-entry to unemployment
- *Direct job creation*

● *Subsidies to regular employment*: these are usually selective, one common approach being to pay subsidies to firms that hire the long-term unemployed.

Recent research (Gardiner, 1997) reviewed 42 programmes aiming to help unemployed people to find employment. It suggested that the most effective schemes were Jobmatch (which gives support to those taking part-time work) and Jobfinder's Grant (which gives a cash lump sum to the long-term unemployed when they start a job). Fay (1996) examined a range of programme evaluations across different countries and concluded that schemes that assisted with job-searching were among the most effective. Active policies seemed particularly beneficial for women but made little difference to the prospects of the young unemployed.

Unemployment benefit in other countries

Kvist and Ploug (1996) identify three different types of benefit typically paid to the unemployed. First, there are contributory (social insurance) benefits for the unemployed. In most cases, this tier of support is time limited, and levels of payment may be relatively high and linked to previous earnings (although not in Britain). The level of contributory social insurance benefit for the unemployment, and its duration of payment, varies across countries. To take two very different cases, in Denmark benefit may be as high as 90 per cent of the previous wage and last for a maximum of some 130 weeks, whereas in the UK amounts of benefit are low, flat rate and last only up to 26 weeks. Second, some countries may have a separate form of 'unemployment support'. This is usually paid at a flat rate (although in Germany the relevant benefit, *Arbeitslosenhilfe*, is related to earnings) and may be means-tested. Third, the unemployed may have to rely on social assistance benefits.

These three systems give rise to two main different structures of support. In some countries (as, for example, in Denmark and the UK until the introduction of Jobseeker's Allowance in 1996), a period of claiming the insurance element is followed directly by a move on to social assistance. In other countries (Germany, France and the UK since 1996), there may, after the insurance element, be a move on to unemployment support. For some countries (UK), unemployment support will continue indefinitely, while in others (such as Germany) this will also be exhausted, and the unemployed person may then have to turn to the general social assistance system.

In many European countries, the receipt of unemployment insurance is falling, while unemployment assistance is rising. This appears to be the case in UK, Denmark, Germany and the Netherlands, and has resulted from a mix of:

- Tighter rules
- More young unemployed who have not qualified for contributory benefits
- More long-term unemployed who have exhausted entitlement to contributory benefits.

6

Benefits to Meet Specific Costs of Living

Introduction

This chapter considers the benefits designed to meet the costs that are not met (or not expected to be met) out of the basic social security benefits. These extra-cost benefits include those which are designed to help meet the costs of housing and local taxes, and those which provide assistance with meeting special or exceptional needs. Before looking at each area, we consider some of the issues surrounding the balance of provision between paying money and meeting certain costs at source, and the appropriate means of meeting special needs. Although the Disability Living Allowance is designed to provide extra support for some disabled people, we considered it in the previous chapter rather than here because there is no link between the potential costs that Disability Living Allowance might be used to meet and its value. It is also only available to disabled people whereas the other benefits mentioned in this chapter are available to all types of claimant.

There are two main pertinent issues. First, as discussed in Chapter 1, there is the question of what should be paid for by weekly social security benefits and what might be provided by other areas of social policy, or which goods should be provided by some form of guarantee. For example, should poor families be provided with benefits to pay for housing, or should they instead be provided directly with housing at a low or subsided rent? Should weekly benefits be expected to include the cost of vital utilities (such as water), or should benefits meet the direct costs of such services? Second, to what extent should decisions about meeting extra costs either be based on fixed rules of entitlement or instead be determined by discretionary rulings by officials?

Generally speaking, social security benefits such as Income Support provide people with an income from which they have to meet particular costs of living such as clothing, food and transport. Most of this expenditure depends on the individual and how much he or she wishes to spend on each item. However, some expenses, for example rent and local taxes, vary according to the geographical region in which people live and over which they may have only limited control. Benefits, however, are paid at national rates, which means that those living in areas where rents and other costs are high would be much worse off than others if there were no specific help to meet the variable local costs of housing and local taxes.

The choice between providing services or products at zero cost instead of cash benefits can, therefore, have important consequences. It raises questions concerning the desirability, or otherwise, of allowing people to spend their incomes on goods as they see fit. Closely associated with this are the so-called 'passport' benefits that meet the costs of particular goods, such as school meals for children, dental treatment and optical check-ups, for those receiving means-tested benefits.

Of course, discussion about which goods might be provided for free, or through a separate scheme, presupposes some knowledge about which goods are ordinarily paid for. In the USA, unlike the UK, health care must usually be paid for, typically in the form of health insurance, but families on a low income may be exempted from such costs through the Medicaid programme. The USA also has a large centrally funded programme of 'food stamps', which act something like a negative income tax, consisting of vouchers that may be exchanged only for food. In the UK, the question of meeting health care costs does not arise since the NHS aims to provide health care that is free at the point of use.

Economists have traditionally assumed that people are their own best judges of their welfare and should, therefore, be free to spend their income as they like. This would imply that the state should seek to maximise the cash element of support and leave people to spend their income in the ways in which they choose.

Against this, there is a strong element of paternalism running through many of the benefits provided in kind, including free school meals for children and milk tokens for the mothers of younger children. It might be argued that society should override free choices to ensure that an adequate minimum is maintained because, without such measures, people might, for example, choose to buy alcohol and lottery tickets rather than food and clothes for their children. If people choose not to pay rent, an eviction may simply shift problems from one area of social policy to another (from social security to housing or possibly the social services).

A further set of issues concerns public support for a system. The media image of the heavy-drinking, heavy-smoking man or woman frittering away benefits relies on their spending publicly provided *cash*. It is more difficult to demonise the receipt of free goods, although the size of houses provided by local councils for some large families on benefit has admittedly sometimes come under media scrutiny.

Help with housing costs

As discussed in Chapter 3, Beveridge was much occupied with the 'problem of rent' – or how to meet housing costs that differed widely across the country without paying all of people's rent and thereby encouraging them to move to more expensive properties. The system of housing benefits that existed until the 1980s was another particularly puzzling part of the benefit system, with overlaps between schemes run by local authorities and housing payments included as part of Supplementary Benefit. Since the mid-1980s, however, there has been a centrally fixed formula for calculating Housing Benefit. For those on Income Support, rent is paid in full. This is rare in the housing benefit systems of other countries (described below), and it is argued that 100 per cent payment of rent encourages people to live in expensive accommodation. The British system tackles this potential problem, to some extent, by introducing a maximum rent that will be paid in full.

It is worth noting that privately rented housing in particular forms a much lower proportion of the housing stock in the UK than in most European countries (Goodlad and Gibb, 1994: 50). In contrast, owner-occupation is more common than average, and social housing remains (despite large-scale sales of council housing) highly significant by European standards.

In the 1980s, the government introduced two major overhauls of Housing Benefit. The government has also acted to increase rents in public sector housing and eagerly promoted the sale of council houses at reduced prices via the 'Right to Buy' policy. However, it can be strongly argued (Berthoud, 1989) that each change in policy has been considered in isolation so that no government has ever examined as a whole the impact and interactions of rent levels, council house sales, housing benefit and other aspects of housing finance.

The government provides support for people's housing costs in three main ways, as follows (Berthoud, 1989; Hills and Mullings, 1990):

- Tax relief to owner-occupiers
- 'Bricks and mortar' subsidies (public contributions to the current costs of local authorities and housing associations)
- Social security benefits, comprising Housing Benefit (also known as Rent Rebate and Rent Allowance) and Income Support for mortgage interest.

The following sections look at each of these types of support.

Help with mortgage costs

The majority of people now live in owner-occupied housing. There is no equivalent to Housing Benefit to help to pay mortgage costs. For those out of work, help with mortgages is currently available only for those on Income Support. It has been argued that this provides some disincentives to work for owner-occupiers since they will lose this help if they find a job (and if the job is low paid, they may be worse off than if they were on benefit). Webb and Wilcox (1991) have argued for an extension of help with mortgage costs to low earners as well. However, far from increasing support for owner-occupiers, the response of government has been to withdraw from provision in this area – new mortgages (those taken out from October 1995) are no longer covered through Income Support. Therefore, it is expected that the private provision of insurance will need to cover the departure of state support from this area.

Although there is no social security benefit to help to meet mortgage payments for low-paid workers, tax relief on mortgage interest is currently available to all tax-payers. Kay and King (1978), and other economists, have argued that the true subsidy to home owners is the lack of payment of tax on 'imputed rent' rather than the more obvious tax break on mortgage interest. Tax was imposed on imputed rent until 1963, under Schedule A of income tax. Unlike mortgage interest relief, the tax concession on imputed rent increases in proportion with the value of the house occupied. The argument for this view is, perhaps, a little difficult for non-economists to appreciate on first reading. It is based on a comparison of the situation of a home owner living in his or her own property compared with a home owner who lets out the same accommodation for rental income. While, in the latter case, the landlord/owner would pay tax on the rental income, an owner-occupier who effectively lets the property to himself pays no tax at all on the implicit rental income. In any case, tax subsidies to home owners go to all owners rather than just those on a low income. Also, if the true benefit is the lack of a tax on imputed rent, the greatest gains go to those with the most valuable properties and, therefore, likely to be on the highest incomes.

'Bricks and mortar' subsidies

Council housing was started by the 1919 Housing Act at a time when 90 per cent of households rented their accommodation from private landlords and when there were concerns about the scarcity of the stock of homes in adequate condition. Housing construction was particularly buoyant in the years 1945–75, when financial concerns began to play a much larger role in policy development. Since then, particularly since 1980, housing policy has been directed towards a number of objectives. First, the government has encouraged a general rise in rent levels so that rents for social housing have moved closer to commercial levels of rent. Second, the introduction of the 'Right to Buy' policy has generated increasing polarisation in the housing market between different housing tenures.

As a result, the mix of different tenures in England and Wales has changed drastically over the course of the twentieth century (Malpass and Murie, 1994). Private renting was the dominant tenure in 1914, accounting for nine dwellings out of every ten. Since the early 1970s, owner-occupation has been the majority housing tenure.

In effect, subsidies to 'bricks and mortar' have been reduced so that public support to tenants is being restricted to means-tested Housing Benefit for the poorest. Of course, as subsidies have been reduced, one would expect rent levels to rise, causing more families to claim Housing Benefit. Government expenditure on the benefit would, therefore, rise, although we might expect there to be some non-take-up because some people are unaware of their entitlement to benefit or are unwilling to go through a complex application process. We might also expect a greater number of families to face reduced incentives to work – as more of their benefits will be calculated on the basis of any earnings from paid work.

Social security benefits to meet rent

Benefits for tenants to help with the costs of rent have had a long and complex history. There have been several attempts at reform, but significant problems with the current system of Housing Benefit remain (Kemp, 1992), and official policy has identified a high level of fraud with this benefit (Department of Social Security, 1998c). Local authorities have been able to provide reductions in rent levels since the Housing Acts of 1930 and 1935 if they choose to do so, and several have developed such schemes. Reductions in the cost of social housing were, however, often unavailable to recipients of National Assistance (and then Supplementary Benefit), who could instead gain help with housing costs through additions to their assistance benefits.

This split in housing support between those on Supplementary Benefit and those on low incomes continued to be a problem for several decades (effectively until 1988). At least one advantage of support through Supplementary Benefit was that a single national scheme applied, whereas local authorities could invent schemes of different types, until national legislation changed this.

In 1972, the Housing Finance Act made a national scheme mandatory for local authorities. Further changes in 1974 tried to tidy up some of the needless complexities that had been included. After 1972, *Rent Rebate* acted to reduce rent for council tenants, and *Rent Allowance* provided cash assistance to help with the rents of private tenants.

This post-1974 system came under a number of criticisms (Hill, 1990: 113–122). The twin approach for recipients of means-tested benefits and for everyone else remained, leading to several problems. First there was the so-called 'better-off' problem. The rent element of Supplementary Benefit was calculated according to a formula set within the social security system, which was different from the formula for Rent Rebates paid by local authorities. Some people were on the border between means-tested benefits and Rent Rebates, and had a choice of which to apply for – one which had a material impact on their final level of income. However, they did not always choose their best option, such was the complexity of the situation. Second, the system was opposed by the Supplementary Benefits Commission on the grounds of complexity (Supplementary Benefits Commission, 1980: 24):

> The inclusion of housing costs in supplementary benefit adds considerably to the complexity of the scheme and the cost of administering it... It would be a major simplification if housing costs were removed from the scheme completely and

covered by a single comprehensive scheme which applied to all people on low incomes... We think that the local authorities would be best suited to administer such a scheme.

The views of the Supplementary Benefits Commission held sway, and Housing Benefit was introduced in 1982. The main idea behind Housing Benefit was to stop taking the payment of rent out of Supplementary Benefit. Instead, local authorities would be responsible for help to tenants whether or not they were on means-tested benefits. This was probably a good idea, but the system failed to harmonise rules between those receiving and those not receiving social assistance, so that two different sets of rules continued ('certificated' and 'standard' Housing Benefit). The reduction in the workload of the DHSS was more than offset by additional problems created in local authority housing departments.

It was not until 1988 (through the 1986 Social Security Act) that a new Housing Benefit scheme was finally introduced that cleared away this type of problem. This scheme is founded on a formula based on principles similar to those of the Income Support calculation. This has removed any 'better-off' problems, where the choice of different packages of benefit income could lead some people to take the route meaning that they were worse off than if they had made the 'correct' choice.

The rising cost of Housing Benefit continues to position it as a candidate for reform, even if the main reason for higher costs is a switch away from 'bricks and mortar' housing subsidies. In fact:

> In real terms, the total value of housing support is lower now than it has been for most of the time since the end of the 1970s. If tax reliefs are excluded, housing subsidies are higher now than during most of the 1980s, although they are still lower than in 1979. (Department of Social Security, 1998b, Fact File 05: 1)

Housing Benefit has been the subject of criticism for a number of reasons. First, the rapid withdrawal of Housing Benefit as people earn more is seen as reducing the incentive to work. Like other in-work benefits, Housing Benefit works on the basis that a person on a low income receives a maximum award – usually all of their eligible rent. As their income rises, a proportion of that benefit is taken away. For families on low earnings, additional income may lead to additional tax and national insurance, then less Working Families Tax Credit and less Housing Benefit. The combined effect of all these reductions (or 'tapers') could be to take more than 90 pence out of each pound of higher earnings. This might be expected to affect, in particular, the 16 per cent of recipients who are unemployed and the 19 per cent who are lone parents (Department of Social Security, 1998b, Fact File 05), although perhaps not the 40 per cent who are elderly. The introduction of Working Families Tax Credit makes some changes to the interaction between this benefit/credit and Housing Benefit.

The welfare reform Green Paper (Department of Social Security, 1998c) focuses on Housing Benefit as an important source of fraud, which research puts at a cost of £840 million (Government Statistical Service, 1998), getting on for one-quarter of the total social security fraud. Yet, it claimed, some local authorities have never made a prosecution for Housing Benefit fraud.

It has also been noted that the system of administration and appeals continues to work very differently from the rest of the social security system (Kemp, 1992).

There is limited information about systems of housing support in other countries, on a comparable basis. However, Kemp (1997) identified three different institutional approaches to meeting housing costs that are found in different countries:

- Social assistance allows for some element of housing costs (although special housing allowances may be available on top of this).
- Social assistance is enhanced to meet actual housing costs.
- Housing allowances form a separate scheme.

Britain often meets 100 per cent of housing costs, whereas other countries tend to pay for only a proportion of housing needs under specific schemes.

Help with the costs of local taxes

Housing costs are not the only costs that vary across the country. Local government taxes (rates, Community Charge or Council Tax) also vary considerably. Assistance with local taxes has an even longer history than interventions to help with the costs of tenants. Under a 1925 Rating and Valuation Act, local authorities were able to excuse payment of rates on the grounds of poverty. A national scheme was introduced in the 1966 Rating Act.

Local government finance was a political minefield in the 1980s and early 1990s, particularly with rate-capping and the Poll Tax (Butler *et al.*, 1994). Domestic rates were changed first to a Community Charge (or Poll Tax) and then to the current Council Tax. Each change has been seen to require compensatory changes within social security and a network of rebates to bills that has been actually outside social security. During the days of the Poll Tax/Community Charge, and 1 year prior to that, recipients of Community Charge Benefit could claim only a maximum of an 80 per cent rebate, even if they were living on Income Support. The aim of this was to ensure that everyone paid something towards the tax. However, 100 per cent rebates were re-established when Poll Tax was replaced by Council Tax.

Water rates are another cost that benefit recipients have received help with. Before the water industry was privatised, water rates were covered as part of rate rebates under the domestic rates system. In 1988, however, this system was changed and water charges were meant to be covered by Income Support. This caused problems because of regional variations in the level of charge, which meant that some benefit recipients lost while others gained, and the budgeting difficulties experienced by people unused to having to accumulate the money required to meet fairly infrequent bills. The increase in Income Support that would compensate for the 'average' increase would meet neither problem, and the inevitable result was a surge in rates of non-payment (Herbert and Kempson, 1995).

Benefits to help meet 'special needs'

Before discussing particular social security benefits that are designed to meet 'special needs', we will first of all consider the role that discretion plays in the benefit system. The scope for discretion has been crucial to changes in the ways that special needs may be met.

Discretion

Most decisions about social security involve officials making decisions about whether a person meets the appropriate rules. This will often be based on relatively clear-cut information, such as whether or not a person is (say) aged 24 or 25 years. Sometimes, however, officials will have the guidance of rules and manuals but will still need to make a judgement about whether a person does or does not meet a particular rule. This could include deciding whether a person left his or her previous job with or without *just cause*, and whether he or she is *available for work*. Where there is scope for considerable decision-making about whether a person qualifies for a particular programme, the official may be said to be exercising discretion, although it should be said at once that the use of the term 'discretion' varies in the literature. Spicker (1995: 135, 263) offers a definition of discretion that assumes a very large degree of personal assessment: 'the scope for independent judgment which is left to officials when *no* rules apply' (emphasis added). Hill (1990: 84) uses the term to include decisions 'ranging from ones that are unfettered to ones which are the subject of elaborate regulation'.

Discretion is very much a two-edged sword for benefit recipients. It may be helpful to some applicants to have their circumstances decided on an individual basis. A structure of rules will tend to deal with average or typical situations, which may not apply in all instances. Thus, a degree of discretion may mean that resources are directed to areas where they may have the greatest impact. The downside is that discretion is likely to lead to inconsistency in making decisions, as different officers apply different principles or judgements, and may lead to discrimination against certain types of applicant. For example, Benefits Agency officers may have taken on board images of the 'deserving' and 'undeserving' that influence their decisions. These official staff are good examples of 'street-level bureaucrats' (Lipsky, 1980), whose day-to-day actions not so much thwart public welfare policy as become it.

It may be worth noting that the exercise of discretion is often associated with having a 'professional' status or role, such as in the decisions taken by doctors and social workers. The administration of social security, in Britain, has lacked the kind of professional career that might command the authority to exercise a wide degree of discretion (Adler *et al.*, 1991: Chapter 1).

In the context of meeting extra needs, approaches based on both rules and discretion have been tried. Each has been the subject of reform. The aim has generally been to curtail costs and reduce administrative loads rather than to invest in an approach thought to be logically superior to the other.

The existence of benefits to meet special needs is a distinctive feature of the UK. Since 1935, the authorities administering benefits have had the power to make extra provision over and above the basic scale rates used in benefits. There would seem to be clear reasons for such provision. Benefits are paid at a relatively low level that seeks to meet day-to-day costs. It would be difficult to meet the costs of large consumer durables (such as cookers and refrigerators) from weekly benefit. Some families may also experience different needs that are not adequately captured within uniform rates of payment (Walker *et al.*, 1992).

In general, two types of additions may be made. First, amounts could be added to weekly benefit in recognition of some continuing need. This could take account of the need for a more costly special diet, for example. These additions have, since 1988, largely been abolished in favour of amounts (premiums) reflecting the type of group receiving benefit (for example, premiums for disabled people and those aged 60 or older). Second, there are one-off, lump-sum payments that meet special needs that are not expected to re-occur (at least, not very often). These could be the breakdown of a cooker, a stolen wallet or some other unanticipated event.

A short history of methods to meet special needs

The long history of extra provision for special needs has seen a variety of changes to the type of system used. At various times, there has been pressure to contain rising costs, but until the advent of the Social Fund in 1988, such attempts had met with only temporary success. As Figure 6.1 shows, there has been an inexorable rise in the number of lump-sum grants made for additional or special needs since the late 1940s. Only part of this may be explained by general rises in the caseload of means-tested benefits – the number of grants per 100 claimants has risen sharply too, especially since the early 1980s. Not only has the total caseload risen, but concern has been expressed that a disproportionate share of the available resources goes to a small proportion of the caseload (Department of Health and Social Security, 1985). This might indicate that they are better informed or better able to present a case, but alternatively it might indicate that need is highly concentrated among such a group.

From 1966 until 1979, there was a scheme known as 'exceptional needs payments' for one-off grants to people with special needs, and 'exceptional circumstances additions' for continuing amounts. People receiving Supplementary Benefit could apply for such payments, which were made at the discretion of staff in benefits offices. They had the guidance of an unpublished and supposedly secret code. They were not generally affected, however, by any particular budgetary limits on their exercise of discretion. Hill (1969) explains that regional approval for larger grants was required, but this could be circumvented by giving 'a number of smaller grants in fairly quick succession' (Hill, 1993: 413). Copies of the guidance notes appear to have been available to at least some parts of the welfare rights community. The discretion to make additions was framed by the Supplementary Benefits Commission.

A review of this system was set up by the Labour government in 1976, and the main findings were enacted by the Conservative government in the 1980 Social Security Act. This introduced a system of one-off 'single payments' (plus even more last resort 'urgent payments') and additional payments for particular weekly needs. These were paid out as legal entitlements and were designed to meet specific needs that were laid down in published legislation and regulations. The main aim was to reduce the role of discretion, which was seen as operating to too great an extent, with serious implications for the costs of running the system and for office workloads. The new scheme also sought to simplify the administration of the system for staff and increase the understanding of the system for claimants (Walker, 1983). The Act also saw the end of the Supplementary Benefits Commission, which had previously set policy, and the introduction of the Social Security Advisory Committee, which continues to have a purely advisory (although wide-ranging) role.

As Figure 6.1 shows, the 1980 legislation led immediately to a dramatic reduction in the number of lump-sum grants awarded, but the effect lasted barely 2 years. It has been argued that this reduction reflected tougher legislation rather than any straight comparison of the discretion versus rules-based systems (Berthoud, 1984). In time, benefit recipients and their advisers learnt which needs could successfully be met and which were effectively proscribed by legislation. It has been suggested that some urgent needs could not be met, simply because they had not found expression in the legislation. This led to the perverse situation of people arguing for extra payments on the grounds of a specified need (which they did not in fact have) in order to be able to spend the money on a different but more urgent need (see, for example, Walker, 1993: 119–20). Such criticisms remain true of today's system, as it is known that certain requests for extra help are more likely to succeed than others.

After 1982, the number of grants was back to the 1980 level and then continued to shoot upwards. This partly reflected the ability of welfare rights workers to help recipients to claim the benefits that were, now, their legal entitlement. Hill (1990: 61) has described the 1980 changes

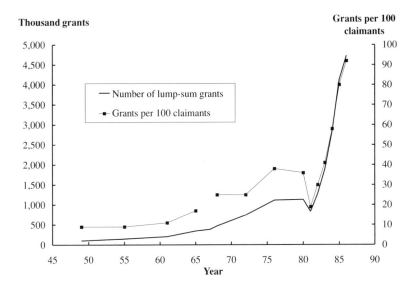

Figure 6.1 Number of lump-sum grants for special needs
(Walker *et al.*, 1992)

as 'with the benefit of hindsight, a victory for welfare rights', going on
to describe what came next as 'a backlash against that victory.' The
system that came next, through the 1986 Social Security Act, was the
Social Fund. In the meantime, various cuts were made in August 1986
to single payments (particularly furniture grants) to reduce their
growing cost (Cohen and Tarpey, 1988).

The Social Fund

The Social Fund was one of the most controversial changes of the mid-
1980s and has been the subject of considerable adverse criticism (Bradshaw, 1987; Craig, 1989; Lister, 1989; Berthoud, 1991). The Social
Fund was introduced in full by 1988. It took over the payment of one-
off sums that had formerly been single payments. Weekly additions for
particular requirements were stopped in favour of premiums for particular client groups within the Income Support system that replaced
Supplementary Benefit.

The Social Fund may be divided into two different sections. The
regulated Social Fund pays out benefits as of right and includes

Maternity Payments, Funeral Payments and Cold Weather Payments. These are grants, although the amounts paid for funerals may be recovered from the estate of the deceased person. The *discretionary* Social Fund pays out benefits that depend, in part, on the discretion of staff in local benefit offices. This part of the social fund pays out Community Care Grants, Crisis Loans and Budgeting Loans. As their names suggest, the latter two forms of assistance are paid through loans rather than being met by grants, as special needs have been in the past. Loans from the Social Fund are interest free and are usually repaid by deductions from benefit. Box 6.1 provides a summary of the types of help on offer, the figures in brackets showing the average size of each award made in 1996.

Loans that are made are subsequently recovered from recipients, generally through deductions from their weekly benefit. Since loans are interest free, it might be better to regard these loans as a form of 'advance' on benefit. They do not give the recipient any extra resources but merely allow people to alter the rate at which they receive payment. However, applicants may only receive loans if the deductions from

Box 6.1

The Structure of the Social Fund

Basis of decision

Type of payment	Discretion	Entitlement
Grant	Community Care Grants (£320)	Maternity Payments (£100) Funeral Payments (£750) Cold Weather Payments (£8.50)
Loan	Budgeting Loans (£290) Crisis Loans (£67)	

their weekly benefit are less than a specified level. This has led to the charge that some people are refused help if they are thought to be 'too poor' to afford the repayments (Berthoud, 1991). It is generally agreed that amounts paid in Income Support barely provide an adequate standard of living, so the deductions made to cover Social Fund loans mean that the weekly benefit will appear to be even lower.

The actual cost of the Social Fund is, therefore, rather less than the amount of money that is paid out. Most of the money paid in the form of loans is successfully recovered – almost 95 cent of the cost of Crisis Loans and 90 per cent of Budgeting Loans were recovered in 1996. This means that the most expensive element of the Social Fund, in net terms, is Community Care Grants (Figure 6.2). In 1996–97, the total net cost of Social Fund payments made (grants and net loans) was around £240 million.

Another new element from 1988 was the removal of any independent right to appeal against Social Fund decisions, which exists within most social security law (Lister, 1989). Instead, there is a separate review process. Cases may be reviewed first within the local office and then by a Social Fund Inspector centrally based if the appellant wishes to take matters further.

The discretionary part of the system is cash limited at the local level. Districts are required to observe budgetary limits and to manage resources so that a similar level of need may be accommodated throughout the financial year. However, this does mean that access to benefits will depend partly on how many others are making applications and, potentially, the district in which someone lives rather than just the level of need. Districts may also set local priorities in deciding which types of claim receive the highest priority.

Research into the Social Fund has been conducted by various groups. Some large-scale research was commissioned by the DSS to compare those who were granted awards with those who applied but were rejected. We would expect, if the system were working well, that those rejected would have lower levels of need than those who were successful in gaining a loan or grant. However, Huby and Dix (1992: 127) found that:

we cannot show that those who got awards were in greater need than those who did not.

Ways forward for meeting extra needs

While the Social Fund has now been functioning for 10 years, there remain considerable problems with the system. The administration of the system is very complex for what is a relatively small sum of money actually paid out. People's needs for extra income are not necessarily being met consistently, nor are resources being targeted to areas of greatest need.

One means of tackling both problems would be to make the loans paid more of a 'right' rather than being subject to an extensive discretionary decision-making process. After all, the Benefits Agency is particularly successful in recovering the money that is loaned out. So why should not more people be able to make use of the 'service' of having benefits paid in advance? This argument falters, at least in part, on the basis of the treatment of loans within the government's national accounts. A greater amount of money given as loans (student loans being another example) apparently counts as additional government borrowing. The probable return on these loans is not counted until they are repaid, meaning that government borrowing appears to be higher –

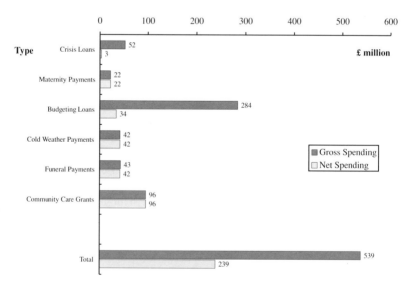

Figure 6.2   Expenditure on the Social Fund in 1996 (Department of Social Security, 1997)

and recent governments have put great store by minimising their overall level of borrowing.

However, the argument that loans must be rationed in some way but that there are simpler means of making decisions appears to have been accepted. The 1998 Social Security Act amended regulations for Budgeting Loans. Assessment is moving away from discretion and towards a 'fact-based' approach. It is worth noting that 'point-scoring' systems are often used in making credit decisions, and these could provide a useful parallel. An approach based on point-scoring would need to include features that applicants could do little to alter (such as the length of time on benefit).

It certainly seems unlikely that a greater use of discretion is on the agenda. However, to return to an important theme of this chapter, it is probably the net resources dedicated to this area that are the most important point when reform is considered. The precise means by which decisions are made about who benefits from those resources is important but historically something of a second consideration.

7

Delivering Benefits

Introduction

The administration of benefits in Britain is a mammoth undertaking involving a third of all government spending. A number of organisations are involved in this administration, including the DSS, the Benefits Agency, local authorities, the Employment Service and the Post Office. This chapter reviews how these organisations attempt to pay 'the right amount to the right people'. Various issues relating to the delivery of benefits are discussed. For example, some people who are entitled to benefit do not receive it, and the chapter considers the issue of non-take-up of social security. Equally, some people do receive benefit even though they are not entitled to it, and the chapter also looks at the issue of fraud.

The administration of benefits

Although the DSS has responsibility for developing social security policy, the responsibility for implementing policy is left with various organisations, including several Next Steps Agencies. Next Steps Agencies were introduced by the Conservative government in the 1980s as a way of 'semi-privatising' various public organisations and enshrining a distinction between policy and practice. The degree of openness practised by these agencies has at times been an issue: at first, questions to DSS Chief Executives were not published in *Hansard* in response to parliamentary questions, but now, after pressure, they are being published. Although Next Steps Agencies are still in public hands, the Chief Executives have a greater degree of autonomy from ministers than was previously the case for managers within the DSS.

The 1998 Comprehensive Spending Review projected the following costs (£million). The costs of administration are large and are expected to remain at 3.3–3.4 per cent of spending on benefits:

	1998–99	*1999–2000*	*2000–2001*	*2001–2002*
Benefit spending	92,267	97,119	99,529	105,274
Administration costs	2,880	3,330	3,410	3,490
Total	95,147	100,449	102,939	108,764

The Benefits Agency

The largest of the Next Steps Agencies responsible for benefit administration (and in fact the largest Agency across all the government) is the Benefits Agency, which in 1996–97 spent more than three-quarters of the overall social security budget (Benefits Agency, 1997). In 1996–97, it employed 72,333 (full-time equivalent) staff.

In 1996–97, the Benefits Agency was divided into two territorial directorates, with 13 area directorates containing 148 districts. In addition, each of the districts had two or three branch offices. The Benefits Agency offices one might find in the high street tend to be either district or branch offices. It is common for more complex specialist work (such as calculating mortgage interest and dealing with 16–17-year-olds) to be centralised to the district office. Alongside these offices, there are also:

- 3 benefit centres (in Ashton-in-Makerfield, Belfast and Glasgow) handling transactions from selected London offices
- 4 benefit directorates (in Blackpool, Newcastle, Preston and Washington) responsible for a range of centrally administered benefit; for example, the Blackpool office is mostly responsible for disability benefits
- 6 central service directorates responsible for services such as accounts and personnel.

In 1996, the senior management structure of the Benefits Agency was reorganised. Alongside the Chief Executive, Peter Mathison, the Benefits Agency Management Team included two non-executive directors from the private sector and eight other senior managers from within the Benefits Agency.

Other agencies within the DSS

Other agencies within the DSS include:

● The *Child Support Agency* (dealing with most child support issues), and the first Next Steps Agency to be established from scratch
● The *War Pensions Agency* (which, as its name suggests, administers War Pensions)
● The *Information Technology Services Agency* (which deals with the IT needs of the DSS and Next Steps Agencies).

In Northern Ireland, the administration of benefits is not handled by the Benefits Agency but by the Social Security Agency. Some hostels for homeless men ('resettlement units') were run by the *Resettlement Agency* until 'community care' legislation meant that the government withdrew from direct care provision. The *Contributions Agency* (which administers National Insurance contributions) is to merge with the Inland Revenue as a finance-collecting body from 1999, having been part of DSS until then.

Performance targets

Each agency has performance targets set by central government. The targets for the Benefits Agency in 1996–97 are set out below in Table 7.1.

These targets are interesting in a number of ways. First, they demonstrate the priorities that the Secretary of State has for benefit administration. For example, there are targets for the speed and accuracy of processing claims, so these are clearly seen to be important, but there is no target for ensuring a certain rate of benefit take-up. Second, it is interesting to consider how the level for each target is set. Third, it is worth contemplating how accurately the performance of the Benefits Agency is measured. Finally, it is unclear what happens if an Agency fails to meet its target, although the performance pay and continuing job of the Chief Executive probably rests, at least to some extent, on meeting the Agency's performance indicators. The following sections consider some of these issues.

Table 7.1   Benefits Agency performance targets in 1996–97

Activity	1996–97 target	Achievement
Claims clearance times		
Social Fund Crisis Loans	Same day	98%
Income Support	63% in 5 days	64%
	87% in 13 days	88%
Incapacity Benefit	65% in 10 days	79%
	85% in 30 days	96%
Child Benefit	68% in 10 days	75%
	94% in 30 days	94%
Disability Living Allowance	65% in 30 days	64%
	85% in 53 days	91%
Family Credit	90% in 5 days	92%
Accuracy		
Income Support	87%	81%
Incapacity Benefit	94%	90%
Family Credit	91%	91%
Disability Living Allowance	96%	98%
Unemployed sign-offs	156,700 within 10 days	140,300
	189,000 within 28 days	181,200
Financial management		
Recovery of Social Fund loans	£278m	£299m
Security savings	£1,500m	£1,524m
Recovery of overpayments	£91.5m	£102.6m
Financial control		
Deliver business plan within gross allocation		Achieved
Keep the Social Fund cash limit		Achieved
Customer satisfaction		
Percentage of customers that regard the service as satisfactory or better	85%	86% in 95–96

Claims clearance times

As we can see from Table 6.1, five areas are singled our for targets for the Benefits Agency. Claims clearance time is the time taken from someone submitting a claim to a decision being made about the claim. The importance of this target is twofold: from the claimants' perspective, it is clearly desirable to know the outcome of a claim as soon as possible; from the perspective of 'efficiency', a shorter time spent sorting out a claim should save money in terms of expenditure on administration.

Claims clearance targets vary depending on the type of benefit. It might be thought that benefits that are simple to administer would be sorted out most quickly. However, the targets for Income Support and Family Credit are the toughest, yet these are both means-tested benefits, which are, therefore, complicated to administer. The reason for the difference in targets is because it is more important for claimants to have their Income Support and Family Credit worked out quickly. In the case of Income Support, this may be their only source of income. In cases of Family Credit, some people may not take a low-paid job unless they can be sure of receiving their top-up from Family Credit within days rather than weeks.

In virtually all cases, the Benefits Agency achieved its claims clearance targets in 1996–97. This could be seen as positively demonstrating the success of the Benefits Agency's administration, but it is also important to consider whether the targets were set too low. For example, the target for Disability Living Allowance (two-thirds of claims to be cleared in 30 days) seems woefully low. However, this should perhaps be put in the context of the Disability Living Allowance's history. When the benefit was introduced in 1992, the Benefits Agency came in for major criticism for poor administration of the benefit, some claimants waiting many months before their entitlement had been calculated. The Benefits Agency explained this by the unexpectedly high number of claims that were received and the complexity of their administration. Whatever the initial problems, Disability Living Allowance has now been in existence for more than 5 years, so it is surprising that the clearance times are still rather slow.

Accuracy

If Benefits Agency staff are under pressure to administer claims within certain time periods, there is likely to be some concern that they will make mistakes in calculating a claimant's entitlement to benefit. This may explain the reason for the second area for targets: 'accuracy'. Accuracy targets look fairly high, but, for Income Support, the government is accepting the fact that more than one person in 10 on the main safety net benefit will be receiving an incorrect award. This may mean that some people receive more money than they should and others receive less; this could be because of error by staff, error by the claimant or fraud. However, it is worth adding that not all inaccuracy affects the level of award. Error may occur if a claim is incorrectly 'adjudicated', meaning that inappropriate legislation or regulations have been referred to in settling a benefit application.

The Benefits Agency is not quite as successful with these targets compared with clearance times and, in particular, fails to meet the target for Income Support: one recipient in five had received an incorrect Income Support award in 1996–97. Reviews of benefit claims are made to check for errors and fraud, but these are not without measurement error themselves, so the figures relating to achieved targets presented can only be used as a guide (independent figures are shown later in this chapter).

Under the broad term 'accuracy' comes an interesting performance target called 'unemployed register sign-offs'. In 1996–97, the Benefits Agency aimed to sign 156,700 people off the unemployment register within 10 days of their signing on. This target could, once again, be seen positively if people were signing off because they had found work with the help of Benefits Agency staff, but the fact that this target comes under 'accuracy' gives a clue to the underlying reason for the target. Moving into paid work is only one reason for a person signing off from unemployment-related benefits, other possibilities including being sanctioned or being persuaded to sign off. Indeed, the staff of the Employment Service are believed to have have targets for the number of benefit sanctions that they apply. The target should be seen in the context of the politics surrounding the monthly unemployment count, which has received widespread publicity and which governments are obviously keen to reduce.

Financial management and control

The next area for targets is 'financial management'. Two of the targets under this heading relate to the recovery of money – first from those who are given Social Fund loans, and second from those who have previously been overpaid benefit because of either error or fraud. In the case of staff error, it is not clear that the claimant should have to repay the money and, therefore, effectively be penalised. In the case of error or fraud more generally, this target relates back to accuracy because, if people were initially paid the correct amount of benefit, there would be no erroneous or fraudulent overpayments to recover. As we saw in the last chapter, the recovery of Social Fund loans and overpayments is a controversial area because, in most cases, money will be deducted from Income Support payments that already provide a bare minimum for

someone to live on. Some of those who owe money to the Benefits
Agency may have managed to find jobs, so these people should be
more able to repay any money owed, but it is more difficult for the
Benefits Agency to track these people and ensure that the repayments
are made.

The targets on 'security savings' relate to various anti-fraud initiatives, but it is difficult to measure how much has been saved through
these initiatives because we cannot know how much money would
have been defrauded had these initiatives not existed.

Customer satisfaction

The existence of this target at least acknowledged that the Benefits
Agency should take a more 'customer-orientated' approach to its oper-
ations. A biennial survey of benefit recipients was carried out to
measure satisfaction, but the difficulty in measuring and interpreting
the results of this survey has been given as a reason for dropping this as
a Secretary of State performance target in the future. The Benefits
Agency has, however, introduced a 'milestone target' relating to
customer satisfaction, and research is being carried out to improve the
measurement of this factor. Nevertheless, the removal of this as a key
performance indicator could signal a change in the overall importance
of a customer-orientated approach within the Benefits Agency.

Cutting back on administration

As we have seen, the administration of benefits is a major business,
involving almost £100 billion and approaching 100,000 staff in
various organisations. Pressure to reduce the benefits bill has recently
been applied to cutting the cost of administration, and in 1996 the
government announced the 'Change' programme, which aimed to cut
administrative running costs by 25 per cent in real terms over the
following 3 years. Costs of this scale were to be achieved in a number
of ways. The DSS would concentrate on its main ('core') business and
would cut out what was seen as non-essential – the free benefits
advice line was stopped in July 1996, for example. New computer
systems would remove the need to collect the same information on
more than one occasion. There were also plans radically to change the
way in which the DSS made decisions about cases and dealt with
appeals (see below).

The Employment Service

The system of benefits for unemployed people has traditionally involved staff from the government department concerned with employment issues. Today, benefits for jobseekers are funded by the DSS but administered at job centres run by the Employment Service, itself an Agency of the DfEE. The Employment Service is also responsible for monitoring people to ensure that they are taking sufficient action to get back into work. Some Benefits Agency staff now also work within Employment Service job centres.

The role of the Employment Service is also wider than just dealing with benefit recipients: it also runs a vacancy advertising and filling service that is available to anyone wanting to find a different job.

Local authorities

Local authorities administer Housing Benefit and Council Tax Benefit. The UK system is heavily centralised in terms of benefit levels and rules. Other countries allow regional or local governments to determine these key aspects of the system, and indeed there used to be separate local Rent Rebate systems in Britain. Local authorities also run social services and may set up welfare rights units to encourage local people to claim their benefit entitlements.

The Post Office and the ACT system

Benefits are generally paid in one of two ways. The most common route is to have a book of Giro credits that may be handed over for cash at Post Offices on set dates. The frequency of payment varies but may be as common as weekly for some benefits. Payment on a fortnightly and 4-weekly basis is also common. The vast majority of benefits are paid in this way. The process of queuing up for benefits might be thought to be stigmatising, but it appears to suit those used to dealing mostly with cash, which encompasses a sizeable proportion of British adults (Kempson, 1994). The main alternative is for benefit to be paid into a bank or building society account through Automated Credit Transfer (ACT). Payment is typically made on a 4-weekly basis.

The process of 'cashing' Giros provides significant work for the Post Office. Suggestions to move towards ACT, which might save money in administration and reduce fraud, are often opposed on the grounds of decimating the wide network of rural Post Offices in Britain.

Claimants, customers or recipients?

The words used to describe the social security system and its users are rarely neutral and often reflect views on the validity of people's behaviour. Labels are also subject to change: until recently, what we have called means-tested benefits were invariably referred to in official writings as income-related benefits. The word 'poverty' also seems to be enjoying a partial resurgence in official documents.

The term used to describe people receiving benefits has long been that of 'claimant'. On the positive side, this term emphasises the individual's right or claim to social security. One of the problems with the term, however, is that some people claim, or apply for, benefit but are not awarded it (either because they are not entitled to benefit or because there is a mistake in the decision to award benefit).

More recently, the Benefits Agency has moved away from using the term 'claimant' in favour of the term 'customer'. This reflects more general moves in industry and the service sector to be more customer orientated. The term should, therefore, emphasise customers' rights and needs, and be a step forward in the way in which the agencies handle claims. It has been criticised in the context of social security because, in most situations where the term is used, customers are able to choose between different companies or services so can exercise a degree of customer choice; those dealing with the Benefits Agency, however, have little or no ability to 'shop around' for the best deal in benefits. Thus, the term is frequently seen as inappropriate, even if it does indicate that change in the relationships between staff and 'customers' is important.

The latest moves to improve service quality and streamline administration are evident with the Benefits Agency's attempt to introduce an 'Active Modern Service' (Benefits Agency, 1998). This emphasises the ministerial objectives of Active Services, Customer Focused, Transforming, Integrity and Security, Valuing and Developing Staff, and Efficient Services.

We have tried to keep an open mind and to use more neutral terms in this book. The word 'claimant' is used to refer to people receiving social security benefits (this is a rather natural usage for those writing in this area), but we also use the term 'recipients', which we regard as less value laden and ambiguous than 'claimants' or 'customers'.

Equal access to benefits for all?

People who face disadvantage in the labour market and elsewhere may be expected to have a greater reliance on social security benefits. However, some of the reasons for that disadvantage may carry over into the structure and administration of benefits, exacerbating existing inequalities. Some disadvantaged groups have received relatively little attention from both social security researchers and social security policy-makers (Williams, 1989). In this section, we briefly discuss some of the interactions between disadvantage in wider society and the implications for social security.

As discussed in Chapters 1, 3 and 4, social security in Britain has long been based on strong links with paid work – the 'contributory principle'. By definition, those not in paid work at all, or in intermittent forms of employment, cannot build up entitlement as easily as those in secure jobs. This alone will mean that many groups are unable to access social insurance and will instead rely on the means-tested elements of provision. Those not in paid work will include:

- Those, mostly women, who are performing other tasks incompatible with paid work, such as caring
- Disabled people and minority ethnic groups who are excluded from work for various reasons, including discrimination
- Those in particular occupations and social class categories whose seasonal and temporary jobs are highly insecure
- Young people with limited work experience
- Some older people who are on the margins of early retirement, part-time work and long-term unemployment.

Taking the first of these groups, the place of women in relation to the social security system has received some attention. Chapter 3 discussed how the British social security system developed out of the vision of Beveridge, which made various assumptions about the roles of men and women. The essence of Beveridge's social insurance approach is that paid work is the gateway to most benefits, and those not in paid work are expected to depend on a partner or someone else. Alternatively, there is recourse to the safety net of means-tested benefits. Women's dependence on male benefit recipients and their lower likelihood of being in employment mean that the amount of money that goes *independently* to women is about half as much as goes to men (Duncan *et al.*, 1994).

Since the Second World War, there has been a substantial increase in the employment of women (particularly married women and mothers), but women still have a more restricted access to the labour market compared with men so are less likely to receive contributory benefits. Their low level of economic resources, however, means that they are more likely to be receiving means-tested benefits. They are also the main recipients of some contingent benefits (such as for disability and caring), and there are specific provisions for women as widows and mothers (Department of Social Security, 1998d).

In the very recent past, however, quite direct forms of discrimination against women were part of social security regulations. (For example, married women were disallowed from claiming Invalid Care Allowance, apparently on the grounds that they would be normally expected to carry out such care, while there would be no such expectations of married men, so they could claim.) Equal treatment legislation in European law has been used to remove such restrictions. There are also instances of sex discrimination against men in the social security system as widowers have long been treated differently from widows, to the disadvantage of the former. The government is considering benefit changes to remove the anomalous treatment of widowers.

Policy changes around lone parenthood and child support seem to have raised the stakes in comparing the situations of men and women. The benefit cuts for lone mothers may indicate the continuing power of negative stereotypes in driving through reform. However, it is also true that persistent cuts to insurance benefits have adversely affected mostly men, long their principal beneficiaries (Millar, 1997).

The issue of 'race' has received much less attention in the development of recent policy and in social security research. The disadvantaged position of minority ethnic groups in the labour market, relative to whites, has been well documented (Jones, 1993; Sly, 1996; Modood *et al.*, 1997), but the welfare reform Green Paper mentions ethnic minorities just twice, each time in the context of health services rather than social security (Department of Social Security, 1998c: 46, 47).

Only since the mid-1990s has there been information about income and benefits for different minority ethnic groups (Berthoud, 1997). Bloch (1997) describes policy changes for immigrants and asylum-seekers from the mid-1980s onwards and points out that many benefits contain residency tests. While immigration status is quite different from 'race', it is possible that such reforms affect UK residents differentially on the basis of their skin colour (Bolderson and Roberts, 1995).

A group not mentioned in the list above is gay couples, yet benefit policy is predicated on heterosexual relationships. There are benefit regulations that in rare circumstances recognise polygamous marriages (when they took place in jurisdictions where this was legal), but lesbian and gay couples are never treated as couples but always as single people. This would be a financial advantage for most means-tested benefits, since the single rate is more than half the couple rate (and a lone parent plus a single person receive more than do a couple with children). The situation with Working Families Tax Credit, however, is more complex, and it would be a financial disadvantage for benefits contingent on the death or status of a partner. Of course, issues of equal treatment concern rather more than the particular financial circumstance in a system where they are the arbitrary outcome of recognising only some types of relationship.

As discussed in Chapter 5, disabled people are particularly likely not to be in paid work: perhaps only one-third of those of working age are actually in employment (Martin and White, 1988). Contributory benefits for disabled people may be higher than for the unemployed but depend on a previous record of employment and, therefore, exclude those disabled from a young age. Cash benefits may contribute towards maintaining independence but do not address wider features of society that may constitute some of the main problems confronting disabled people.

Decision-making and appeals

The 1998 Social Security Act makes important changes to the legal basis for making decisions about benefit applications and to the appeals process for those wanting to challenge particular decisions. This set of changes has been controversial among those involved in this area (see Adler and Sainsbury, 1998) but has attracted much less attention than have other changes in the Act, especially cuts to benefits for lone parents.

From 1911 onwards, decision-making on initial claims had generally been split between decisions that were made by an Adjudication Officer (or officials with similar titles in areas of disability, Social Fund and child support matters) and those made on behalf of the Secretary of State (for Social Security) – actually by officials with this delegated authority. In general terms, decisions on many procedural matters (such as when and whether a claim had been made) were taken by the Secretary of State. Most matters of fact concerning entitlement to social security benefits were made by Adjudication Officers. In practice, the same person might act in both capacities. Historically, decisions by an Adjudication Officer could be challenged by an independent appeal, whereas Secretary of State decisions were subject only to internal review, with the possibility of judicial review in the courts.

The Adjudication Officer was considered to be somewhat impartial, with standards of decision-making within the remit of a Chief Adjudication Officer supported by an independent Central Adjudication Service. The 1998 reforms simplified the system so that all decisions are now taken on behalf of the Secretary of State, and the role of the Chief Adjudication Officer is given over to the Chief Executives of the Agencies. The legislation also aims to introduce simpler claim forms and to provide clearer guidance about the respective roles of applicant and Agency in providing necessary information to decide a claim and at what time.

The system of appeals has also changed. The government was concerned that the process of appeals often took too long and that many people were pursuing cases with no prospect of success. In 1996, 38 per cent of appeals were won by the appellant, and the average clearance time was almost 6 months (see Sainsbury, 1998, for an analysis of the case for change).

The right of appeal to an independent appeal has been retained. The appeals process has been 'unified' to form one rather than the five separate systems under the remit of the Independent Tribunal Service. However, Housing Benefit appeals remain a local authority matter, so unification is far from complete.

There are several important, if rather technical, changes to the ways in which tribunals operate and to their composition. The consideration of matters of fact will now relate to the time of claim rather than the time of tribunal, as before, and to the particular point of issue rather than to the whole claim. There are particular provisions for holding 'paper-based' hearings that the person does not attend.

Non-take-up of benefits

Not everyone who is entitled to receive a social security benefit necessarily receives it. For people to receive a benefit, they generally need to apply for it and to supply all of the relevant information. Therefore, if they do not recognise that they are eligible, or do not want to apply for a benefit even if they believe themselves to be eligible, they will not receive the benefit. For some benefits, this will affect the situation of individuals, but for many benefits, it will be a matter for a family or household.

Various studies have attempted to determine the main reasons why people do not claim benefits. Studies have also investigated whether some people are more likely to claim than others, and the types of benefit subject to the lowest and highest levels of take-up. One of the strongest conclusions has been that means-tested benefits have lower levels of take-up than more universal benefits. It is generally reckoned that the take-up of the Retirement Pension and of Child Benefit tends towards 100 per cent. In contrast, the take-up of Family Credit is in the region of 70 per cent, and the take-up of Income Support by some groups, particularly pensioners, may also be as 'low' as 70 per cent. Take-up is generally measured in two ways. First is as a 'case-load measure', which is the proportion of eligible people who receive a benefit. However, many of these are entitled to only small amounts – the higher the level of entitlement, the more likely it is that people will claim a particular benefit. To capture this difference, take-up may also be expressed as an 'expenditure measure', which is the proportion of eligible money that is claimed by those taking up their entitlement. The expenditure figure is generally at least as high as the case-load-based measure (Table 7.2).

Table 7.2   Take-up of means-tested benefits

Benefit	By caseload	By spending
Income Support	76–93%	88–92%
Family Credit	69%	82%
Housing Benefit	90–96%	93–97%
Council Tax Benefit	70–78%	71–79%

Source: Department of Social Security (1997: section H)

Some commentators have suggested that non-take-up is an inherent feature of means-tested benefits. However, the situation may not be quite as simple when the figures are examined in greater detail. The rate of Income Support take-up for lone parents is virtually 100 per cent, so perhaps some groups do not appear to experience take-up problems.

It is also difficult to measure the rate of take-up of some universal benefits, such as disability benefits. A large-scale follow-up survey of disabled people who had taken part in a wider survey found that rates of take-up were approximately 50 per cent (Craig and Greenslade, 1998), and apparently higher for those dealing with mobility rather than with care needs.

It remains true that means-tested benefits are among the most likely to face problems of non-take-up, and there are good reasons to pay most attention to the non-take-up of these benefits. Most of the means-tested benefits are designed to provide a safety net so that people's living standards do not slip below a certain level. If a significant number of eligible families are not receiving these benefits, we might conclude that their quality of life is being particularly badly affected. An alternative is that they have other forms of support that protect their lifestyle, such as in-kind or financial support from their family.

Early research on take-up brought a range of disparate concepts to the study of people's claiming behaviour. People were leaving benefits unclaimed for a mixture of reasons relating to ignorance, complexity and stigma. If people were not informed about the types of benefit available, or their rules, it might be their *ignorance* that was preventing them from claiming. Alternatively, if they had the relevant knowledge, they might be dissuaded from taking their claim further forward because of the range of difficult application forms and the *complexity* of the whole process. A third possibility is that people valued their ability to live independently and did not want the *stigma* of being a recipient of state support. Older people might have retained memories of the harshness of the means tests of the 1930s (Deacon and Bradshaw, 1983) or might have picked up such messages from family members.

These ideas have a good deal of intuitive appeal. The system is relatively complex, and people tend to have a limited understanding of the relevant rules and application process. The point about stigma could explain the lower take-up level of Income Support compared with Retirement Pension as the means-tested benefit carries connotations of people being unable to support themselves and, therefore, being dependent upon the state. The Retirement Pension is the expected return for years of contributing to National Insurance and may be more likely to be seen as a right that people have. It is also easy to see how some of these ideas might interact: those concerned about stigma might take less notice of information about benefits.

However, a few ideas do not amount to a useful model of claiming behaviour. Moreover, studies that have attempted to use these ideas have not met with complete success. Campaigns seeking to encourage claiming by providing greater information have achieved some success but have not perhaps been as successful as one might expect (Alcock and Shepherd, 1987).

It is also clear from surveys that those in receipt of benefits are not really better informed than non-claimants – everyone, whether claiming or not, has a relatively low level of knowledge. A study of the take-up of Family Credit in 1991 found, contrary to expectations, that eligible non-recipients were generally in better conditions than recipients: they were more likely to be owner-occupiers and indeed seemed to have a higher standard of living (Marsh and McKay, 1993). One of the explanations put forward by this study and a subsequent follow-up (McKay and Marsh, 1995) was that claiming required self-identification of eligibility. People often assumed that benefits were only available to the very badly off and would, therefore, not recognise themselves as eligible if they felt themselves able to manage on their existing resources.

Various attempts have been made to arrive at more systematic accounts of people's claiming behaviour. The most sophisticated has sought to combine the concepts of 'thresholds', 'trade-offs' and 'triggers'. Kerr (1983) put forward a model based on thresholds: in order to claim, people had to pass six thresholds that included recognising that they were eligible and believing that they would benefit from making a claim. This approach has been seen as particularly influential in the field (Craig, 1991) but did not convince all, and indeed the empirical evidence presented did not rule out that a model based on trade-offs could provide good predictive power. A model based on trade-offs suggests that people may claim, even if they do not pass a particular threshold, if one of the key factors is very strong. If their need is great, this may be enough to overcome deep-seated feelings of stigma.

To this field may be added the concept of 'triggers' (van Oorschot, 1995). An application may be more likely to be made if a definite event precedes it. Thus, losing a job, retiring or having a child may precipitate a person into considering applying for benefits. In contrast, those facing a more gradual change in circumstances might not benefit from such a 'triggering' effect. Such an effect could also help to explain some of the known differences between different benefits and client groups in their rates of take-up of benefits. Those becoming lone parents might deal with various aspects of their financial arrangements, including claiming benefits, at one time, which would contribute to high rates of take-up. Among pensioners, a more gradual erosion of private sources of income (such as occupational pensions that were not regularly uprated) might not trigger an awareness of the benefits that could be claimed.

A concern with rates of take-up appears to be most important in Britain. When other countries have conducted research studies, it has been rare for take-up rates to exceed 80 per cent, and rates of around one-half are not unknown. According to van Oorschot (1995: 25):

> very little, if anything, is known about the non-take-up of benefits, except in Britain and, to a lesser degree, the USA, the Netherlands and... Germany.

This general picture is complemented by the study of Eardley *et al.* (1996b: 106).

Fraud and error

Perhaps the other side of the coin from non-take-up is fraud – where people are claiming money to which they are not legally entitled.

In October 1992, Peter Lilley, the then Secretary of State for Social Security, made the crackdown on fraud part of a personal crusade, when he told the Conservative Party conference: 'Be in no doubt, this government and this Secretary of State will not tolerate fraud... I've set a target of £500 million and I mean to get it back.' According to government figures, the Benefits Agency recovered £558 million in 1992–93. This emphasis on fraud has been at least matched by the New Labour government, which has said, in a Green Paper devoted to the subject, that 'Social security fraud is a threefold evil' (Department of Social Security, 1998e: 1).

This section considers the nature and extent of benefit fraud, the causes of benefit fraud and the official response to fraud.

How much benefit fraud is there?

Benefit fraud is a crime. According to the Social Security Administration Act 1992, it occurs when 'a person for the purpose of obtaining benefit or other payment... makes a statement or representation which he knows to be false'. It may be committed by individuals on a fairly small scale or by organised groups on a large scale. Consequently, benefit fraud covers a wide range of activity.

It is, of course, very difficult to measure the true extent of many criminal or deviant activities. In 1992–93, the Sector Fraud branch of the Benefits Agency (which deals with frauds by individuals) investigated 560,000 cases, of which 219,000 (39 per cent) ended in some form of calculated saving or discovery of an overpayment. As a result, the Benefits Agency claims that savings of £516 million were achieved. However, these figures represent notional rather than actual savings; in other words, they relate to an estimate of how much money would have been defrauded had the fraudster not been caught. They do not, therefore, represent real savings. The activities of the Organised Fraud branch of the Benefits Agency led to the arrest of 1,400 people, with calculated savings of £42 million.

The most recent attempts to measure fraud have been based on samples of particular benefit claims, which are subject to detailed scrutiny and sometimes interview surveys. These Benefit Reviews, which also cover other types of incorrect payment, began in 1994.

Benefits Reviews published prior to the recent Green Paper on fraud (Department of Social Security, 1998e: 12) suggested that:

● a conservative estimate of fraud is £2 billion a year; but
● the figure could be much higher, around £7 billion if all suspicions of fraud were well founded.

These figures are based on 2 per cent of claims being fraudulent, a strong suspicion of fraud in 3 per cent and a low suspicion of fraud in a further 2 per cent.

The results of the most recent reviews of particular benefits are listed in Table 7.3.

Table 7.3   Fraud in the Benefits Reviews

Benefit (in order of publication of results)	Percent of claims where fraud is confirmed or strongly suspected	Total estimated cost (million pounds)
Unemployment Benefit	7.8	86
Retirement Pension	up to 0.13	up to 40
Invalid Care Allowance	6.5	37
Disability Living Allowance	12.2	499
Income Support (2nd review)	11.1	1,774
Housing Benefit (2nd review)	4.9	610

Source: Department of Social Security (1998e: 56) and, for Housing Benefit, Government Statistical Service (1998)

Fraud, like non-take-up, appears most prevalent with means-tested benefits and with some disability benefits. Among Income Support recipients, fraud is apparently more common among lone parents than pensioners or disabled people. The more recent Benefit Reviews for means-tested benefits adopt the classification shown in Table 7.4.

Not declaring earnings is the largest component of fraud. The more recent figures give less weight to cohabitation, and more to fraud relating to address or identities, compared with the first Income Support review.

Table 7.4   Main types of fraud in means-tested benefits

Type of fraud	Fraud (Percent of value)
Earnings	39
Capital/income	22
Address/identity	22
Dependants	7
Other	5
Rent	5
Living together	4

Source: Department of Social Security (1998e: 56)

What causes benefit fraud?

The causes of benefit fraud, like the causes of crime in general, are hotly debated. The main division in such debates is perhaps between those explanations which deal with the individual pathology of the criminal and those which see the causes as being closely related to the society and the systems in which individuals live.

Economists suggest that individuals adopt a cost–benefit analysis. Research on fraud has generally focused on tax evasion (Pyle, 1989), and economists use a model of rational decision-making in conditions that are uncertain. Fraud is seen a rational decision and reflects the likelihood of being caught, the size of the probable gain and the size of the probable penalties.

In contrast, *social psychologists* consider benefit fraud as a combination of instigations and constraints, in terms of both the objective social situation in which people find themselves and their subjective reactions to it. It has been argued that instigations operate in the early stages of considering fraud whereas constraints come into play at a later stage. Once someone feels the need to commit fraud, that person considers the opportunities and constraints (Hessing *et al.*, 1993).

Social policy researchers sometimes argue that the level of benefit payments is inadequate and that this alone may lead claimants to defraud the system in order to provide a satisfactory living standard for themselves or their families. Fraud may also be seen as a preferable option to receiving more stigmatising benefits, such as free school meals. However, poverty seems unlikely to be the whole story. Many people on low incomes do not commit fraud, although, of course, this may be due partly to a lack of opportunity rather than a lack of motivation or need. Indeed, studies of the hidden economy have shown that the very poorest groups, who have most need for cash-in-hand work, have fewest opportunities for finding such work. This is because their neighbours are unlikely to have the spare cash for some of the odd jobs that might be an available option (Jordan *et al.*, 1992).

Another factor to consider is the nature of the social security system. Recent developments in social security have, arguably, resulted in the criminalisation of behaviour that was previously acceptable. For example, the stiffening of regulations relating to 'actively seeking work' raises the likelihood that people will be found to be in breach of such rules. It is also argued that particular aspects of the benefit system make fraud more likely. These include:

- The small amounts of money that recipients can earn before losing £1 of benefit for each pound earned
- The possible disruption to the 'secure' flow of benefit caused by signing off for a short period before signing back on again
- That there is only a crime of 'living together as husband and wife' because of the family-level nature of the calculation of means-tested benefits.

Finally, respect for the system and the perceived fairness (or otherwise) of the system is likely to affect the tendency to commit social security fraud or abuse.

The official response to fraud

In 1995, the Benefits Agency instigated a 'Five Year Security Strategy' to deal with fraud. This comprises a number of policies, including investment in new technology (benefit payment cards to replace order books and centralised computer systems for more cross-checking) along with new detection methods (such as a freephone hotline for members of the public to report suspected fraud). About 200,000 cases are detected each year and about 10,000 people prosecuted. The remainder sometimes pay back the money owed and/or sign off benefit.

In the 1970s, the number of prosecutions for benefit fraud rose, and this was seen as a measure of government success in the fight against fraud. However, prosecution is very expensive, and there is no evidence that prosecution acts as a deterrent against fraud (Rowlingson *et al.*, 1997). In the 1980s, the emphasis shifted away from prosecution and on to the achievement of financial savings, through removing benefits from fraudulent claimants and through recovering overpayments. In the 1990s, the emphasis has shifted again – this time towards preventing and deterring fraud.

Attacking benefit fraud has always been popular with the electorate, so various governments have made the issue a priority. Much less attention is given to fighting tax fraud even though this probably accounts for more lost government revenue than does benefit fraud (Cook, 1989). Less attention has also been given to errors made in assessing benefit claims (Rowlingson and Whyley, 1998), although it has been estimated that more people on Income Support have erroneous claims than make fraudulent claims (Benefits Agency, 1995).

Error

Alongside fraud and non-take-up, there is error, in which mistakes are made in the process of calculating the entitlement to benefits. These may result in non-payment, underpayment or overpayment. Official estimates suggest that overpayments amount to £750 million and underpayments to £600 million each year. About half of the overpayments are the result of departmental mistakes (Department of Social Security, 1998e: 12). While the inclusion of these figures in the fraud Green Paper is interesting, much less attention is given to reducing errors than to the more popular cause of attacking fraud (Rowlingson and Whyley, 1998).

Standards of adjudication of benefits and child support maintenance orders are subject to detailed investigation by the Chief Adjudication Officer and Chief Child Support Officer (albeit, in 1998, the same person – Ernie Hazlewood). The system changes in 1999 (as described above). Standards of decision-making vary markedly across different benefits, and a high proportion of decisions is incorrect. The most recently available evidence for selected benefits is shown in Table 7.5 (Chief Adjudication Officer, 1998). Note that it is possible for the benefit award decided to be correct even if the legal basis of the decision was not sound.

Table 7.5 Chief Adjudication Officer comments on benefit decisions

	Adjudication incorrect and payment incorrect	*Adjudication incorrect and payment in doubt*	*Adjudication incorrect but payment not affected*	*Decision correct*
Income Support	10	20	5	65
Jobseeker's Allowance	8	41	7	44
Family Credit	5	15	1	79
Social Fund Funeral Payments	14	36	14	36
Retirement Pension	1	0	9	90
Widow's Benefits	0	0	3	97
Child Benefit	0	0.5	0.5	99
Disability Living Allowance	3	9	9	79

Source: Chief Adjudication Officer, 1998: various charts

The likelihood of an entirely correct decision was lowest among the means-tested benefits, and highest for the contingent and contributory benefits. The high level of doubtful Jobseeker's Allowance cases reflects the benefit being in its first year of operation – although those affected might take a dimmer view.

Results for Maintenance Assessments within Child Support appear much worse, although the Chief Child Support Officer has said:

In plain terms, however, my monitors found 43% decisions correct and 57% deficient in some way. But it would be unfair to judge the Agency on such a basis, hence our amplification of findings to provide details in cash terms. This changes the figures to 62% correct, 22% wrong and 15% where, because of lack of evidence, it was impossible to tell. From this, one may conclude that MAs [Main-tenance Assessments] may have been correct in 77% of cases. Viewed against a figure of only 25% correct three years earlier, such improvement is dramatic. (Chief Child Support Officer, 1998: second page in Foreword)

Benefit fraud in other countries

There is rather limited evidence concerning the importance of fraud and mechanisms to recover funds in other countries. In the area of social assistance, Eardley *et al.* (1996b: 88–92) detect a growing role for computerised checking and the use of home visits as a way of providing regular monitoring. The DSS (1993a: 27–8) has argued that there is growing activity in this area, particularly to reduce illegal employment.

8

The Effects of Social Security

Introduction

One of the most important debates about social security provision concerns its effects on people's behaviour: does it cause them to act in particular ways? There are several different areas in which there may be effects. The most often talked about are:

- The effect of benefits on people's willingness to take paid work or to work longer hours
- The effect of benefits on the types of family that people form, in particular whether they are more likely to become lone parents or to have more children
- The effect of pensions and some other benefits on people's willingness to provide for themselves, such as through saving.

The types of question raised in this debate are not purely technical. Instead, they go to the heart of debates about the proper roles that should be played by individuals, their families, the local community and wider society. They introduce the language of morality into discussions of state welfare. For example, it is often suggested that the sorts of value system that people hold have been affected by the availability of social security. In particular, it is argued that there has been a growth in 'welfare dependency' or a 'dependency culture'. The existence of widespread unemployment and the perceived breakdown of the family are attributed by some to the development of the welfare state, social security provision being identified as the central problem. The development of an 'underclass' is but the most extreme form of this view.

The purpose of this chapter is to describe these arguments in more detail and to consider competing theories. Empirical evidence is also considered.

Disincentives to work: is it worth working?

People receive earnings when they work and may receive benefit income when they do not. This suggests, if people respond to simple financial incentives, that unemployment may become an attractive option. It will be all the more desirable for those who expect to have relatively low earnings in work and higher benefits out of work (Bryson and McKay, 1994). Within economic theory, these views attain a greater degree of formality. It is argued that individuals face a choice between work and leisure. Earnings may make it worthwhile to abandon leisure (which is desired for its own sake) to take paid work (which is usually treated as not inherently rewarding). When there is extra payment for not working, the balance of the choice is affected: some may be induced to prefer leisure to work. For any given wage, and level of non-work income, people will make a decision about whether or not to work and for how many hours.

This theoretical approach is contentious, and there are various criticisms that may be made of it. First, criticisms may be made about some of the details, and many of these criticisms come from within the economics discipline (Blundell, 1992). It may be argued that people do not have all the information necessary to make appropriate judgements, work may be a reward in itself, work and leisure are not the only two options and so on. However, these do not really question the underlying logic of the model (Bryson and McKay, 1994), which is that people make rational decisions based on maximising their expected level of happiness.

A further set of criticisms relates to the real-world application of the model in a labour market with a wide range of institutional features very different from those of the model presented (Atkinson and Micklewright, 1991). Instead, employers are important actors. Benefits are often denied to those leaving work voluntarily or taking insufficient action to move back into work – people cannot simply choose to remain on benefits and do nothing without the risk of losing those benefits. A more philosophical critique questions how far the utility-maximising approach is valid at all (Broome, 1992).

The importance of this debate is not confined simply to the world of theory – unemployment is a major problem for the individuals and families affected as well as more generally for society. Not only does unemployment cost money directly in terms of benefits and other support for the unemployed, but there is also a very large indirect cost. This comprises the cost of the lost production or lost tax revenue, not to mention the large degree of social distress that unemployment can cause. Research in Britain has shown that unemployment is regarded as 'just about the worst thing that ever happened to me' by about half of those becoming unemployed (Daniel, 1990: 82). White (1991: 18) emphasises that this question was posed some 5 months after unemployment began, by which time many people had left unemployment. Moreover, those leaving unemployment quickly were just as likely to give the most negative answers about the experience.

However, it is crucial to realise that unemployment (being without paid work but being able to and wanting to work) is not the only status a person may have when not working. In addition to being employed, self-employed or unemployed, people may be described as 'retired', looking after children, disabled relatives or a household, or unable to work through sickness or disability. Indeed, as we saw earlier in this book, the total of benefits paid to people when they are unemployed is small compared with that paid to those who are sick and disabled (some of whom do have paid jobs), and to the retired. In looking at whether the social security system discourages paid work, we are considering jobless people in a range of different situations, including:

- Being unemployed
- Being 'sick' or 'disabled'
- Looking after children, family and/or the home
- Becoming retired or taking early retirement.

As well as considering the unintended consequences of benefits such as Jobseeker's Allowance on incentives to work, some benefits are specifically intended to alter behaviour in ways in which society or government deems appropriate. For example, Family Credit is available to families with children, in paid work, whose earnings are low enough to qualify. This is partly a matter of providing social assistance, ensuring that this group has enough on which to live, but it is also designed to overcome the 'unemployment trap' and encourage people to move into paid work at lower levels of earnings than they would otherwise be willing to accept. Pensions are, presumably, there partly to encourage people to leave the labour market at a particular age, earlier than would be the case without benefits. Indeed, with support from employers, the policy may be said to have been particularly successful. The proportion of people remaining in paid employment after the official state pension or retirement ages is very low and has been declining over a long period of time despite rising life expectancy and better overall health among those reaching state pension age. In France, it is accepted that the benefits policy should be used to encourage people to have more children, and it is generally believed that such a policy is likely to be successful.

In Britain, the rising number of people on disability benefits has called into question the legitimacy of some claims. The key question is how far the system encourages people to put themselves into the box marked 'disabled' rather than that marked 'unemployed'. There are currently some advantages to doing so (as discussed in Chapter 5): the 'insured' element of benefit lasts much longer, the benefit levels are higher and the extent of monitoring is much less.

Whether or not the consequences are intended, the main question is how far policy is able to alter people's behaviour. Is social security an important factor in influencing behaviour (and, if so, in what areas?), or is it relatively insignificant in its effects? Most research has been in the area of incentives to work among able-bodied people of working age. These studies have generated caution about assigning social security benefits a straightforward effect. In several areas, they have signalled the need for more precise statements of the types of effect that might be expected, but we may summarise many of the main conclusions from this body of research.

One of the conclusions is that individuals should not be considered in isolation. Instead, decisions about whether people work are likely to be made in the context of their family circumstances (Millar, 1994). In Britain, indeed, the benefits system is largely based on links between people who form couples. When one partner loses a job, it may make sense for the other partner also to cease work (Cooke, 1987). This will be particularly true if the second earner is relatively low paid or perhaps working only part time.

Second, social policy researchers have suggested that people have to deal with various risks when they move in and out of work. Coping with risk is more difficult for people used to low incomes, who may have scant resources on which to fall back. For this reason, a great deal of value may be attached to the certainty of different sources of income (Millar, 1994). A life on Income Support may mean a low standard of living, but at least the level is constant and the money can (generally) be relied upon to turn up. If a person within the family then moves instead into paid work, the delicate balance of budgets may be upset. There is a strong chance that income will rise, but even a small chance that the person will be worse off might be enough to dissuade people from making the transition. There might also be particular problems in the *transition* from non-work to paid work. Some items may need to be purchased, and there could be a time lag while benefits are recalculated to take account of the new circumstances.

Politicians have been sufficiently convinced by these arguments to introduce specific policy measures to address these problems. Under 'fast-track' provisions, Family Credit can generally be paid on the Friday if someone starts work on the Monday. Certain benefits that people receive when not working (Housing Benefit and Council Tax Benefit) are permitted to 'run on' for 4 weeks when people move into work. Such changes to rules have sought to remove any institutional features that might be inhibiting people, particularly families with children (including lone parents), from making the jump into paid employment.

McLaughlin (1991b) has argued that there is increasingly a serious mismatch between the types of job on offer and the types of work that are being sought by a large proportion of those unemployed. Most of those looking for work are men, and the jobs they are looking for are typically full time with high earnings and status, preferably in traditionally 'male' jobs (such as manufacturing and construction). A large proportion of vacancies, however, are for part-time, and perhaps temporary, work in the services sector, which is the main expanding part of the economy. This may often be thought of as 'women's work' and would generally be paid relatively low hourly rates of pay.

However, the changing nature of the labour market may easily be exaggerated. Beatson (1995) shows that Britain has fewer temporary workers, for example, than many European countries. The greatest evidence of flexibility is perhaps provided by the very high proportion of people working part time, itself often undertaken because people only want to work part time. Elsewhere, part-time work is often taken because people cannot find full-time work.

The *level* of benefits is not the only variable relating to the benefits system. There are many requirements placed on recipients of Jobseeker's Allowance and its predecessors, meaning that a simple model of economic behaviour is inaccurate. Recipients are not able to 'sit back' while on benefits and turn away all offers of assistance, possibilities of interviews and job offers. The introduction of the Restart interview after 6 months (White and Lakey, 1992) provides a degree of monitoring and seems effective in increasing the rate of outflow from benefits at this point in time (Dolton and O'Neill, 1996). This does not directly address the argument that unemployment benefits discourage working, but it does provide an important counterpoint to armchair theorising assuming that benefits merely pay out cash to people without requiring certain actions from them in return.

From theory to evidence

Theories about the choices of individuals may or may not be correct. However, a key criticism of such views is their apparent mismatch with the observed workings of the labour market. Over the past two decades, unemployment has risen rapidly and then fallen back, only to rise again substantially and then fall back again rather quickly. This suggests that some economy-wide process is likely to be at work and is more important than individual decision-making or the workings of the social security system. The OECD 1994 *Jobs Study* provides evidence for this. During the 1950s and 60s, the total number of unemployed averaged under 10 million. From 1972 to 1982, this number more than tripled. A subsequent prolonged economic expansion meant that unemployment was reined back, although only to 25 million. Since then, overall unemployment seems to have risen to the levels of the early 1980s, with 35 million, about 8.5 per cent of the labour force, unemployed in 1994.

It is possible to consider differences in different regions of the OECD. North America is distinguished by the experience of the late 1980s and early 1990s in that unemployment did not return to the levels of the early 1980s. Japan managed to keep unemployment low throughout this period. Thus, looking to North America provides one picture – looking to Japan might provide a rather different story. In nearly all OECD countries, young people continue to have a much higher rate of unemployment than do adults. However, countries with traditionally strong apprenticeship systems do not have such high levels. These changes do not appear to mirror, at least not in any obvious way, alterations in either people's 'preferences' for work or the prevailing system of benefits.

A clear 'real-world' feature of unemployment is its dynamic character. Unemployment is experienced by many different people over time, but many stay unemployed for only a relatively short time. Among a group of people becoming unemployed in 1995, half had ceased being unemployed 14 weeks later, approximately two-thirds of this group moving into paid work rather than into education, on to training schemes and so on (McKay *et al.*, 1997: Chapter 6).

A characteristic feature of most of Europe seems to be a relatively high rate of long-term unemployment. However, the risk of becoming unemployed at any one time is quite low. In the USA and Canada, in contrast, there is a much greater risk of becoming unemployed but, once unemployed, a much greater chance of avoiding long-term unemployment – and less support from social security for those who do. It is, therefore, sometimes argued that this signifies inflexibility in the European labour markets. Europe has also been much less successful in creating new jobs than have other OECD regions. This is despite the fact that male labour force participation has fallen the most quickly and female participation risen the most slowly. Any job growth that has taken place in Europe has been largely a product of growth in the public rather than the private sector.

Unemployment itself may be measured in two main ways: first, as the number of working-age people who are registered as unemployed or receiving benefits for this reason (the 'claimant count'); and second, as the number looking for work and available to take paid work (with some refinements, the 'ILO measure'). It has increasingly been argued that measures of registered unemployment are a very partial measure of potential labour supply. One problem with them is that the unemployment count is affected by differences in rules governing access to benefits such that if unemployment benefits are restricted to fewer people, the unemployment count will go down even though there may be no change in the number of jobless people looking for work. The New Labour government has introduced monthly measures of International Labour Office unemployment, while the previous Conservative governments tended to rely on the claimant count.

Research studies have looked at a range of areas. Qualitative studies have suggested that unemployed people are particularly keen to find jobs but may be dissuaded from taking some available work because of certain inflexibilities in the benefits system (McLaughlin *et al.*, 1989). Studies that have looked at replacement rates – how much better or worse off people are on benefits – tend to find that relatively few people would be better off not working. Until recent changes in mortgage protection, there might have been problems for home owners, who could only receive help with mortgage payments when not working, unlike tenants, who could receive Housing Benefit whether or not they were in paid work. Surveys also tend to show that the unemployed are at least as work orientated as those in employment – and often more so.

A concern about incentives has been central to policy (see below). However, the empirical evidence suggests little effect from the level of

benefits. There may be effects, however, caused by the structure of the
benefits system.

Policy towards unemployment compensation

Cuts in benefits for the unemployed and increases in in-work benefits
were an important part of the 1985 Fowler Review of social security
(DHSS, 1985) and of the 1988 White Paper *Training for Employment*.
This paper argued that the unemployed contributed to their own situation by:

● Inefficient and ineffective job-searching
● A lack of skills and a failure to develop these
● A lack of flexibility regarding the types of job they would accept and
  their realism in expecting particular levels of wages.

Policy has, therefore, aimed at ensuring that:

● People are financially better off in work than out of work, by
  providing benefits such as Family Credit to workers
● The unemployed are remotivated and the genuineness of claims is
  checked
● Unemployed people, especially young people, are reskilling through
  training.

Research on specific groups

Overall, the case for there being strong disincentives to work generated
by social security seems weak, particularly when looking at the general
population of those unemployed. However, there may be some groups
for whom the situation is rather different, who could confront quite
severe financial disincentives to work as a result of social security.
Research has looked in particular at lone parents and the partners of the
unemployed, especially the labour market behaviour of women married
to men becoming unemployed.

Partners of the unemployed

It has long been realised that the proportion of women in work is much lower among those married to (or living with) unemployed men compared with women whose partners are in paid work. A wide range of surveys has provided information about this feature. In the 1980 Women and Employment Survey (Martin and Roberts, 1984), 33 per cent of women married to unemployed men were in paid work compared with 62 per cent of wives whose husbands were in paid work. Davies *et al.* (1994) have termed this difference (62 − 33 = 29 per cent) the 'employment shortfall'. A figure for the employment shortfall for the wives of unemployed men in the region of 30 per cent is consistent across a range of survey information collected during the 1980s and 90s (Kell and Wright, 1990; Pudney and Thomas, 1993; Davies *et al.*, 1994; McKay *et al.*, 1997). The figure for the husbands of unemployed women seems to be about half this figure (Elias, 1997).

It has often been suggested that it is the benefits system that is creating this correlation between the working patterns of men and their partners. It is argued that, as a particular feature of disincentives to work, women are encouraged by the benefits system to cease working if their partners are unemployed, and the effect is expected to be particularly strong for those on means-tested benefits (Dilnot and Kell, 1989).

This effect is expected to occur, in part, because of the 'aggregation' present in the benefits system. Benefits are often based on the circumstances of the whole household rather than of individuals. If we take the system that existed up to 1996, an unemployed man would, under Unemployment Benefit, receive an allowance for a dependent wife (who need not be looking for work) that would be lost if her earnings exceeded a certain level. Under the means-tested Income Support, benefit would be withdrawn pound for pound as a woman's earnings increased past a nominal level. Benefit would be denied altogether if she worked for 16 or more hours a week (irrespective of the earnings level).

There are, however, alternative reasons why women married to (or cohabiting with) unemployed men might have lower than average rates of economic activity (Cooke, 1987). The first is that each person in the couple is likely to face the same local labour market conditions. This means that we might be observing the effect of different locations – an above-average rate of male unemployment is associated with depressed local conditions, which is in turn generally associated with a high rate of female unemployment (or perhaps inactivity). A second factor is that people tend to have partners with characteristics similar to their own (including similar qualifications and socio-economic background). This may mean that men with a higher risk of unemployment tend to live with women who also have a high risk of being without paid work. This similarity of couples would also affect the links between couples in their rates of being in paid work. A third factor might be the effects of different values and norms of working. Traditionally, men have worked and women's employment has been somewhat secondary. This could mean that women leave paid work in order not to undermine traditional roles, or to provide moral support to an unemployed partner.

An important means of distinguishing between some of these different theories is to look at the same people over time. If it is true that the benefits system is affecting women's work status, we would expect changes in women's work when their partners became unemployed or moved on to means-tested benefits at 1 year's unemployment (or, after April 1996, at 6 months). The fact that both face a similar labour market would have much less effect, or at least a less immediate effect, on *transitions* into and out of work. However, even if such transitions were to take place, they would not necessarily prove that the benefits system had the greatest effect.

Research has suggested that the rate of women leaving paid work as their husbands become unemployed is rather low. Instead, a great deal of the correlation between the employment of partners is the result of their sharing similar characteristics and cannot be directly attributed to the effect of one of them becoming unemployed.

If we look at a particular group of people becoming unemployed in 1995, 53 per cent of their partners were in paid work. If they were just like people in work, we would expect around 64 per cent of their partners to have been in paid employment (McKay *et al.*, 1997). However, if we take a look at the stock of all those unemployed in 1995, at the start of their unemployment just 30 per cent of their partners were in paid work. In other words, at the start of unemployment for this group, there are already wide differences between the employment rates of the partners of unemployed people and those of employed people. This suggests that a great deal of the 'employment shortfall' is caused by differences in the characteristics of couples rather than the effects of continuing as unemployed.

Research using 1987 data on six localities estimated that, of a total employment difference of 27 per cent for the wives of unemployed men, just 10 per cent was attributable to their husband's unemployment (Davies *et al.*, 1994). A similar size of effect was found for data collected in 1993–96 (Elias, 1997).

We should be clear what is meant by these results. Most of the difference in the rates of partners working, based on their husband's (or partner's) status, appears to be related to shared characteristics of the couples. The remaining proportion – about 10 per cent – seems to be directly related to the partner becoming and remaining unemployed. However, this does not mean that it is caused by the benefits system: it could reflect non-financial factors that couples take into account when deciding on work strategies. However, this figure of 10 per cent is significant and may be regarded as the maximum effect that the system of unemployment benefits is having on the labour supply of women married to unemployed men.

Lone parents

Lone parents in Britain are characterised by very low levels of employment and high levels of reliance on Income Support. At present, there are no rules that require lone parents to be available for work, or looking for work, as long as at least one child is aged 16 or less, or 18 or less and still in full-time education.

The rules of Income Support, as described above, apply in a similar way to lone parents. They may earn £15 a week and retain all of this income. Any earnings above this level mean a pound-for-pound deduction in Income Support. In other words, while on Income Support, earnings of £75 per week lead to the same final income as earnings of £15 per week – and that assumes that there are no additional costs of working for the higher amount through travelling or childcare.

Disincentives to work are potentially great in that lone parents receive much higher benefits than single people and tend to have fewer labour market skills. A potential means of alleviating problems is through Family Credit, a benefit designed to increase the income of families with children in lower-paid work of at least 16 hours a week. This benefit is supposed to work as outlined in Figure 8.1. When moving into paid work of at least 16 hours a week, the combined income from earnings and Family Credit should exceed that of Income Support (and some earnings) even after changes in entitlement to Housing Benefit and Council Tax Benefit have been taken into account. While accurate, the shape of this graph takes a number of things for granted. In particular, it ignores the potential role of 'in-work costs'. Being in work may lead people to have higher costs than when not working. For example, they may need a certain type or standard of clothing, may perhaps need to purchase tools and may have to pay the

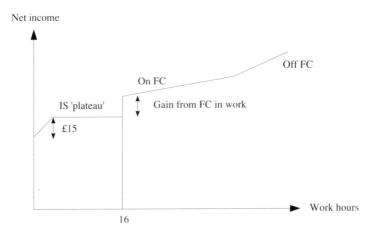

Figure 8.1   The effects of earnings on net income: schematic picture.
IS = Income Support; FC = Family Credit

costs of travelling to and from work. Arranging childcare of a desired flexibility and quality may also present particular problems, and the proportion of lone parents in paid work rises strongly when children go to school and are able mostly to look after themselves.

Lone parents have traditionally faced the particular difficulty of paying for childcare. Given that the gain from moving on to Family Credit might be, for example, £30–£50 per week, childcare costs might eliminate this benefit. At least, that was the case until childcare costs began to be taken into account when calculating a person's income. Now, the costs of registered childminders and local authority childcare provision may be deducted, up to a maximum of £100 per week, for children aged up to 11 years old.

Viewed internationally, the total lack in Britain of an obligation for lone parents to be available for work is highly unusual. In most countries, lone parents would face similar tests to those claiming as unemployed, at least once the youngest child had reached a particular age (often linked to schooling or childcare provision). There are some signs that this liberalism is being reconsidered. The New Deal for Lone Parents, which invites lone parents to visit Employment Service job centres to receive advice on work, continues to move the emphasis towards encouraging lone parents to seek and take paid work. So far, the approach remains entirely voluntary: there is no compulsion to attend and no penalties for not accepting the advice (or the offer of advice).

This is the current situation. A historical perspective provides an interesting counterpoint in the USA. Whereas now lone mothers in the USA face particular pressure to work, when benefits for lone parents were introduced in the 1930s, it was partly to ensure that they stayed at home. Forcing mothers to work was perceived, at the time, as just as much of a problem as was the absence of a father (Garfinkel and McLanahan, 1986: 34)

As with the wives of unemployed men, there are a number of different factors, and not just the social security system, that need to be taken into account when looking at the employment rates of lone parents. A recent analysis of the Family and Working Lives Survey (McKay and Heaver, 1997) found that the low rates of working among lone mothers were matched by low rates of working *prior* to becoming a lone mother and relatively low rates of paid work once people had ceased to be lone mothers (when they formed a couple or their children stopped being dependent). This is strong evidence that there is much more than the social security system driving the low employment rates of lone mothers.

And what of Family Credit, which is designed to promote work incentives among lone parents? This does seem to be having an important effect. The number of lone parents on this benefit is around 300,000, having risen from around half that number in 1988. This tends to demonstrate that financial incentives and the structure of various benefits can be important: policy changes have moved a significant number of lone parents from Income Support to Family Credit. How far this reflects the longer-term interests of recipients is less clear (Bryson and Marsh, 1996; Bryson, 1998).

Disincentives to marry? Incentives to have larger families?

Most research into the effects of the social security system have looked at incentives to work, but it has also long been thought that benefit structures might affect people's choices of living arrangements. For example, Deacon and Bradshaw (1983) argue that the household-based means test of the 1930s caused some families to split up rather than have to support dependent relatives. However, a recent review of available research argued that 'an area that remains particularly obscure is that of the effects of welfare benefits on families' (Gauthier, 1996: 297). Two particular questions are whether welfare benefits encourage the formation of lone-parent households and how far benefits affect the timing and number of births to women. Once again, these are not purely technical questions. On them ride strong views about the appropriate role of state welfare and the extent to which the traditional family is being 'undermined' by the (unintended) effects of income maintenance policies.

Work on the 'underclass' and the formation of lone-parent households has generally been stronger in the USA than in Britain. It is, therefore, crucial to appreciate that, in the USA, 'welfare' has generally treated lone parents quite differently from two-parent families. The main American programme is now Temporary Assistance for Needy Families (which replaced Aid to Families with Dependent Children following legislation in 1996; see Waldfogel, 1997). The Aid to Families with Dependent Children rules had long required that a household has low income and assets, and a child under 18 years old, and be 'deprived of support due to death, incapacity or absence of a parent' (Hoynes, 1996: 3). Although the system has been extended to two-parent families (mandatory for states since 1988), couples with children (where a parent is unemployed) still face greater hurdles in gaining eligibility. The argument that social security benefits affect family structures is, in the US context, very clear. From the point of view of women in particular, there may be financial incentives to have children without a regular partner or to separate from an existing partner. Since Temporary Assistance for Needy Families generally pays more for larger families, there might also be incentives to have more children – although states are now permitted to introduce a 'family cap', which means that benefits do not increase for those having children while receiving Temporary Assistance for Needy Families. A more formal theoretical justification may be found in the work of Becker (1981).

An obvious response would be that the USA has very high rates of lone parenthood – the highest in the developed world – while at the same time paying them among the lowest benefits (Whiteford and Bradshaw, 1994). However, it could then be argued that it is the difference in support between one- and two-parent households that is the operative factor. In principle, the ideal way to consider the effects of welfare benefits on any outcome (fertility or family formation) would be to pay different benefits to people who were otherwise identical and then observe any differences that resulted. All other factors would have to remain equal in such an experiment. For good ethical and practical reasons, this method has not been open to researchers. Instead, research has employed several different methods of considering the links between levels of benefit and the incidence of lone parenthood. Each attempts to restore the kind of 'experimental control' that would be used if conditions were ideal.

First, it is possible to look at differences between various countries in their rates of benefit and the resulting differences in outcome. Second, one could look in the same country over time to consider how far changes in benefits and family changes were linked. Third, one could consider differences between individuals, linking benefit entitlement to subsequent decisions about families. Fourth, there have been experiments that have changed the prevailing benefit rules in certain localities.

Each method is open to criticism of various kinds and, to carry conviction, would need to deal with various competing explanations and potential effects (Gauthier, 1996, contains a detailed scrutiny of this). It should be noted that welfare benefits comprise just one aspect of state intervention that could affect the costs of different family structures. As was explored in Chapter 1, there are other concessions, including those provided by the direct and indirect taxation systems. In the USA, direct benefits may be low, but tax concessions for those with dependent children are available. The costs of raising children will also be reduced if various services – such as day-care nurseries or health care – are provided at a reduced cost. Including these state benefits in the calculation of total support may give a picture very different from that based solely on direct cash benefits. Further realism may be introduced by considering that not all of those covered by a benefit necessarily receive it. As discussed in Chapter 7, many social security benefits are not claimed by all those eligible. Rates of take-up lower than 50 per cent have been known, particularly for means-tested benefits.

The costs of motherhood are also affected by the involvement of employers, who may provide maternity pay – and indeed may be forced to do so by government legislation, Of course, such benefits will only go to those covered by the appropriate rules and regulations. Thus, it cannot be assumed that all women face exactly the same mix of financial costs and benefits from having children.

In many studies, the 'direction of causation' should also be considered, that is, whether it is higher benefits affecting changes in families, or changes in families, that are altering policy. It is not implausible to argue that the high rate of benefit for lone mothers in some Nordic countries reflects their pressure and needs, rather than there being more lone mothers as a result of welfare policy.

In addition to these general points, there are technical questions about each type of method. Moreover, the results from various studies using different types of approach (mostly for the USA and Britain) have tended to be mixed and rather inconclusive. An American review was more specific than most when it said that 'increases in benefits account for about 9 to 14 percent of the increased prevalence of families headed by women' (Garfinkel and McLanahan, 1986: 167).

Disincentives to save?

Another area of individual behaviour that might be affected by the social security system is personal saving. Feldstein (1974) argued that social security significantly depressed private savings because there was little need to make precautionary saving if the system provided income in time of sickness or old age. However, people pay National Insurance and income tax towards social security, so they are, in this way, saving, and even if social security depressed precautionary savings, this might mean that money was diverted to savings for other purposes – perhaps house purchase. Various economists have investigated this issue, developing mathematical models based on economic principles of the 'permanent income rational expectations hypothesis', but little empirical research has been carried out to test these theories.

There is considerable disagreement about the effect of social security on saving. Cagan (1965) and Katona (1975) found that occupational pension scheme members saved slightly more than non-members, but Munnell (1976) found contrary results. There is certainly evidence, however, that the social security has a retirement effect, inducing earlier retirement than would be the case without the system. In turn, this 'retirement effect' might actually have led to greater incentives to save, since if people are likely to be retired for longer periods, they may save more money for use during that time. The effects of a social security system on saving may, therefore, be complex.

Another way in which the social security system may affect saving behaviour is in the particular rules of the system. For example, the capital rules on most means-tested benefits act, in theory at least, to discourage saving since those with more than a certain amount of capital (not including housing wealth) are either ineligible or eligible for only a reduced amount of benefit. Similarly, there is also a disincentive to invest in an occupational pension since this is then offset against pensioners' Income Support and Housing Benefit, leaving some people no better off than if they had not taken out an occupational pension at all. This has been referred to as the occupational pension trap (Walker *et al.*, 1988).

There have been various empirical studies that have investigated the role of means-tested benefits in creating a disincentive to *work*, but the disincentive to *save* has received less attention. The extent of the disincentive to save will depend partly on knowledge of the rules on capital limits: clearly, those who do not know about these rules will not be discouraged from saving because of them. Also, there will only be a disincentive for those who have the ability to save; many people do not have enough income to be able to save, regardless of whether or not there is a theoretical disincentive.

In recent years, the state has increasingly withdrawn from areas of welfare provision, including earnings-related pensions and mortgage interest payments for unemployed people. Many people do not have enough income to build up assets, but, for those who do, assets may have become increasingly important as one form of private 'insurance' against the future uncertainty of income.

In a study on the links between income, wealth and the lifecycle (Rowlingson *et al.*, 1998), 40 in-depth interviewees were asked about their knowledge of how the social security system treated assets. Most people had an idea, or at least guessed, that some social security benefits were unavailable to people with a certain level of savings. Most of those who had some ability to save money, however, had never claimed means-tested benefits so had not personally come across the savings rule. Those who had received means-tested benefits in the past thought that they might need to do so at some point in the future because of the insecurities of their employment. However, they had such difficulties in saving as a result of their low income that their awareness of the capital rules was not a factor in their savings behaviour.

There may also be disincentives to save and accumulate housing wealth because elderly people with property and other forms of wealth may have to use up these assets to pay for local authority care. This issue was addressed in the 1995 budget with a change to the rules on capital for care. This means that those with less than £10,000 (previously £3,000) in assets (including housing wealth) do not have to pay anything towards their care, and only those with more than £16,000 (previously £8,000) have to pay the full amount. Rowlingson *et al.* (1998) found strong popular criticism of these rules but little evidence of any real effect on behaviour. This was mainly because the prospect of needing care seemed so far off to those of working age that it did not affect their economic behaviour.

9

Social Security Reform

Introduction

In this chapter, we look at the main challenges currently faced by the social security system in Britain today, radical ways of addressing some of those problems, and the developing policy agenda of the New Labour government elected in 1997.

The system has, of course, been subject to more or less constant reform over the past few decades, reflecting both short-term and long-term appraisals of the need for change at each point in time. Thus, we should not believe that reform is something entirely new. The 1980s and 90s have witnessed significant changes in social security, at times adopting both 'big bang' styles of reform (such as the Fowler Review of the mid-1980s) and more 'gradualist' styles (such as the changes introduced by Tony Newton and Peter Lilley in the early and mid-1990s).

While further reform seems inevitable, the size of particular long-term problems is often exaggerated, as we now discuss.

Problems facing the social security system

There now appears to be widespread agreement that a major reform of social security in Britain is inevitable. The cost is seen as extremely high, high enough to prevent spending that is desirable in other areas of the welfare state, particularly education and health. More and more people are receiving benefits, yet many people still fail to claim what they might (for example, the one million retirement pensioners not claiming top-ups from Income Support), and many argue that levels of benefits are not adequate for those who rely on them. Those receiving benefit may be trapped rather than helped by high rates of benefit withdrawal that make paid work less attractive (Chapter 8) or by the very complexity of the system.

The direction that reform should take is not clear, but we outline some current thinking, the context in which ideas about change have arisen and the principles on which reform should be based.

Changes in the structure of families and working life

A common starting point for looking at reform is to emphasise the significant changes in family and working arrangements that have taken place in the second half of the twentieth century against a social security system that was designed for the conditions expected to prevail at the middle of that century. This perspective takes the following form.

As we saw in Chapter 3, the social security system we know in Britain was developed out of the social insurance vision of Beveridge, whose findings were published in 1942. This system was designed at a time when there were particular certainties that could be relied upon. Men would work full time for all or almost all of their working age years, and few would have many years of retirement. Women would tend to work only until they were married, or had children, and would then be expected to rely on men for income security. Families would stay together in most circumstances, married couples typically for life. The payment of benefits would generally be linked to risks such as retirement, unemployment and death or disablement of the main bread-winner, events that were, then, closely associated with becoming poor. Workers would typically earn enough to support themselves (himself, generally speaking) and a small family, so benefits for those in work would not be needed, although there would need to be some benefits for larger families whether or not they worked. Against such a background, the system of social insurance was able to function at relatively low cost compared with today's social security system.

The key problem, according to this line of reasoning, is that this vision of society and the economy is no longer true. Changes in family structure have seen the rise of the single-person household, more non-marital cohabitation between couples, greater family disruption and (the most costly in social security terms) the increasing importance of the lone-parent family (McRae, 1999).

These changes in family circumstances have been accompanied by economic changes. Women are more likely to work, a particularly marked increase being seen in the number returning to work after the birth of children. Unemployment has risen for men, and work is much less secure and more 'flexible'. There can be no reliance on lifelong employment, and wages at the lower end of the labour market are often insufficient to support a family. More people seem to have impairments affecting their ability to work. Additionally, the link between insured contingencies and poverty is much less clear; in particular, many older people and some widows have enough income from private sources to be able to live comfortably without the basic state Retirement Pension or benefit for widows. The conclusion is then drawn that the social insurance vision of temporary interruption to earning power is no longer consistent with today's world. Instead, social security needs to respond to a changing world.

This mismatch between the context of the Beveridge report and the context faced by social security today forms an important, implicit element of many people's thinking about social security. There are, of course, several details where the argument is oversimplified. The Beveridge vision was written in wartime, during a war that came soon after a period of mass male unemployment, which meant that full employment need not have been a feature of post-war society. It may be fairer to Beveridge to say that the full employment of men and the expected inactivity of wives and mothers are a mix of requirements for the Beveridge system to work and assumptions about the likely development of Britain after the Second World War.

As we saw in Chapter 8, changes towards a more 'flexible' labour market may also be exaggerated. Temporary work is still relatively uncommon, although the loose nature of employment law means that people on apparently 'permanent' contracts can be hired and fired relatively easily. Some of the demographic developments, such as the increase in the number of lone-parent families, seem particularly significant, although there has previously often been a large number of widowed mothers during periods of war.

Social security: unsustainable growth?

It is worth analysing the contention that the system is likely to outstrip the ability of the nation to pay for social security. This seems to have been a main preoccupation of both the Conservative and the Labour governments of recent times. While this has not been the *only* argument used to justify reform, it has clearly been one of the most powerful incentives to make changes.

There are at least three distinct arguments for saying that the current rate of growth *can* be met without severe economic problems.

First, it has been shown (in Chapter 2) that the proportion of national income spent on social security benefits is lower in Britain than in many comparable OECD countries. Other countries seem to manage to devote a greater share of their income to transfer payments on social security without incurring particularly noticeable economic penalties. It is also true, however, that many of those countries are concerned about high levels of spending, although it seems unlikely that they will attempt to reduce spending to levels similar to those seen in the UK.

Second, the extent of growth (at least in the short term) is easily exaggerated. Projections that are based on amounts of money are likely to sound particularly worrying. However, the best basis for examining the potential of the economy to meet the apparently growing cost perhaps is to express the resources needed as a percentage of national income. A DSS publication from Peter Lilley, which set the scene for subsequent reform and aimed to encourage public debate, argued that 'it is not possible for the system to continue indefinitely to grow more rapidly than the economy as a whole' (Department of Social Security, 1993b: 3). It is worth commenting that this review did not say that social security *was* going to be unaffordable in the near future. However, a case was made for current action to reduce the long-term real growth of social security spending. Indeed, the actions taken by Peter Lilley did reduce the real growth of social security spending, from 3.3 per cent per annum to around 1.5 per annum – somewhat less than the long-term growth rate of the economy. In 1992–93, benefit spending accounted for 12.3 per cent of the GDP. Depending on assumptions about the growth of unemployment and government spending, by 1999–2000 the level of benefit spending was projected as likely to be between 11.3 and 13.5 per cent. The next section looks at longer-term trends.

Third, commentators have used historical comparisons to put any projected growth into perspective. It has been argued that spending on the overall welfare state (including health, housing, social services and education) has been relatively stable as a proportion of national income over the medium term (Hills, 1993). There has been marked growth since the founding of the welfare state, but apparently with little effect on the economy's ability to absorb such growth.

These three arguments are important in tempering any fears that current rates of growth will lead to an economic crisis, but they do not mean that rising social security spending can simply be ignored or will have no consequences. However, much of the debate about social security spending is political in nature and relates to attempts to keep the rate of income tax as low as possible. Once again, British rates of income tax are already low compared with those in many other European countries (Hirsch, 1997), but it has become generally accepted that the electorate places a high priority on low taxation when deciding which party to vote for. Moreover, if there is any extra government money available for spending, the electorate would seem to prefer it to go on education or health rather than social security (Lipsey, 1994).

A demographic time bomb?

Another potential problem often raised, one linked to fears about the rapid growth of spending, is that of the ageing of the population. Over time, there are likely to be dramatic changes in the structure of Britain's population – and that of other countries at a similar level of development. In particular, there will be a higher proportion of older people and fewer people of working age (as well as perhaps fewer children).

This may lead to difficult decisions about the level of pension income and perhaps other types of spending, such as that for long-term care, that may be supported. Even if the prospect of a sudden crisis (the 'bomb' metaphor in 'timebomb') is unlikely (Hills, 1995a), demographic changes still seem likely to have distributional consequences. For a given level of resources, this could mean either a reduced share going to each older person, perhaps achieved by tighter entitlement conditions such as a higher pension age, or the young keeping less of their income in order to finance pensions.

A great deal of the ageing of the population has already taken place. Those countries which were among the first to industrialise saw their birth rates decline and life expectancies increase. Generally, these processes took place over many years. By 1960, the UK had one of the lowest proportions of young to old people of any country – around five people of working age for every person aged 65 and older. This ratio will 'worsen' to about three to one by 2030 (Figure 9.1). However, in most of the large industrial countries, the degree of ageing anticipated is greater than, or at least as great as, that in Britain.

The dependency ratio described here is very crude. A more appropriate measure would be to look at the number of older people compared with the number actually in work, and their level of earnings. While this may be done for the past and for the current year, it is difficult to project employment and earnings patterns far into the future. However, is it precisely these factors that determine how large a welfare state will then be affordable. A rise in the proportion of women in work, or a change in the declining proportion of the over-50s in

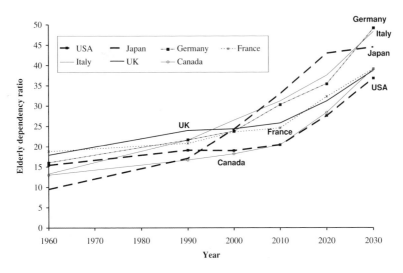

Figure 9.1   Elderly dependency ratios in the G7 population aged 65 and older as a percentage of the working-age population: (*Ageing in OECD countries,* Copyright OECD, 1996: Table A3)

employment, could, at least to some extent, offset the apparent fall in simple dependency ratios.

One element often mentioned in concerns about an ageing population is the nature of the state pension system, which in most countries is based on the 'pay-as-you-go' principle. The state pensions of today's older generation are financed by the contributions to National Insurance made by today's working population. The image of 'insurance' is just that – imaginary. People may think that they (or the state, on their behalf) are putting away money each month when working to pay for their retirement pension. This is not happening.

This is in contrast to personal and occupational pension schemes. In popular parlance, these private schemes invest money in companies both here and abroad in order to pay out returns to people when they retire. A 'fund' is accumulated; hence, this type of scheme is often said to be 'funded' rather than 'pay-as-you-go'.

However, this is a rather misleading representation of the differences between state and non-state schemes. No matter what the system, the resource demands of today's older and retired generation must be met from the ability of today's workers to produce. There is no easy means of taking resources out of the system only to re-inject them in later years when people retire, although investment abroad is perhaps the nearest equivalent. Under a pay-as-you-go system, pensions are met by taxing the incomes of workers. Under a funded system, pensions are paid from the profit margins of companies (through their large shareholdings of publicly quoted companies), which might otherwise have benefited other groups. A pay-as-you-go system emphasises taxes on labour, while funded systems are based on taking part of the returns to capital. Funded schemes are often regarded as superior to pay-as-you-go systems because they are not linked to the dependency ratio and, in the past, the profits from investment have been good. However, there are no guarantees that funded schemes will be quite as successful in the future.

Britain is in a rather different situation from many other countries, with the result that the state pension demands created by population ageing are less significant than in many other countries. This is because the pension system in the UK is predominantly flat rate rather than based on people's previous earnings, and the level of the basic state pension is set to grow in line with prices rather than with growth in the economy as a whole.

As a result, the pension obligations of the British state pension system are a rather more modest share of national income than is seen in other industrialised nations. Projections of the cost of the state pension system up to the year 2070 are shown in Figure 9.2. There is a general 'peak' in the expected share of resources going to pensions in the years 2030–40, with a sharp rise from now until then. After 2040, the size of obligations is more stable or even falling.

Two features of the UK are clear. First, it is towards the bottom of the list (of the 'G7' group of industrialised countries) in terms of the size of current state pension obligations. Second, over time, the share of pension spending from the GDP is stable and even ultimately on a decline. This reflects, of course, the less generous than average nature of state pension provision in the UK.

Possible radical reforms

We have so far looked at some of the main problems with the current system. These may be exaggerated, but there remains a perceived need for reforming the system. Reformers may aim at either large-scale or more gradualist change. In this section, we consider some of the more thorough-going reforms that have been suggested, which attempt to cut

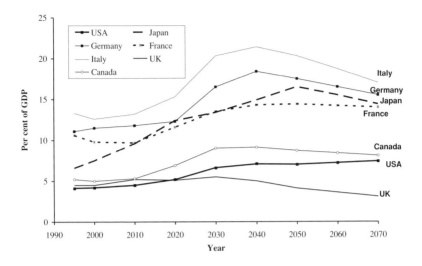

Figure 9.2   Pension expenditure as a percentage of Gross Domestic Product (*Ageing in OECD ccountries*, Copyright OECD, 1996: Table 2.3)

through the complexities of the current system. Indeed, it is often their simplicity that makes such proposals appealing, and each has been supported by informed commentators over recent years. In comparison, more incremental styles of reform may appear ill principled. Major structural reform could follow one of three main routes:

- First, there could be a return to, and enhancement of, the principles of social insurance.
- Second, there could be further growth in the extent and importance of means-testing, perhaps involving some integration of benefits with the system of direct taxation.
- Finally, one could propose a radical move towards contingent benefits, as is proposed by supporters of a Basic Income scheme.

A return to social insurance

The rallying call 'back to Beveridge' has been in use for at least the past 30 years (Atkinson, 1970: 105). This strategy involves extending the insurance principle. Supporters tend to argue that some of the key elements of the Beveridge plan were not implemented, especially that contributory benefits were never set at levels high enough to prevent widespread dependence on means-tested National Assistance. However, they also recognise that insurance of the Beveridge model has various flaws.

An approach based on insurance principles needs to incorporate all the new types of risk into the areas traditionally covered by social insurance, to include part-time work and family breakdown. It also needs to find ways to cover those who are not in a position to make contributions (Webb, 1994), such as those providing full-time care, the lowest paid and those unable to work. This usually means a combination of lowering the threshold at which contributions are paid and crediting-in those who are not in work. This currently happens with Home Responsibilities Protection for the Retirement Pension, for which caring for children or disabled adults may count. In the context of the basic pension, such an approach has been criticised as creating needless complexity purely in the name of insurance: 'what is the point in having a complex set of contributory requirements... when there are so many special provisions that virtually everyone becomes eligible no matter what their employment and contribution history' (Johnson *et al.*, 1996: 86).

An approach based on modernising social insurance was advocated in various writings by Frank Field before he became Minister for Welfare Reform (Field, 1995, 1996). A detailed argument in favour of social insurance was also provided by the Dahrendorf Committee (1994), of which Frank Field was a member. A stance supporting social insurance was also taken by the Commission on Social Justice. This group was set up by the Labour Party and included the experienced social security analysts Steve Webb (now a Liberal Democrat MP), A. B. Atkinson, Ruth Lister and Eithne McLaughlin, among others. This latter group proposed that 'a modern social security system should be built upon the foundation of social insurance'. They also argued that 'Means-testing... encourages dependence on benefits, rather than independence' (Commission on Social Justice, 1994: 247).

More means-testing and tax-benefit integration

For those who believe that social security exists (or should exist) to alleviate poverty, the policy prescriptions are very clear: simply design a system that identifies those who are poor (or those with income below a certain level) and then pay this group enough money to bring them up to this level. Those with incomes above this level would pay tax on their incomes to fund benefit payments. In practice, such a threshold income would be set by reference to the different sizes of household. In extreme versions of this system, there would be no need for any other types of benefit.

Such a system is attractive if the sole purpose of social security is to relieve poverty. If so, the only information that is of relevance relates to current income level. However, in most social security systems, there are a multiplicity of different aims. We would, perhaps, be keen to ensure that disabled people were treated more generously than the non-disabled, perhaps that retired people should receive more than those of working age, and that amounts should be varied to reflect other priorities. In other words, some information about people's circumstances, which change over time, would also be required.

Critics of enhanced means-testing are often concerned about maintaining incentives to make self-provision under such a system. Among those receiving benefits, extra income would probably mean losing benefits very rapidly. Taking money away more gradually would mean paying them benefits even when they moved above the poverty threshold, weakening the apparent degree of targeting in such systems.

A view that only income-related benefits are required is often accompanied by the idea of integrating the system of benefits with the direct tax system (for example, as is used for income tax). This is sometimes called a 'negative income tax', since it would involve making payments as well as collecting taxes. According to three economists writing in the mid-1980s:

> an explicit abandonment of the national insurance concept and the pursuit of a single, properly integrated tax and benefit system provide the only promising direction of reform. (Dilnot *et al.*, 1984: 2)

This integration is seen as beneficial for at least two reasons. First, it prevents a situation in which some people both receive means-tested benefits and also pay income tax. The group most affected at present are those 700,000 families receiving Family Credit as low-earning workers. Second, it is an attempt to avoid the criticism that means-tested benefits are inevitably very costly to administer and subject to high levels of non-take-up.

In the British context, such integration faces a number of problems because differences between cash benefits and tax credits run very deep. Income-related benefits are usually associated with family or household units, whereas income taxation is based on the incomes of individuals. One of these two principles (that welfare depends on a couple's joint resources, particularly among those on low income, and that people should be taxed as individuals) would almost certainly have to be compromised if this type of model were to be adopted.

Tax liability (and rebates) depends ultimately on income over a given financial year. In contrast, entitlement to benefits is generally based on an assessment of weekly income over a short time period. One concern is that low-earning families require support immediately and cannot afford to wait for standard tax calculations based on the financial year, but the tax system would have difficulties with more rapid assessments.

Ideas about using the tax system to provide social security remain popular, as discussed below, although usually in the context of more limited reform.

Basic income schemes (or Citizen's Income)

Under basic income schemes (increasingly known as Citizen's Income but sometimes known as 'social dividend schemes'), everyone of sufficient age receives a set level of benefit. The idea 'is to provide everyone with a guaranteed income that remains constant regardless of economic circumstances. In this sense it would be a means of preventing poverty, as opposed to alleviating it' (Stevens-Strohmann, 1997). This income would be paid for by taxes rather than contributions.

Such a scheme is administratively very simple. It is also set at the level of individuals rather than being based on some notion of a 'family' or 'household'. Critics point out that the cost of a full basic income would require extremely high rates of taxation, which would be unacceptable – at 'acceptable' rates of tax, the value of the basic income benefit would be insufficient to meet people's needs. Supporters suggest that there are a range of different options, some short of a 'full' basic income, that would deliver significant advantages while still being workable and publicly acceptable (Parker, 1990).

A further problem for supporters of basic income schemes, and one that also afflicted Beveridge, is how to deal with widely varying housing costs. It is hard to see how housing costs could be met, other than on a household basis, and presumably subject to a means test of some kind.

It could be argued that, the negative income tax represents an extreme form of means-testing, and basic income schemes represent the full extension of universal benefits. However, some economists have argued that the outcomes for household income are similar between the two schemes – each provides a minimum level of income for those with none, and taxes or takes some away as people earn past a certain point. Economic analysis also suggests that incentives to work are not affected by issues such as whether we call a system one of benefits or instead one of tax credits or Citizen's Income (for an elementary treatment, see Brown and Jackson, 1990).

An assessment of radical alternatives

Recent reports from, for example, the Commission on Social Justice (1994) and the Joseph Rowntree Foundation Inquiry into Income and Wealth (Barclay, 1995; Hills, 1995b), have proposed less sweeping reforms than the extreme versions discussed above. This may show some recognition of the range of different objectives within the social security system, which seem to require greater complexity than some of the more 'elegant' reforms listed above.

Major reforms are also difficult to handle politically and practically. They are certain to create both gainers and losers, and it is often assumed that the trouble created by the losers tends to outweigh the gratitude of the gainers. In the face of such problems, an approach based on incremental reform becomes more attractive (Lilley, 1993).

New Labour and social security: a developing agenda

At the time of writing (mid-1998), much of the social security system is the subject of various reviews, and a number of commissions are in the process of receiving evidence or writing reports. A flurry of Green Papers has discussed welfare reform (Department of Social Security, 1998c), child support (Department of Social Security, 1998a) and fraud (Department of Social Security, 1998a), with another on pensions expected after Autumn 1998. Proposals on sharing non-state pensions between divorcing couples are the subject of consultation. Reform is clearly a high priority, and the Prime Minister is chair of the committee seeking to achieve this.

It is possible to discern a number of themes that have influenced current measures and seem likely to inform future changes. In the *Case for Welfare Reform*, (Department of Social Security, 1998f) it is argued that:

> Beveridge's principles will remain central:
> 1. Society has a responsibility to help people in genuine need, who are unable to look after themselves;
> 2. Individuals have a responsibility to help provide for themselves when they can do so;
> 3. Work is the best route out of poverty for people who are able to work.
>
> In addition fraud and abuse should be minimised and rooted out wherever found.

Later the same year, in *The Government's Annual Report 1997–98* (p. 50) the strategy is identified as:

- Work as the best route out of poverty for those who can.
- Once in work to make sure work pays.
- For those who cannot work... we offer security.
- Greatest help should go to those in greatest need – with an attack on fraud.
- Services such as health and education are as important as cash benefits.
- Innovation in tackling these problems.

The clear emphasis is on meeting need and the avoidance of poverty. Wherever possible, people should take steps to provide for themselves, in particular by engaging in paid work, which is the centrepiece of the strategy. This clearly falls short of a wider role of maintaining people's living standards in times of relative adversity.

We will now consider some of the specific programmes and ideas that the New Labour government has been formulating.

The New Deals: gateways, personal advice and compulsion

In recent years, the phrase 'Welfare-to-Work' has been increasingly advocated and implemented in various programmes, particularly in Australia and some American states. The largest new element in the New Labour reforms undertaken to date is the New Deal for the young unemployed, although there are several other programmes that go under the 'New Deal' label and which include related policies. These are new programmes dealing not just with those aged 18–24, but also lone parents, disabled people, excluded communities, the long-term unemployed and partners of the unemployed. The first of these is the furthest developed, having been implemented nationally from April 1998 and reflecting pre-election planning by the Labour Party.

The New Deal for the young unemployed is the enactment of a Labour Party pre-election commitment to move off benefit 250,000 people aged from 18–24 who had been unemployed for 6 months or longer. The total cost, of £3.5 billion, was raised from a once-off wind-fall tax on the privatised utilities. The programme consists of a number of elements.

At 6 months' unemployment, there is a 'gateway' to New Deal. This consists of in-depth advice and assistance with job-searching provided to young people. After they have been through this process, there is then the choice of four options:

- Paid work, possibly subsidised by the state at £60 per week
- Work in the voluntary sector
- Work with the environmental task force
- Full-time education or training for the less qualified.

A crucial element is that there will be 'no fifth option of an inactive life on benefit' (Finn, 1998: 32). The programme is compulsory for young people unemployed for at least 6 months, with short benefit sanctions for those refusing (without 'good cause') to comply.

Many of the other New Deals involve some type of gateway process – an intensive period of advice about finding paid work or ways to facilitate the move back into employment. There is often an emphasis on personal advice. The degree of compulsion does vary, with the New Deal for lone parents being entirely voluntary and that for disabled people including many innovative small-scale projects. From April 2000 there may be pilot schemes where working age benefit claimants *must* attend an interview about work prospects. Perhaps another common element is a proactive approach, in which the benefit system is seen as an active means of promoting independence rather than a 'passive' machine for paying out cash benefits.

Making work pay: support for low-earners

Another key area of welfare reform is 'making work pay'. This mostly involves support to families in employment whose earnings are judged to be insufficient to give a good standard of living. This group includes a large number of lone parents in low-earning work (perhaps of part-time hours). The thorough-going approach of the Conservative governments since 1988 had been the idea of means-tested wage supplements, usually paid in the form of cash benefits to the mother and known as Family Credit. This has become a very significant benefit, being paid to over 700,000 families, of whom around half are lone parents.

In the USA, to take a very different type of system, support for low earnings is instead paid via a tax credit – the Earned Income Tax Credit. This is not a benefit as such but instead either amounts to a reduction in direct taxation or gives rise to a tax rebate at the end of the financial year. Such an approach seems appealing on simple efficiency grounds. In Britain, it is common for those receiving Family Credit to be paying income tax, so that the state appears to be both taking away money and returning it in another way (Walker and Wiseman, 1997).

In Britain, Taylor has investigated a number of ideas for promoting work incentives, including the possibility of a tax credit for low-earning workers (Taylor, 1998). This quickly abandoned the American approach of Earned Income Tax Credit in favour of retaining the structure of Family Credit but delivering it through the tax system, to become, from October 1999, Working Families Tax Credit. This is available for payment through the wage packet (from April 2000), which is seen as reducing the stigma of both working and being on a (means-tested) benefit; however, it may also be paid directly to the mother in line with the Family Credit approach. Administration is by the Inland Revenue rather than the Benefits Agency. The newer Credit has much more generous levels of payment and more assistance with certain childcare expenses (Strickland, 1998). Disabled people in work will have a similar tax credit scheme – Disabled Person's Tax Credit.

In this policy area, two New Labour ideas have been combined: first, a view that extra resources needed to be channelled to low earners; and second, a view that the tax system might provide a more acceptable delivery mechanism than the benefits system, largely through its association with paid work.

Making work pay: a minimum wage

One of Labour's firmest commitments was to a minimum wage of some kind. This was recommended to be set, from April 1999, at £3.60 per hour for workers over the age of 21 (Low Pay Commission, 1998). Its implementation is anticipated. Introducing a minimum wage should mean that people will be aware of the lowest level of wages that they might expect to attain on moving into work.

It may be thought that a minimum wage will remove the need for benefits like Family Credit and the Working Families Tax Credit, but in fact the numbers taken out of benefit *completely* are likely to be small. Analysis suggests that there is only limited overlap between low hourly wage rates and low family income. Low wages appear to be most common among young (often single) people and women who are second earners in households with other sources of income. Given that many recipients, especially lone parents, work relatively few hours, there is likely to be an effect on the size of awards but rather less impact on the total number receiving benefit/credits.

A statutory minimum wage has no effect (or only an indirect effect) on the income of the self-employed. This group forms a significant proportion of working families on low incomes and one in seven of those receiving Family Credit (Department of Social Security, 1997).

Pensions reform

This is a crucial area for reform because pensions are the largest element of social security spending and are an important point of concern for the future level of spending as the population continues to age. Changes to the pensions market were discussed by Labour in opposition, and one of their first acts in government was to establish a Pensions Review and to consult on changes to the pension system. The Pensions Provision Group was charged with reporting on methods of reforming pension provision; a Pensions Education and Awareness Working Group has sought to develop ways of improving 'financial literacy and economic awareness'. Both groups reported in 1998.

The two main instruments of reform for future pensioners seem to be the Stakeholder Pension (designed for workers not covered by a good occupational pension) and the Citizenship Pension (a second pension for those with significant caring responsibilities).

The vision behind the Stakeholder Pension seems to be that there are a large group of people who do not have adequate second pensions. Large numbers of people may not have the opportunity of joining occupational schemes – the coverage of occupational pensions has been around 50 per cent of employees since the late 1960s – leaving non-workers, the self-employed and the remaining half of employees who are not members. Personal pensions, as they currently operate, are often regarded as a poor deal for those on lower earnings.

That leaves some people who are not covered by a private second pension. It is expected that this will disproportionately include women, who are most affected by low earnings and long interruptions to employment, and those with rather mixed patterns of working over their lifetime. The aim of the Stakeholder Pension is to create a new instrument that suits this group. They are supposed to offer good value for money for those on relatively low incomes, and not penalise those who take breaks from work for example to raise a family or care for disabled adults.

Important though Stakeholder Pensions undoubtedly are in Labour thinking, they face an uphill battle in reforming the pensions system. If it were possible to make profitable business from low-paid earners who changed job frequently, and who spent large amounts of time not able to make contributions to pensions, such a product would probably already have been offered by existing private sector providers. Instead, it must overcome some of the key problems faced by groups with more limited pension provision. Left alone, many people will make too little non-state pension provision and will start too late.

A new pension product also raises the question of transfer values for those who move between jobs with different benefits. It is difficult to see how all advice, which is often costly, could be eliminated from what is often a particularly troublesome area.

Another key issue raised is that of compulsion. There is no simple choice between compulsion and freedom, but in what is made compulsory. Compulsion is already present, first, in the basic state pension for those with earnings above the lower earnings limit. Second, there is compulsion – the self-employed and non-workers aside – in second-tier pensions: workers must be either in SERPS, an occupational pension or a personal pension.

Stakeholder Pensions may, therefore, represent the introduction of an additional element into an already complex market for pensions. They are aimed at filling a clear gap, but one which appears particularly difficult to fill adequately.

Current pensioners benefit from a new guaranteed minimum income level through increased means-tested benefits.

'Affluence testing'

Suggestions for reforming the social security system have recently put forward the idea of 'affluence testing'. This new phrase appears to denote means-testing in which the test of resources is pitched at the higher rather than the lower end of the range. While means-testing Child Benefit might be taken to imply paying it solely to people on Income Support or an equivalent income, affluence-testing would seem to mean removing it from higher earners – perhaps those paying the highest rate of income tax. This might be seen as attractive because it would save money on benefits but affect only those with such a high level of income or savings that they could scarcely claim to be badly affected by the change.

This approach has been mentioned in connection with Maternity Benefits but most firmly in connection with Child Benefit. This was raised, significantly, in the 1998 budget but with the comment that any future rises could fairly introduce taxation of Child Benefit for higher rate tax-payers (Greener and Cracknell, 1998).

The central dilemma of 'affluence-testing' is that if the level of affluence were set too high, the amount of money saved might be relatively small and yet require a good deal of administrative effort. If the level were set too low, many 'middle income' people might well be affected, who might argue that they either needed the money or might have arranged their finances such that they expected such benefits to be available.

Removing benefits from middle-income groups runs the risk of undermining support for welfare (Goodin and Le Grand, with others, 1987). The more that the system is geared only to the needs of the poorest, and the more residual that the scheme becomes, the less likely is it that welfare will command popular support.

Conclusion

In 1993, the eminent academic David Ellwood was appointed to head welfare reform in the United States. He tells the following story about arriving in Washington:

Senator Daniel Patrick Moynihan... said, 'So you've come to do welfare reform...
I'll look forward to reading your book about why it failed this time'. (Ellwood,
1996)

The task of reforming welfare depends on the political considerations of the day and changes in the structure of society and the
economy. The prevailing mood seems to be that social security, if not
actually creating problems, is failing to address the aims it is set. The
idea that social security should exist to cover only temporary interruptions to earning is back with us, with a new view that the system should
be promoting the return to work rather than relying on the natural
course of events, such as job-searching and an economic upturn, to do
that for us. The emphasis within welfare is changing to an active rather
than a passive stance. The consequent job for social security adminis-
trators should, therefore, be changing away from one of calculating
entitlements to benefits and delivering cheques, and towards an ethos
that seeks to move people back into the 'normal' state of working.

Reform during the 1990s has certainly shown that changes to benefit
rules can restrict the rate of growth of spending on social security. To
rein back spending to a greater extent is likely to involve either very
radical changes in the structure of the system or cuts in benefits to a
much greater extent than has previously been tried.

10

Conclusions

The social security system in modern Britain affects the lives of virtually everyone in the country. It is a simple fact that we will all spend most of our lives either receiving or paying for benefits. In spite of this, the system itself is far from simple, and most of us understand very little about what it aims to do, how it operates and what its effects are. This book has tried to provide an overview of social security in Britain while also introducing readers to some of the important details.

In the first chapter, we argue that there are two main aims of social security policy in Britain today: insurance against certain 'risks' and the alleviation of poverty. Whereas many books link social security primarily to issues of poverty, we argue that a concern for insuring against the risks of unemployment, sickness and retirement provided the historical impetus for the development of social security in this country. In addition, although the importance of the insurance principle has declined in recent decades, insurance benefits still play a major role in the current system. The system of social insurance, however, has always left gaps through which those without adequate employment records have fallen, so a system of social assistance has developed to provide a safety net and alleviate the poverty of the most vulnerable groups. The success of social assistance in providing this safety net is also discussed in this book.

Although insurance and poverty alleviation are the most important aims of social security policy, the issue of redistribution is also mentioned. Despite some exceptions, the system does not particularly perform a 'Robin Hood' function of redistributing resources from the rich to the poor but does provide a significant 'savings bank' mechanism, forcing people to save when they are in employment for those times when they need extra income, such as when they retire. The system, therefore, redistributes money over time more than from one individual to another. Finally, the system tries to 'compensate' people for certain extra costs of living, such as having children or being disabled.

The functions of the state social security system could be, and at various times in the past have been, provided by employers, charities, voluntary associations and family members. Thus, if we take a very wide definition of social security, there is no necessary reason why the state should itself be the provider of ways to help people insure against risk and alleviate poverty. As well as looking outside the state, it is also important to consider the role of wider government policies, such as those relating to the tax system or the economy (for example in prioritising full employment). Such policies will also have an important impact on risks, income and poverty.

Chapter 2 of this book takes a comparative perspective on social security. By so doing, we can see what is distinctive about our own system. For example, the British system combines universality of coverage with low levels of benefit. This in contrast to the Scandinavian model, which has universal coverage but higher benefit levels funded from general taxation. The Bismarckian model (in Germany and Austria) relies heavily on insurance benefits but has some social assistance, often locally based, to plug any gaps. Social security in Southern Europe also relies heavily on social insurance but has very little social assistance, and continues to rely on family ties.

A comparative perspective can also help us explain why certain types of social security system develop in different countries, and we can learn lessons from abroad about the impact of different benefit regimes or policies. For example, it is often argued that the problems with the system of child support introduced in Britain in the early 1990s could have been significantly reduced had the lessons of the Australian child support system been studied.

As well as taking a comparative perspective, a historical perspective also throws light on the current social security system. The system we have today is built on foundations that go back four centuries to the Elizabethan Poor Law. It was changes in the nineteenth century, however, that provide the firmest foundations. The spread of industrialisation and urbanisation led to demands for social reform to alleviate the problems of the new working class. The Poor Law Amendment Act of 1834 provided such reform, and important policy changes then occurred in the early twentieth century under Lloyd George's influence. Beveridge, however, stands out as the main architect of today's social security system. The early emphasis on social insurance is clear, but Beveridge knew that his system could only work if full employment were secured. The failure of successive governments to deliver this from the 1970s onwards caused enormous strains on the Beveridgean system. Changes in gender roles and the growth of more flexible forms of employment have also caused major cracks to appear in the current system, but governments in the past three decades have merely tried to paper over these cracks rather than attempt to build a new structure from first principles.

The system today is, therefore, a highly complex organism that has evolved over time and which very few people understand in its entirety. For every possible generalisation about the system, there are myriad caveats that need to be made. It is thus difficult to give a brief overview without oversimplifying the system and, therefore, possibly giving misleading information. Nevertheless, some attempt at giving an overview is made in Chapter 4. This chapter broadly categorises benefits into three types: contributory benefits (or social insurance), means-tested benefits (or social assistance) and contingent benefits. Benefits can also be categorised into two dichotomies: universal versus means-tested, and contributory versus non-contributory. Another way of categorising benefits is in terms of who receives them, and Chapter 5 discusses each of these different types in turn.

Pensions account for the largest share of benefits spending – one-third of spending in 1996/97, the equivalent of £30 billion. The state Retirement Pension was fundamental to the development of social security early in the twentieth century, but the concept of retirement was relatively new at that time. It is now taken for granted, but it is also a particularly male concept – as there is little opportunity for (mostly) women to retire from work in the home. The state Retirement Pension is based on contributions made during employment (or self-employment), so women are less likely to qualify for the benefit in their own right, despite separate provisions for caring since 1978. Nevertheless, women are much more likely than men to receive state Retirement Pension because they often receive it when they become widows.

The second largest area of benefit expenditure goes to sick or disabled people. This is for two reasons: insurance against sickness and disability is a keystone of Beveridge's system; and disabled people face major disadvantages in the labour market that force them to rely on social security. However, labour market disadvantage does not always mean that a group will receive particular benefits. Disability benefits are a particularly complex part of the benefit system and can be divided into the following types of benefit: earnings replacement, means-tested benefit, compensation for injuries, compensation for extra costs and benefits for carers.

Family benefits are rather different from other types of benefit as they do not relate directly to insurance or poverty alleviation. Child Benefit acts to recognise the extra costs of having children, although it goes nowhere near meeting the full cost. Other benefits exist to make sure that people with children are better off in employment than receiving social security. Without the existence of in-work benefits, families with children are likely to be part of the working poor because wages do not take into account family size. Increasingly, lone parents are an important group for social security purposes. Most of the 1.7 million lone parents in Britain receive social security, only 40 per cent being in paid work, often low paid and supplemented by in-work benefits.

Unemployed people are a relatively small group on benefit. The typical unemployed benefit recipient is a young, single man without qualifications. A significant number of the unemployed move into work very quickly, but another large group remain on benefit for a considerable amount of time. For these long-term unemployed, the contributory part of their benefit will end after 6 months. If eligible, they will then go on to receive the means-tested part. Unemployed people also have to meet certain obligations to qualify for benefit – they have to be actively seeking a job and available for work.

Alongside benefits for different groups, there are also benefits to help people to meet specific extra costs of living. These are discussed in Chapter 6. Housing Benefit exists to help people pay their rent if they are on a low income. The cost of this benefit has increased dramatically in the past two decades because there has been a deliberate policy shift from subsidising 'bricks and mortar' (in terms of low council rents) to subsidising individuals (by raising rents and paying benefit to those on low incomes). While low-paid renters can receive help, those with mortgages are mostly denied assistance with their housing costs. Those on a low income can also receive help with their Council Tax. The other major benefit to help meet extra costs is the Social Fund. This is another distinctive feature of the British system, although social workers in some other countries can give out money to people in need. The Social Fund is a much criticised part of the system, particularly as claimants are mostly given loans rather than grants.

There is no point in talking about social security policies without also considering how the policies are put into practice. Chapter 7 covers the delivery of benefits, a huge task employing over 72,000 staff in the Benefits Agency alone. Performance targets are set to guide and review the workings of the Agencies that implement policy. For example, they check that claims are cleared quickly and accurately. However, despite the emphasis on accuracy, a significant proportion of claims are incorrect as a result of either error or fraud. In addition, as well as considering error and fraud, a number of people do not receive the benefits to which they are entitled – the problem of non-take-up.

The New Labour government that came into power in 1997 has continued previous Conservative government policies attempting to cut back on expenditure on benefit administration. This has included fundamental changes to the system of decision-making and appeals.

As well as reviewing the aims of the system and how it works, this book also investigates the effects of social security. It is often argued that the system provides disincentives to work because it is possible to survive financially without taking a job. This idea has influenced policy in terms of tightening the obligations of the unemployed to look for, and take, paid work. It is also thought that the effects of the system may be felt by the partners of unemployed men as they have particularly low rates of employment. However, it is more likely that these women are similar to their partners in having poor employment opportunities. Lone parents are another group that might be discouraged from taking paid work because the costs of childcare do not make employment particularly worthwhile financially.

Disincentives to work are only one possible effect of the system. It is also possible that the system may discourage people from saving for themselves, and there may also be effects on non-financial aspects of people's lives. For example, there may be disincentives to live as part of a couple or get married, and there may also be incentives to have large families as benefit rates are linked to the number of children in a family.

Chapter 9 weighed up the extent of the problems facing the system and considered possible reforms. Governments now seem to shy away from root and branch reform. Instead, they plan changes that use the existing structure of benefits as a starting point. Such change may still, however, be radical. The key elements of current thinking and policy development seem to lie in the active approach typified by the various New Deal programmes, the use of the tax system and a minimum wage to help 'make work pay', and an increased emphasis on support for families with children. The emphasis on reducing fraud and reducing spending on some disability benefits continues policies associated with the previous government. More resources have gone to current pensioners, but longer-term reform (for future pensioners) is proving a more difficult subject.

One of the difficulties in describing and explaining social security policy and practice is that it is continuing to evolve. Each year, new complexities and issues develop, while others retreat into the background. However, the underlying issues and structures generally remain the same. We hope that this book has enabled readers to increase their understanding of social security matters and to appreciate the difficulties in adapting the system to the challenges it faces, both today and in the future.

Appendix

Data Sources Relevant to Social Security

There are a number of sources of information for people concerned to keep in touch with developments in social security. This short guide covers the most important printed material and those available on-line. An increasing volume of information is now becoming available on the internet, particularly in the form of pages on the World Wide Web. A short list of some of the most important websites is provided at the end of this appendix for those with access to the Internet and a web browser (Netscape Navigator, Microsoft Internet Explorer, Mosaic, Lynx, and so on).

Information provided by the government

An important annual source of information is the DSS's own *Social Security Statistics*, published by the Stationery Office. This includes details of total spending on each benefit and the number of recipients in each of a number of recent years. Most of the Agencies forming part of the DSS also produce Annual Reports. These usually indicate performance against various targets while also giving information about levels of staff, new initiatives and so on. The annual report of the Benefits Agency is the one most directly concerned with issues related to social security benefits.

Social Security: The Government's Expenditure Plans is published every year around the time of the budget. This provides a detailed breakdown of current and projected future spending on social security benefits.

Figures on 'poverty' may be found in *Households Below Average Income*. This is a large volume of tables showing the proportion of individuals falling below certain proportions of the average income, adjusting for differences in family size. There has been a long and wide-ranging debate about many of the technical questions involved in measuring low income and how far low income may be said to represent 'poverty' (see Oppenheim and Harker, 1996, for more detail).

Early in 1998, the DSS brought out *The Case for Welfare Reform.* This was accompanied by seven 'Focus Files' providing considerable factual information about social security and how it has developed over time. These form a particularly useful set of documentation.

The DSS also commissions research projects of various kinds. The findings from these studies are typically published in either its Research Report Series (published by the Stationery Office) or more informal in-house reports (published by the Social Research Branch of the DSS). Full details of their annual research programme and resulting publications may be found in the *Social Security Research Yearbook.*

The DSS is also responsible for a large annual survey of people's incomes, known as the *Family Resources Survey.* This provides a good source of information about the proportions of different families receiving particular benefits, different levels of income and savings, the importance of different types of family and many other areas. For regular information on areas such as economic activity, caring, disability and so on, the principal surveys (for Britain) include the *General Household Survey,* the *Labour Force Survey* and the *Family Expenditure Survey.* Those with data analysis skills can access the raw data from these surveys from the Economic and Social Research Council (ESRC) data archive based at Essex University.

The headquarters of the DSS may be found on the World Wide Web at http://www.dss.gov.uk/hq. This site contains a regularly updated set of press releases, information about the ministerial team, publications and details about the structure of the department.

The DfEE produces a monthly magazine known as *Labour Market Trends* (still sometimes referred to by its former name, the *Employment Gazette*). This contains detailed data on unemployment, earnings, price changes and vacancies, as well as articles describing issues related to the labour market in considerable detail. The DfEE is also an important funder of externally conducted research on labour market issues, including research on unemployment, youth, retirement and incentives to work. Four-page summaries of their funded research, called *Research Briefs,* are often freely available. Copies are also available from their website.

From time to time, reports relevant to social security are produced by the appropriate parliamentary committees, the Social Security Select Committee (that is, MPs) and the Social Security Advisory Committee (containing independent experts). The Social Security Advisory Committee provides advice to the Secretary of State on proposed new legislation and regulations. The National Audit Office, which scrutinises all public expenditure, often produces a report when a particular aspect of the system has been reformed.

Non-official sources

The Child Poverty Action Group produces a number of guides to the social security system. These concentrate on particular benefits and provide very detailed descriptions that might be most useful to welfare rights advisers. The two main sources are the *Rights Guide to Non-Means-Tested Benefits* and the *National Welfare Benefits Handbook*. The *Child Support Handbook* is also produced each year, and other Child Poverty Action Group guides cover (among other areas) Jobseeker's Allowance, Council Tax, debt advice and immigration. The Disability Alliance produce a *Disability Rights Handbook*, and the Unemployment Unit an *Unemployment and Training Rights Handbook*.

There are few academic journals with a strong coverage of social security matters. *Benefits* is dedicated to the area, covering a range of academic and practical matters as well as book reviews and a round up of research in the social security area. The journal is produced three times a year. Students and the unwaged benefit from lower-rate subscriptions. Further details may be found at their website, maintained by one of the authors of this book (McKay), at http://pages.hotbot.com/edu/benefits. This website also contains a useful list of links to other Internet locations concerned with social security issues.

Other journals frequently including coverage of social security issues include:

- *Fiscal Studies*, produced at the Institute for Fiscal Studies on a quarterly basis, with an emphasis on an economic perspective, although the articles are mostly accessible to more general readers
- The *Journal of Social Policy*, which deals with all the traditional areas of social policy rather than just income maintenance
- The *Journal of European Social Policy*, although this includes other social policy areas and contains articles on countries other than Britain

- The *International Social Security Review*, published by the International Social Security Association
- *Policy and Politics*
- *Critical Social Policy*, which adopts a more radical (typically left-leaning) approach to social policy issues.

Research particularly relevant to social security matters is often funded by the Joseph Rowntree Foundation, whose headquarters are based in York. They produce particularly helpful four-page summaries of each research project (*Findings*, copies of which are available from the Foundation, or on its website – http://www.jrf.org.uk). A regular journal, *Search*, summarises particular projects and those research ideas selected for future support.

Useful websites for social security information

Web address (http://)	Organisation
pages.hotbot.com/edu/benefits	*Benefits* journal. Includes an extensive set of links to other websites, including many of those listed here
www.dss.gov.uk	Department of Social Security
www.dss.gov.uk/hq	Headquarters
www.dss.gov.uk/ba	Benefits Agency
www.dss.gov.uk/csa	Child Support Agency
www.dfee.gov.uk	Department for Education and Employment
ns.hm-treasury.gov.uk	The Treasury
www.ssa.gov/international/links.html	Social security websites around the world, mostly national offices
dawww.essex.ac.uk	ESRC data archive at Essex University
www.cyberpoint.co.uk/asi	Adam Smith Institute
www.iea.org.uk	Institute for Economic Affairs
www.ifs.org.uk	Institute for Fiscal Studies
www.ippr.org.uk	Institute for Public Policy Research
www.jrf.org.uk	Joseph Rowntree Foundation
www.psi.org.uk	Policy Studies Institute
www.scallywag.com/nacsa	National Association for Child Support Action, a counterpoint to the Child Support Agency

References

Abel-Smith, B. and Townsend, P. (1965) *The Poor and the Poorest*. London: Bell.

Adler, M. and Sainsbury, R. (eds) (1998) *Adjudication Matters: Reforming Decision Making and Appeals in Social Security*. New Waverley Papers, Edinburgh: University of Edinburgh.

Adler, M., Bell, C., Clasen, J. and Sinfield, A. (eds) (1991) *The Sociology of Social Security*. Edinburgh: Edinburgh University Press.

Alcock, P. (1987) *Poverty and State Support*. London: Longman.

Alcock, P. (1993) *Understanding Poverty*. London: Macmillan.

Alcock, P. and Shepherd, J. (1987) 'Take-up campaigns: fighting poverty through the post', *Critical Social Policy*. **19**: 52–67.

Atkinson, A. (1970) *Poverty in Britain and the Reform of Social Security*. Department of Applied Economics Occasional Papers No. 18. Cambridge: Cambridge University Press.

Atkinson, A. and Micklewright, J. (1991) 'Unemployment compensation and labour market transitions: a critical review', *Journal of Economic Literature*, **29**: 1679–727.

Atkinson, A., Rainwater, M. and Smeeding, T. (1995) *Income Distribution in OECD Countries*. Social Policy Studies No. 18. Paris: OECD.

Baldwin, P. (1990) *The Politics of Social Solidarity: Class Bases of the European Welfare State 1875–1975*. Cambridge: Cambridge University Press.

Baldwin, S. (1985) *The Costs of Caring: Families with Disabled Children*. London: Routledge & Kegan Paul.

Bane, M. and Ellwood, D. (1986) 'Slipping in and out of poverty: the dynamics of spells', *Journal of Human Resources*, **21**(1): 1–23.

Barclay, P. (1995) *Joseph Rowntree Foundation Inquiry into Income and Wealth*, Volume 1. York: Joseph Rowntree Foundation.

Barr, N. (1993) *The Economics of the Welfare State*. London: Weidenfeld & Nicolson.

Beatson, M. (1995) *Labour Market Flexibility*. Research Series No. 48. London: Employment Department.

Becker, G. (1981) *A Treatise on the Family*. Cambridge, MA: Harvard University Press.

Becker, S. (1997) *Responding to Poverty: The Politics of Cash and Care*. London: Longman.

Benefits Agency (1995) *Benefit Review (Income Support and Unemployment Benefit): Report on Methodology*. Leeds: Benefits Agency Security.

Benefits Agency (1997) *Annual Report and Accounts 1996/7*. London: Stationery Office.

Benefits Agency (1998) *Benefits Agency Business Plan 1998–99*. Leeds: Benefits Agency.

Berthoud, R. (1984) *The Reform of Social Security*. London: Policy Studies Institute.

Berthoud, R. (1989) 'Social security and the economics of housing', in Dilnot, A. and Walker, I. (eds) *The Economics of Social Security*. Oxford: Clarendon Press.

Berthoud, R. (1990) 'The extra costs of disability', in Dalley, G. (ed.) *Disability and Social Policy*. London: Policy Studies Institute.

Berthoud, R. (1991) 'The social fund – is it working?', *Policy Studies*, 12(1): 4–25.

Berthoud, R. (1993) *Invalidity Benefit: Where Will the Savings Come From?* London: Policy Studies Institute.

Berthoud, R. (1997) 'Income and standard of living', in Modood, T., Berthoud, R., Lakey, J. *et al.* (1997) *Ethnic Minorities in Britain*. London: Policy Studies Institute.

Berthoud, R. (1998) *Disability Benefits: A Review of the Issues and Options for Reform*. York: Joseph Rowntree Foundation.

Berthoud, R., Lakey, J. and McKay, S. (1993) *The Economic Problems of Disabled People*. London: Policy Studies Institute.

Beveridge, W. (1942) *Social Insurance and Allied Services*. London: HMSO (Cmd 6404).

Bieback, K. (1992) 'Family benefits in Australia, Britain and Germany', *Journal of European Social Policy*, 2(4): 239–54.

Bloch, A. (1997) 'Ethnic inequality and social security policy', in Walker, A. and Walker, C. (eds) (1997) *Britain Divided: The Growth of Social Exclusion in the 1980s and 1990s*. London: Child Poverty Action Group.

Blundell, R. (1992) 'Labour supply and taxation: a review', *Fiscal Studies*, 13(3): 15–40.

Bolderson, H. and Mabbett, D. with Hudson, J., Rowe, M. and Spicker, P. (1997) *Delivering Social Security: A Cross-national Study*. DSS Research Report No. 59. London: Stationery Office.

Bolderson, H. and Roberts, S. (1995) 'New restrictions on benefits for migrants: xenophobia or trivial pursuits', *Benefits*, 12: 11–15.

Booth, C. (1889) *The Life and Labour of the People*. London: Williams & Norgate.

Bottomley, D., McKay, S. and Walker, R. (1997) *Unemployment and Jobseeking: A National Survey in 1995*. DSS Research Report No. 62. London: Stationery Office.

Bradshaw, J. (1987) 'The Social Fund', in Brenton, M. and Ungerson, C. (eds) *The Yearbook of Social Policy 1986/87*. London: Longman.

Bradshaw, J. (1994) 'Simulating policies: an example in comparative method', cited in Eardley, T., Bradshaw, J., Ditch, J., Gough, I. and Whiteford, P. (1996) *Social Assistance in OECD Countries: Synthesis Report*. DSS Research Report No. 46. London: HMSO.

Bradshaw, J. and Chen, J.-R. (1997) 'Poverty in the UK. A comparison with nineteen other countries', *Benefits*, 18: 13–17.

Bradshaw, J. and Millar, J. (1991) *Lone Parent Families in the UK*. London: HMSO.

Bradshaw, J., Ditch, J., Holmes, H. and Whiteford, P. (1993) *Support for Children: A Comparison of Arrangements in Fifteen Countries*. DSS Research Report No. 21. London: HMSO.

Brittan, S. and Webb, S. (1990) *Beyond the Welfare State: An Examination of Basic Incomes in a Market Economy*. Aberdeen: Aberdeen University Press.

Broome, J. (1992) 'Deontology and economics', *Economics and Philosophy* , 8(2): 269–82.

Brown, C. and Jackson, P. (1990) *Public Sector Economics*, 4th edn. Oxford: Basil Blackwell.

Brown, J. (1984) *The Disability Income System*. London: Policy Studies Institute.

Brown, J. (1990) *Victims or Villains: Social Security Benefits in Unemployment*. York: Joseph Rowntree Memorial Trust.

Brown, J. (1994) *Escaping from Dependence. Part-time Workers and the Self-employed: The Role of Social Security*. London: Institute for Public Policy Research.

Bryson, A. (1998) 'Lone mothers' earnings', in Ford, R. and Millar, J. (eds) *Private Lives and Public Policy: Lone Parenthood and Future Policy in the UK*. London: Policy Studies Institute.

Bryson, A. and McKay, S. (1994) 'Is it worth working? An introduction to some of the issues', in Bryson, A. and McKay, S. (eds) *Is it Worth Working? Factors Affecting Labour Supply*. London: Policy Studies Institute.

Bryson, A. and Marsh, A. (1996) *Leaving Family Credit*. DSS Research Report No. 48. London: HMSO.

Bryson, L. (1992) *Welfare and the State: Who Benefits?* London: Macmillan.

Burchardt. T. and Hills, J. (1997) *Private Welfare Insurance and Social Security: Pushing the Boundaries*. York: Joseph Rowntree Foundation.

Butler, D., Adonis, A. and Travers, T. (1994) *Failure in British Government: The Politics of the Poll Tax*. Oxford: Oxford University Press.

Cagan, P. (1965) *The Effect of Pension Plans on Aggregate Saving*. New York: Columbia University Press.

Central Statistical Office (1997) *Social Trends*. London: Stationery Office.

Chief Adjudication Officer (1998) *Annual Report of the Chief Adjudication Officer 1997–98*. Leeds: Central Adjudication Services.

Chief Child Support Officer (1998) *Annual Report of the Chief Child Support Officer 1996–1997*. Leeds: Central Adjudication Services.

Child Poverty Action Group (1997a) *Rights Guide to Non-Means-Tested Benefits 1997/98*. London: CPAG.

Child Poverty Action Group (1997b) *National Welfare Benefits Handbook 1997/98*. London: CPAG.

Child Poverty Action Group (1997c) *Jobseeker's Allowance Handbook 1997/98*. London: CPAG.

Child Poverty Action Group (1997d) *Child Support Handbook 1997/98*. London: CPAG.

Clarke, J. (1993) 'Comparative Approaches and Social Policy', in Cochrane, A. and Clarke, J. (eds) *Comparing Welfare States: Britain in International Context*. London: Sage.

Clarke, K., Glendinning, C. and Craig, G. (1994) *Losing Support: Children and the Child Support Act*. London: Children's Society.

Coates, K. and Silburn, R. (1970) *Poverty: The Forgotten Englishmen*. Harmondsworth: Penguin.

Cohen, R. and Tarpey, M. (eds) (1988) *Single Payments: The Disappearing Safety Net*. London: CPAG.

Commission on Social Justice (1994) *Social Justice: Strategies for National Renewal* (chair: Sir Gordon Borrie). London: Vintage.

Cook, D. (1989) *Rich Law, Poor Law*. Milton Keynes: Open University Press.

Cooke, K. (1987) 'The withdrawal from paid work of the wives of unemployed men', *Journal of Social Policy*, **16**: 371–82.

Craig, G. (ed.) (1989) *Your Flexible Friend: Voluntary Organisations, Claimants and the Social Fund*. London: Social Security Consortium/Association of Metropolitan Authorities.

Craig, P. (1991) 'Costs and benefits: a review of research on take-up of income-related benefits', *Journal of Social Policy*, **20**(4): 537–65.

Craig, P. and Greenslade, M. (1998) *First Findings from the Disability Follow-up to the Family Resources Survey*. Research Summary No. 5, March, Social Research Branch. London: DSS Analytical Services Division.

Creedy, J. and Disney, R. (1985) *Social Insurance in Transition: An Economic Analysis*. Oxford: Clarendon Press.

Dahrendorf, R. *et al.* (1995) *Wealth Creation and Social Cohesion in a Free Society*. Commission on Wealth Creation and Social Cohesion.

Daniel, W. (1990) *The Unemployed Flow*. London: Policy Studies Institute.

Davies, R., Elias, P. and Penn, R. (1994) 'The relationship between a husband's unemployment and his wife's participation in the labour force', in Gallie, D., Marsh, C. and Vogler, C. (eds) *Social Change and the Experience of Unemployment*. Oxford: Oxford University Press.

Deacon, A. (1976) *In Search of the Scrounger*. London: Bell.

Deacon, A. and Bradshaw, J. (1983) *Reserved for the Poor: The Means Test in British Social Policy*. London: Martin Robertson.

Department of Health and Social Security (1985) *Reform of Social Security*. London: HMSO.

Department of Social Security (1990) *The Way Ahead: Benefits for Disabled People*. London: HMSO.

Department of Social Security (1991) *Children Come First*. London: HMSO.

Department of Social Security (1993a) *Containing the Cost of Social Security: The International Context*. London: HMSO.

Department of Social Security (1993b) *The Growth of Social Security*. London: HMSO.

Department of Social Security (1995) *Changing Child Support*. London: HMSO.

Department of Social Security (1997) *Social Security Statistics*. London: Stationery Office.

Department of Social Security (1998a) *Children First: A New Approach to Child Support*. Cm 3992. London: DSS.

Department of Social Security (1998b) *Focus Files 01–07*. London: DSS.

Department of Social Security (1998c) *New Ambitions for Our Country: A New Contract for Welfare*. Cm 3805. London: DSS.

Department of Social Security (1998d) *Women and Social Security: A Policy Appraisal by the Department of Social Security*. London: Central Office of Information.

Department of Social Security (1998e) *Beating Fraud is Everyone's Business: Securing the Future*. Cm 4012. London: DSS.

Department of Social Security (1998f) *The Case for Welfare Reform*. London: DSS.

Dewson, S. (1995) *Fiscal Welfare The Hidden Arm of Social Policy – Who Benefits?* Unpublished MSc thesis, Bath University.

Dilnot, A. and Kell, M. (1989) 'Male unemployment and women's work', in Dilnot, A. and Walker, I. (eds) *The Economics of Social Security*. Oxford: Oxford University Press.

Dilnot, A., Kay, J. and Morris, C. (1984) *The Reform of Social Security*. Oxford: Oxford University Press.

Disney, R. (1996) *Can We Afford to Grow Older? A Perspective on the Economics of Aging*. Cambridge, MA: MIT Press.

Dobson, B. and Middleton, S. (1998) *Paying to Care: The Cost of Childhood Disability*. York: Joseph Rowntree Foundation.

Dogan, M. and Kazancigil, A. (eds) (1994) *Comparing Nations: Concepts, Strategies, Substance*. Oxford: Blackwell.

Dolton, P. and O'Neill, D. (1996) 'Unemployment duration and the Restart Effect: some experimental evidence', *Economic Journal*, **106**: 387–400.

Duncan, A., Giles, C. and Webb, S. (1994) *Social Security Reform and Women's Independent Incomes*. Manchester: Equal Opportunities Commission.

Eardley, T., Bradshaw, J., Ditch, J., Gough, I. and Whiteford, P. (1996a) *Social Assistance in OECD Countries: Country Reports*. DSS Research Report No. 47. London: HMSO.

Eardley, T., Bradshaw, J., Ditch, J., Gough, I. and Whiteford, P. (1996b) *Social Assistance in OECD Countries: Synthesis Report*. DSS Research Report No. 46. London: HMSO.

Elias, P. (1997) *The Effect of Unemployment Benefits on the Labour Force Participation of Partners*. Warwick: Institute for Employment Research.

Ellwood, D. T. (1996) 'Welfare reform as I knew it: when bad things happen to good policies', *American Prospect* **26**: 22–9 (*http://epn.org/prospect/26/26ellw.html*).

Esam, P. and Berthoud, R. (1991) *Independent Benefits for Men and Women*. London: Policy Studies Institute.

Esping-Andersen, G. (1990) *The Three Worlds of Welfare Capitalism*. Cambridge: Polity Press.

European Commission (1995) *Social Protection in Europe 1995*. Luxembourg: Office for Official Publications of the European Communities.

Eurostat (1994) *Poverty Statistics in the Late 1980s: Research Based on Micro-data*. Luxembourg: Office for Official Publications of the European Communities.

Falkingham, J. and Hills, J. (1995) *The Dynamic of Welfare: The Welfare State and the Life Cycle*. London: Prentice Hall/Harvester Wheatsheaf.

Family Fund Trust (1996) *Introducing the Family Fund Trust*. York: Family Fund Trust.

Fay, R. (1996) *Enhancing the Effectiveness of Active Labour Market Policies: Evidence from Programme Evaluations in OECD Countries*. Labour Market and Social Policy Occasional Papers No. 18. Paris: OECD.

Feldstein, M. (1974) 'Social security, induced retirement and aggregate capital accumulation', *Journal of Political Economy*, **82**: 905–26.

Field, F. (1995) *Making Welfare Work*. London: Institute of Community Studies.

Field, F. (1996) *How To Pay for the Future: Building a Stakeholders' Welfare*. London: Institute of Community Studies.

Finn, D. (1998) 'Welfare to Work: a new deal for the unemployed?', *Benefits* **21**: 32–3.

Ford, R. and Millar, J. (eds) (1998) *Private Lives and Public Policy: Lone Parenthood and Future Policy in the UK*. London: Policy Studies Institute.

Ford, R., Marsh, A. and McKay, S. (1995) *Changes in Lone Parenthood 1991–1993*. London: HMSO.

Ford, R., Marsh, A. and Finlayson, L. (1997) *Lone Parents, Work and Benefits*. London: Stationery Office.

Fraser, D. (1973) *The Evolution of the British Welfare State: A History of Social Policy Since the Industrial Revolution*. London: Macmillan.

Furniss, N. and Tilton, T. (1977) *The Case for the Welfare State*. Bloomington: Indiana University Press.

Gardiner, K (1997) *Bridges from Benefit to Work: A Review*. York: Joseph Rowntree Foundation.

Garnham, A. and Knights, E. (1994) *Putting the Treasury First: The Truth About Child Support*. London: CPAG.

Garfinkel, I. and McLanahan, S. (1986) *Single Mothers and their Children: A New American Dilemma*. Washington: Urban Institute Press.

Gauthier, A. (1996) 'The measured and unmeasured effects of welfare benefits on families: implications for Europe's demographic trends', in Coleman, D. (ed.) *Europe's Population in the 1990s*. Oxford: Oxford University Press.

Gilbert, B. (1966) *The Evolution of National Insurance in Great Britain*. London: Michael Joseph.

Gilbert, B. (1970) *British Social Policy 1914–1939*. London: Batsford.

Ginn, J. and Arber, S. (1992) 'Towards women's independence: pension systems in three contrasting European welfare states', *Journal of European Social Policy*, **2**(4): 255–77.

Glennerster, H. (1992) *Paying for Welfare: The 1990s*. London: Harverster Wheatsheaf.

Glendinning, C. (1992) '"Community care": the financial consequences for women', in Glendinning, C. and Millar, J. (eds) *Women and Poverty in Britain: The 1990s*. London: Harvester Wheatsheaf.

Glendinning, C. and McLaughlin, E. (1993) *Paying for Care: Lessons from Europe*. SSAC Research Paper No. 5. London: HMSO.

Gold, M. and Mayes, D. (1993) 'Rethinking a social policy for Europe', in Simpson, R. and Walker, R. (eds) *Europe: For Richer or Poorer?* London: CPAG.

Goodin, R. and Le Grand, J., with others (1987) *Not Only the Poor: The Middle Classes and the Welfare State*. London: Allen & Unwin.

Goodlad, R. and Gibb, K. (eds) (1994) *Housing and Social Justice*. London: Institute for Public Policy Research.

Gough, I. (1979) *The Political Economy of the Welfare State*. London: Macmillan.

Government Actuary's Department (1995) *National Insurance Fund Long Term Financial Estimates*. London: HMSO.

Government Statistical Service (1998) *Main Results from the Second National Housing Benefit Accuracy Review*. London: DSS Analytical Services Division.

Greener, K. and Cracknell, R. (1998) *Child Benefit*. House of Commons Research Paper 98/79, July.

Greve, B. (1994) 'The hidden welfare state, tax expenditures and social policy: a comparative overview', *Scandinavian Journal of Social Welfare*, **3**: 203–11.

Hantrais, L. (1995) *Social Policy in the European Union*. London: Macmillan.

Harding, L. F. (1996) *Family, State and Social Policy*. London: Macmillan.

Hauser, R. (1993) 'Approaches to comparative social policy analysis', in Berghman, J. and Cantillon, B. (eds) *The European Face of Social Security*. Aldershot: Avebury.

Hausman, P. (1993) 'The impact of social security in the European Community', in Berghman, J. and Cantillon, B. (eds) *The European Face of Social Security*. Aldershot: Avebury.

Heidenheimer, A., Heclo, H. and Adams, C. (1990) *Comparative Public Policy: The Politics of Social Change in America, Europe and Japan*. Basingstoke: Macmillan.

Herbert, A. and Kempson, E. (1995) *Water Debt and Disconnection*. London: Policy Studies Institute.

Hessing, D., Elffers, H., Robben, H. and Webley, P. (1993) 'Needy or greedy? The social psychology of individuals who fraudulently claim unemployment benefits', *Journal of Applied Social Psychology*, **23**(3): 226–43.

Hill, M. (1969) 'The exercise of discretion in the National Assistance Board', *Public Administration*, **47**: 75–90 (also reprinted as pp. 407–22 in Hill, M. (ed.) (1993) *The Policy Process: A Reader*. London: Harvester Wheatsheaf.)

Hill, M. (1990) *Social Security Policy in Britain*. London: Edward Elgar.

Hill, M. (1996) *Social Policy: A Comparative Analysis*. London: Prentice Hall/Harvester Wheatsheaf.

Hills, J. (with the LSE Welfare State Programme) (1993) *The Future of Welfare: A Guide to the Debate*. York: Joseph Rowntree Foundation.

Hills, J. (1995a) 'Funding the welfare state', *Oxford Review of Economic Policy*, **11**: 27–43.

Hills, J. (1995b) *Joseph Rowntree Foundation Inquiry into Income and Wealth*, Volume 2, *A Summary of the Evidence*. York: Joseph Rowntree Foundation.

Hills, J. and Mullings, B. (1990) 'Housing: a decent home for all at a price within their means?', in Hills, J. (ed.) *The State of Welfare: The Welfare State in Britain since 1974*. Oxford: Clarendon Press.

Hirsch, D. (1997) *Social Protection and Inclusion: European Challenges for the United Kingdom*. York: Joseph Rowntree Foundation.

Holman, R. (1978) *Poverty: Explanations of Social Deprivation*. London: Martin Robertson.

Hoynes, W. (1996) *Work, welfare and family structure: a review of the evidenc.* Institute for Research on Poverty Discussion Paper No. 1103–96.

Huby, M. and Dix, G. (1992) *Evaluating the Social Fund*. DSS Research Report No. 9. London: HMSO.

Hutton, S., Kennedy, S. and Whiteford, P. (1995) *Equalisation of State Pension Ages: the Gender Impact*. Manchester: Equal Opportunities Commission.

Institute for Public Policy Research (1993) *Making Sense of Benefits*. Commission on Social Justice Issues Paper No. 2. London: Institute for Public Policy Research (based on a submission by Pete Alcock).

International Labour Office (1984) *Social Security into the 21st Century*. Geneva: ILO.

Johnson, P., Disney, R. and Stears, G. (1996) *Pensions: 2000 and beyond*. London: Retirement Income Inquiry.

Jones, C. (1985) *Patterns of Social Policy*. London: Tavistock.

Jones, T. (1993) *Britain's Ethnic Minorities*. London: Policy Studies Institute.

Jordan, B. (1996) *A Theory of Poverty and Social Exclusion*. Cambridge: Polity Press.

Jordan, B., James, S., Kay, H., and Redley, M. (1992) *Trapped in Poverty: Labour Market Decisions in Low-income Households*. London: Routledge.

Kamerman, S. and Kahn, A. (1978) *Family Policy*. New York: Columbia University Press.

Katona, G. (1975) *Psychological Economics*. New York: Elsevier.

Kay, J. and King, M. (1978) *The British Tax System*. Oxford: Oxford University Press.

Kell, M. and Wright, J. (1990) 'Benefits and the labour supply of women married to unemployed men', *Economic Journal* (supplement) **400**: 119–26.

Kemp, P. (1992) *Housing Benefit: An Appraisal*. SSAC Research Paper No. 4. London: HMSO.

Kemp, P. (1997) *A Comparative Study of Housing Allowances*. DSS Research Report No. 60. London: Stationery Office.

Kempson, E. (1994) *Outside the Banking System: A Review of Households Without a Current Account*. Social Security Advisory Committee Research Paper No. 6. London: HMSO.

Kempson, E. (1996) *Life on a Low Income*. York: Joseph Rowntree Foundation.

Kempson, E., Bryson, A. and Rowlingson, K. (1994) *Hard Times? How Poor Families Make Ends Meet*. London: Policy Studies Institute.

Kerr, S. (1983) *Making Ends Meet: An Investigation into the Non-claiming of Supplementary Pensions*. London: Bedford Square Press.

Kestenbaum, A. (1993) *Making Community Care a Reality*. Nottingham: Independent Living Fund.

Kvist, J. and Ploug, N. (1996) *Social Security in Northern Europe: An Institutional Analysis of Cash Benefits for the Unemployed*. Working Paper No. 1. Copenhagen: Centre for Welfare State Research.

Large, P. (1990) 'Paying for the additional costs of disability', in Dalley, G. (ed.) *Disability and Social Policy*. London: Policy Studies Institute.

Leibfried, S. (1993) 'Towards a European welfare state', in Jones, C. (ed.) *New Perspectives on the Welfare State in Europe*. London: Routledge.

Leibfried, S. and Leisering, L. (1995) *Zeit in Armut: Lebensläufe im Sozialstaat (Times of Poverty: Life Courses in the Welfare State)*. Frankfurt: Suhrkamp. (As summarised in Brückner, H. (1995) '"Times of Poverty": lessons from the Bremen Longitudinal Social Assistance Panel', *Research in Community Sociology*, **5**: 203–24.)

Lewis, J. (1992) 'Gender and the development of welfare regimes', *Journal of European Social Policy*, **2**(3): 159–73.

Lilley, P. (1993) 'Benefits and costs: securing the future of social security', Mais Lecture 1993. DSS Press Release 93/114.

Lipsey, D. (1994) 'Do we really want more public spending?', in Jowell, R., Curtice, J., Brook, L. and Ahrendt, D., with Park, A. (eds) *British Social Attitudes: The 11th Report*. Aldershot: Dartmouth.

Lipsky, M. (1980) *Street-level Bureaucracy: Dilemmas of the Individual in Public Services*. New York: Russell Sage Foundation.

Lister, R. (1989) 'Social security', in McCarthy, M. (ed.) *The New Politics of Welfare: An Agenda for the 1990s?* London: Macmillan.

Lonsdale, S. and Seddon, J. (1994) 'The growth of disability benefits: an international comparison', in Baldwin, S. and Falkingham, J. (eds) *Social Security and Social Change: New Challenges to the Beveridge Model*. London: Harvester Wheatsheaf.

Low Pay Commission (1998) *The National Minimum Wage: First Report of the Low Pay Commission*. Cm 3976. London: Stationery Office.

Luckhaus, L. and Moffat, G. (1996) *Serving the Market and People's Needs? The Impact of European Law on Pensions in the UK*. York: Joseph Rowntree Foundation.

McDaniel, P. and Surrey, S. (1985) *International Aspects of Tax Expenditures: a Comparative Study*. London: Deverter.

McKay, S. and Heaver, C. (1997) *Family Change and Social Security*. CRSP Working Paper. Loughborough: Loughborough University.

McKay, S. and Marsh, A. (1994) *Lone Parents and Work: The Effects of Benefits and Maintenance*. DSS Research Report No. 25. London: HMSO.

McKay, S. and Marsh, A. (1995) *Why Didn't They Claim?* London: Policy Studies Institute.

McKay, S., Heaver, C. and Walker, R. (1999) *Building up Pension Rights*. London: Stationery Office (in press).

McKay, S., Walker, R. and Youngs, R. (1997) *Unemployment and Jobseeking Before Jobseeker's Allowance*. DSS Research Report No. 73. London: Stationery Office.

McLaughlin, E. (1991a) *Social Security and Community Care: The Case of the Invalid Care Allowance*. DSS Research Report No. 4. London: HMSO.

McLaughlin, E. (1991b) 'Work and welfare benefits: social security, employment and unemployment in the 1990s', *Journal of Social Policy*, **20**(4): 485–508.

McLaughlin, E., Millar, J. and Cooke, K. (1989) *Work and Welfare Benefits*. Aldershot: Gower.

McRae, S. (ed.) (1999) *Changing Families*. Oxford: Oxford University Press (in press).

Mack, J. and Lansley, S. (1985) *Poor Britain*. London: George Allen & Unwin.

Maidment, A., Tu, T., Everett, M. and McKay, S. (1997) *The Effect of Jobseeker's Allowance on 16 and 17 year olds*. London: DfEE.

Malpass, P. and Murie, A. (1994) *Housing Policy and Practice*. London: Macmillan.

Martin, J. and Roberts, C. (1984) *Women and Employment: A Lifetime Perspective*. London: HMSO/Education Department.

Martin, J., Meltzer, D. and Elliot, D. (1988) *The Prevalence of Disability Among Adults*. London: HMSO.

Marsh, A. and McKay, S. (1993) *Families, Work and Benefits*. London: Policy Studies Institute.

Marshall, T. (1950) *Citizenship and Social Class*. Oxford: Oxford University Press.

Martin, J. and White, A. (1988) *The Financial Circumstances of Disabled Adults Living in Private Households*. London: HMSO.

Mendelson, M. (1998) *The WIS that was: Replacing the Canadian Working Income Supplement*. York: Joseph Rowntree Foundation.

Millar, J. (1994) 'Understanding labour supply in context: households and incomes', in Bryson, A. and McKay, S. (eds) *Is it Worth Working? Factors Affecting Labour Supply*. London: Policy Studies Institute.

Millar, J. (1997) 'Gender', in Walker, A. and Walker, C. (eds) (1997) *Britain Divided: The Growth of Social Exclusion in the 1980s and 1990s*. London: CPAG.

Millar, J. and Whiteford, P. (1994) 'Child support in lone-parent families: policies in Australia and the UK', *Policy and Politics*, **21** (1): 59–72.

Minford, P., Davies, D., Peel, M. and Sprague, A. (1983) *Unemployment – Cause and Cure*. Oxford: Martin Robertson.

Mishra, R. (1977) *Society and Social Policy: Theoretical Perspectives on Welfare*. London: Macmillan.

Mitchell, D. (1991) *Income Transfers in Ten Countries*. Aldershot: Gower.

Modood, T., Berthoud, R. Lakey, J. *et al.* (1997) *Ethnic Minorities in Britain.* London: Policy Studies Institute.

Morris, L., with Llewellyn, T. (1991) *Social Security Provision for the Unemployed.* SSAC Research Paper No. 3. London: HMSO.

Munnell, A. (1976) 'Private pensions and saving: new evidence', *Journal of Political Economy,* **84**: 1013–32.

Nove, A., with McKay, S. (1995) *War Pensions Agency Customer Satisfaction Survey 1994.* DSS Research Report No. 42. London: HMSO.

OECD (1994) *Jobs Study.* Paris: OECD.

OECD (1996) *Ageing in OECD Countries: A Critical Policy Challenge.* Social Policy Studies No. 20. Paris: OECD.

Offe, C. (1984) *Contradictions of the Welfare State.* Cambridge, MA: MIT Press.

Oldfield, N. and Yu, A. (1993) *The Cost of a Child: Living Standards for the 1990s.* London: CPAG.

Oorschot, W. van (1995) *Realizing Rights.* Aldershot: Avebury.

Oppenheim, C. and Harker, L. (1996) *Poverty: The Facts,* 3rd edn. London: CPAG.

Parker, H. (1990) 'The tax and benefit systems, and their effects on people with low earnings potential', in Bowen, A. and Mayhew, K. (eds) *Improving Incentives for the Low-Paid.* London: NEDO/Macmillan.

Perry, J. (1993) *Breadwinners or Child Rearers: The Dilemmas for Lone Mothers.* Labour Market and Social Policy Occasional Papers No. 12. Paris: OECD.

Piachaud, D. (1987) 'Problems in the definition and measurement of poverty', *Journal of Social Policy,* **16**(2): 335–51.

Pinker, R. (1971) *Social Theory and Social Policy.* London: Heinemann.

Ploug, N. and Kvist, J. (1996) *Social Security in Europe: Development or Dismantlement?* London: Kluwer Law International.

Przeworski, A. and Teune, H. (1970) *The Logic of Comparative Social Inquiry.* London: John Wiley.

Pudney, S. and Thomas, J. (1993) *Unemployment Benefit, Incentives and the Labour Supply of Wives of Unemployed Men: Econometric Estimates.* Cambridge University: Department of Applied Economics.

Pyle, D. (1989) *Tax Evasion and the Black Economy.* London: Macmillan.

Ritchie, J., with Ward, K. and Duldig, W. (1993) *GPs and IVB.* London: Social and Community Planning Research.

Roll, J. (1991) *What is a Family? Benefit Models and Social Reality.* Occasional Paper. London: Family Policy Studies Centre.

Roll, J. (1992) *Understanding Poverty: A Guide to the Concepts and Measures.* London: Family Policy Studies Centre.

Room, G. (1995) 'Poverty and social exclusion', in Room, G. (ed.) *Beyond the Threshold.* Bristol: Polity Press.

Rose, M. (1972) *The Relief of Poverty 1834–1914.* Basingstoke: Macmillan.

Rose, R. (1991) 'Comparing forms of comparative analysis', *Political Studies,* **39**: 446–62.

Rowlingson, K and Berthoud, R (1996) *Disability, Benefits and Employment.* DSS Research Report No. 54. London: Stationery Office.

Rowlingson, K. and Whyley, C. (1998) '"The right amount to the right people?" Reducing fraud, error and non-take-up of benefit', *Benefits*, **21**: 7–10.

Rowlingson, K., Whyley, C., Newburn, T. and Berthoud, R. (1997) *Social Security Fraud: The Role of Penalties.* DSS Research Report No. 64. London: The Stationery Office.

Rowlingson, K., Whyley, C. and Warren, T. (1998) *The Links Between Income and Wealth.* York: Joseph Rowntree Foundation.

Rowntree, B. (1901) *Poverty: A Study of Town Life.* London: Macmillan.

Sainsbury, D. (1996) *Gender, Equality and Welfare States.* Cambridge: Cambridge University Press.

Sainsbury, R. (1998) 'A critique of the case for change', in Adler, M. and Sainsbury, R. (eds) (1998) *Adjudication Matters: Reforming Decision Making and Appeals in Social Security.* New Waverley Papers. Edinburgh: University of Edinburgh.

Sly, F. (1996) 'Ethnic minority participation in the labour market: trends from the Labour Force Survey 1984–1995', *Labour Market Trends*, **104**(6): 259–70.

Smith, N. (1972) *A Brief Guide to Social Legislation.* London: Methuen.

Smith, P. (1978) *Industrial Injuries Benefits.* London: Oyez Publishing.

Spicker, P. (1993) *Poverty and Social Security: Concepts and Principles.* London: Routledge.

Spicker, P. (1995) *Social Policy: Themes and Approaches.* London: Prentice Hall/Harvester Wheatsheaf.

Stevens-Strohmann, R. (1997) 'Citizen's Income – utopian dream or a sensible approach to a long overdue social security reform?', paper presentation to *Citizenship and the Welfare State: Fifty Years of Progress?,* Ruskin College, Oxford, 18–19 December 1997.

Strickland, P. (1998) *Working Families Tax Credit and Family Credit* House of Commons Research Paper 998/46, April.

Supplementary Benefits Commission (1980) *Report of the SBC for the Year Ended 31 December 1979.* London: HMSO.

Taylor, M. (1998) *Work Incentives. The Modernisation of Britain's Tax and Benefit System Number Two.* Budget 98 Paper.

Thane, P. (1982) *The Foundations of the Welfare State.* London: Longman.

Thornton, P., Sainsbury, R. and Barnes, H. (1997) *Helping Disabled People to Work: A Cross-national Study of Social Security and Employment Provisions.* SSAC Research Paper No. 8. London: HMSO.

Titmuss, R. (1958) *Essays on the Welfare State.* London: Allen & Unwin.

Titmuss, R. (1971) 'Welfare rights, law and discretion', *Political Quarterly*, **42**: 113–22.

Titmuss, R. (1974) *Social Policy.* London: Allen & Unwin.

Townsend, P. (1979) *Poverty in the United Kingdom.* Harmondsworth: Penguin.

Waldfogel, J. (1997) 'Ending welfare as we know it: the personal responsibility and work opportunity act of 1996', *Benefits*, **20**: 11–15.

Walker, A (1986) 'Pensions and the production of poverty in old age', in Philipson, C. and Walker, A. (eds) *Ageing and Social Policy*. Aldershot: Gower.

Walker, A. (1992) 'The poor relation: poverty among older women', in Glendinning, C. and Millar, J. (eds) *Women and Poverty in Britain the 1990s*. London: Harvester Wheatsheaf.

Walker, C. (1983) *Changing Social Policy – the Case of the Supplementary Benefits review*. London: Bedford Square Press.

Walker, C. (1993) *Managing Poverty: The Limits of Social Assistance*. London: Routledge.

Walker, R., with Ashworth, K. (1994) *Poverty Dynamics: Issues and Examples*. Aldershot: Avebury.

Walker, R. and Wiseman, M. (1997) 'The possibility of a British earned income tax credit', *Fiscal Studies*, **18**(4): 401–25.

Walker, R., Hardman, G. and Hutton, S. (1988) 'The occupational pension trap: towards a prelimiary empirical specification', *Journal of Social Policy*, **18**(4); 575–93.

Walker, R., Huby, M. and Dix, G. (1992) *Working the Social Fund*. DSS Research Report No. 8. London: HMSO.

Warwick, D. and Osherson, S. (eds) (1973) *Comparative Research Methods*. New Jersey: Prentice-Hall.

Weale, A., Bradshaw, J., Maynard, A. and Piachaud, D. (1984) *Lone Mothers, Paid Work and Social Security*. London: Bedford Square Press.

Webb, S. (1994) 'Social insurance and poverty alleviation: an empirical analysis', in Baldwin, S. and Falkingham, J. (eds) *Social Security and Social Change: New Challenges to the Beveridge Model*. London: Harvester Wheatsheaf.

Webb, S. and Wilcox, S. (1991) *Time for Mortgage Benefits*. York: Joseph Rowntree Foundation.

White, M. (1991) *Against Unemployment*. London: Policy Studies Institute.

White, M. and Lakey, J. (1992) *The Restart Effect*. London: Policy Studies Institute.

Whiteford, P. and Bradshaw, J. (1994) 'Benefits and incentives for lone parents: a comparative analysis', *International Social Security Review*, **47**: 69–89.

Wilensky, H. (1975) *The Welfare State and Equality: Structural and Ideological Roots of Public Expenditures*. Berkeley: University of California Press.

Williams, F. (1989) *Social Policy: A Critical Introduction*. Cambridge: Polity Press.

Wood, G. (1998) 'Housing tax expenditures in OECD countries', *Policy and Politics*, **16**(4): 235–50.

Index

Act of Settlement 1662 45
Acts of Parliament, *see under* individual Acts
adequacy 87–9, see *also* poverty
Adjudication Officer 153–4
affluence testing 199, *see also* means-testing
ageing population, *see* demographic change
Aid to Families with Dependent Children (AFDC) 178
appeals 154
assessment unit, *see* benefit unit
Attendance Allowance (AA) 107
Automated Credit Transfer (ACT) 149

Basic Income Scheme, *see* Citizen's Income
benefits
  administration 142–3
  cash versus in-kind 17–18, 126–7
  classifications of 72–84
  expenditure on 84–6, 92–3, 184–6
  flat-rate 5–6
  insurance, *see* insurance
  levels of 87–9
  means-tested, *see* means-testing, *see also* affluence testing
  methods of payment 149
  numbers receiving 84–6
  shift from contributory to means-tested 79–81
  see also disability benefits; extra-cost benefits; family benefits; lone parents; pensions; special needs benefits
  see under individual benefit names
Benefits Agency (BA) 143–8
  'Change' programme 148
  customer satisfaction with 148
  performance targets 144–8
benefit unit 77, 89–91

Beveridge, William
  Beveridge model 33, 60–1, 119
  Beveridge report 54–8
Bismarckian system, *see* comparative social security
Booth, Charles 49, 50
Budgeting Loans 138, 139
  see also Social Fund

Carers' benefits 108
Case for Welfare Reform, see Green Papers
'Change' programme, *see* Benefits Agency
charities 17, 48
Chief Adjudication Officer 154
Child Benefit 65, 111–12
Child Poverty Action Group (CPAG) 64, 209
Child Support Act 114
Child Support Agency (CSA) 114, 144
Citizenship Pensions 197–8
  see also pensions; Stakeholder Pensions
Citizen's Income 91, 192–3
claimants 150, *see also* benefits
cohabitation rule 77
Cold Weather Payments 138
  see also Social Fund
Commission on Social Justice 190, 193
Community Care Grants 138, 139, *see also* Social Fund
comparative social security
  Beveridge model 33
  Bismarckian systems 33
  comparing benefits in different countries 35–9
  comparing the mix of benefits 29–30
  comparing whole systems 31–5
  disability benefits 108–9
  lessons from abroad 24–5
  family benefits 115
  pensions 98–9
  problems with comparing countries 25–6
  reasons for studying 22–4
  unemployment benefits 123–4

compensation, *see* disability benefits
complexity of rules 156
contingent benefits 73, 78–9
contributions, *see* insurance
Contributions Agency (CA) 144
Council Tax Benefit 132–3
Crisis Loans 138, 139, *see also* Social Fund

Decision-making 153–4
demographic change 71, 186–8
Department of Social Security (DSS) 142
  information from 207–8
dependency culture 165
dependency ratio 186–7, *see also* demographic change
disability benefits 69
  available benefits 102–9
  compensation benefits 106–7
  expenditure on 101–2
  international comparisons, *see* comparative social security
  rationale for 100, 105
  see also disincentives to work
  see also under individual benefit names
Disability Living Allowance (DLA) 69, 107
Disability Working Allowance (DWA) 69, 107
disabled people 153–4
  see also disability benefits
  see also under individual disability benefit names
discretion 82, 133–5
disincentives to work 166–7
  and disabled people 168
  and Family Credit 169
  and joblessness 166–8, 170–2
  and lone parents 175–7
  and partners of the unemployed 173–5
disregards on income support *see* means-testing

Employers 16–17, 20
Employment Service (ES) 149

errors in benefits
administration 163–4
Esping-Andersen, G 33–4
ethnic minorities 151, 152
European Union 26–7
expenditure on benefits, *see*
benefits
extra-costs benefits 15, 82,
107, 132

Families with children
benefits for families, *see*
family benefits
changes in family structures
71, 183
definition of 'family' for
benefit purposes 77
effects of social security on
family structures 177–80
see also demographic
change
see also under individual
benefit names
Family Allowances Act 1945
58
family benefits 16, 64
available benefits 111–15
expenditure on 109
international comparisons,
see comparative social
security
rationale for 110–11
see also lone parents
Family Credit (FC) 68,
112–13
Family Income Supplement
(FIS) 64–5
food stamps 126
Fowler Review 67
fraud 70, 158–62
causes of 160–2
extent of 158–60
official responses to 167
types of 160
friendly societies 48
funeral payments 138

Gay couples 77, 153
Green Papers
Case for Welfare Reform
194
child support 115
Fowler Review 67
fraud 158
welfare reform 152

Heterosexuality 153
Home Responsibilities
Protection (HRP) 10, 75,
108, 190
homosexuality, *see* gay
couples
housing
help with costs of 127–32
help with costs of rent
130–2
help with mortgage costs
128–9
subsidising council rents
130–2
Housing Benefit (HB) 68,
127, 131–2

Incapacity Benefit (IB) 69,
103
Incentives to work, *see*
disincentives to work
Income Support (IS) 68, 70,
76–7, 87–9
disregards on earnings and
capital, *see* means-testing
for disabled people 107
for families 112
for lone parents 114
for pensioners 95
for unemployed people 119
see also means-testing
independent benefits 90–1
Industrial Injuries
Disablement Benefit
(IIDB) 106
Information Technology
Services Agency (ITSA)
144
insurance 6–10, 73, 74–6
contributions to National
Insurance 9–10, 74–5
entitlement to National
Insurance benefits 75–6
introduction of social
insurance benefits 51–3
social insurance 6–7, 73,
74–6, 79–81, 189–90
state versus private
insurance 7–8
see also National Insurance
Act 1911
see also under names of
individual insurance
benefits

Invalid Care Allowance (ICA)
108
Invalidity Benefit (IVB) 69,
103–5

Joblessness 167, *see also*
disincentives to work
Jobseeker's Allowance (JSA)
70, 118

Labour exchanges 51
labour market flexibility 169,
183–4, *see also*
disincentives to work
less eligibility 47, *see also*
Poor Law
Liberal governments from
1906 50
local authorities 149
lone parents
benefits for 113
expenditure on 114
numbers of 114
see also Child Support
Agency; disincentives to
work; families with
children
low pay 196, *see also* Family
Credit; Disability Working
Allowance; minimum
wage

Maternity Benefit, *see* private
welfare
maternity payments 138
means-testing 6, 73, 76–8,
79–81, 83–4, 107, 190–1
comparative studies 37–9
defining 'means' 76
disregards 76
take-up 155–6
see also affluence-testing
Medicaid 126
minimum wage 197
Mobility Allowance 107

National Assistance Act 1948
59–60
National Insurance, *see*
insurance
National Insurance Act 1911
51–2
National Insurance Act 1946
58–9

National Insurance
Contributions, *see*
insurance
National Insurance (Industrial
Injuries) Act 1946 59
negative income tax, *see*
taxation
New Deal for unemployed
people 122, 194–5
New Labour and social
security 193–9
Next Steps Agencies 142, *see
also* under names of
individual agencies
non-take-up, *see* take-up

Occupational welfare, *see*
private welfare
Old Age Pensions Act 1908
50
One Parent Benefit (OPB)
113–14

Passport benefits 126
pensions
ageing population 187–8
international comparisons,
see comparative social
security
Poor Law 45–8, 50
Poor Law Amendment Act
1834 46–8, 50
Poor Relief Act 1601 45
Post Office 149
poverty 10–14
absolute versus relative
11–12
alleviation of 10
definition of 11–13
dynamics of 13–14
effects of 14
international comparisons
39–43
pensioners 97–8
'rediscovery of' 61–3
private pensions 196–7, *see
also* private welfare
rationale for 93–4
reform of 197–9
SERPS 65, 68
Stakeholder Pension 197–8
state Retirement Pension
50–1, 94–6
see also demographic
change

private welfare 16–17
charitable welfare, *see*
charities
Maternity Benefit 66
occupational welfare 66, 82
Sickness Benefit (SB) 66

Redistribution of resources
14–15
rent, *see* housing; Housing
Benefit
Resettlement Agency, 144
Retirement Pension, *see*
pensions
Rowntree, Seebohm 49
Royal Commission for
Inquiry into the
Administration and
Operation of the Poor
Laws 1832 46
Royal Commission on the
Poor Laws and the Relief
of Distress 1905–9 50

Savings 180–1
separation from social
services 59
SERPS (State Earnings-
Related Pension Scheme),
see pensions
Severe Disablement
Allowance (SDA) 105
single payments 68, 136–7
social assistance, *see* means-
testing
social exclusion, *see* poverty
Social Fund 68, 82, 137–9
social insurance, *see*
insurance
social security
aims of 4–6
definition of 2–4
special needs benefits
135–41, *see also* single
payments; Social Fund
Speenhamland System 45–6
Stakeholder Pension, *see*
pensions
state Retirement Pension, *see*
pensions
stigma 46, 156
Supplementary Benefits
Commission 63

Take-up 154–8
targeting, *see* means-testing

taxation 19–20
negative income tax 64
tax-benefit integration 191
tax credits 19, 196, *see also*
Working Families Tax
Credit
Temporary Assistance for
Needy Families (TANF)
178

Underclass 13, 165
undeserving poor 48
unemployed people
active labour market
policies 122
available benefits 117–18
characteristics of 116
expenditure on 119–21
international comparisons,
see comparative social
security
see also, disincentives to
work; New Deal for
unemployed people
unemployment 170–2, *see
also* unemployed people;
disincentives to work
Unemployment Assistance
Board 53
Unemployment Benefit (UB)
51, 70, 118–19
unemployment trap 164, *see
also* disincentives to work
universal benefits 83, *see
also* insurance; contingent
benefits

War Pensions 106
welfare reform, *see* Green
Papers; New Labour and
social security
Welfare-to-Work 24, 70, 194
Widows' Benefits 110
Widows, Orphans and Old
Age Contributory Pensions
Act 1925 52
work, *see* disincentives to
work; New Deal for
unemployed people;
unemployed people
workfare 25
workhouse 46–7
Working Families Tax Credit
(WFTC) 112, 196